EDUCATING THE PROPER
WOMAN READER

EDUCATING THE PROPER WOMAN READER

Victorian Family Literary Magazines and the
Cultural Health of the Nation

Jennifer Phegley

THE OHIO STATE UNIVERSITY PRESS
Columbus

Copyright © 2004 by The Ohio State University.
All rights reserved.

Library of Congress Cataloging-in-Publication Data

Phegley, Jennifer.
Educating the proper woman reader : Victorian family literary magazines
and the cultural health of the nation / Jennifer Phegley.
p. cm.
Includes bibliographical references and index.
ISBN 0-8142-0967-X (cloth : alk. paper) – ISBN 0-8142-9055-8 (cd-rom)
1. English literature–19th century–History and criticism. 2. Middle class
women–Books and reading–Great Britain–History–19th century. 3. Middle
class women–Books and reading–United States–History–19th century. 4. Periodicals–Publishing–Great Britain–History–19th century. 5. Periodicals–Publishing–United States–History–19th century. 6. Literature publishing–Great
Britain–History–19th century. 7. Women and literature–Great Britain–History–19th century. 8. American literature–19th century–History and criticism.
9. Didactic literature, English–History and criticism. 10. Women in literature.
I. Title.
PR468.W6P48 2004
820.9'9287'09034–dc22
                                          2004007614

Jacket design by Laurence Nosik.
Type set in Baskerville BE.

The paper used in this publication meets the minimum requirements of the
American National Standard for Information Sciences–Permanence of Paper
for Printed Library Materials. ANSI Z39.48-1992.

9 8 7 6 5 4 3 2 1

CONTENTS

CONTENTS

LIST OF ILLUSTRATIONS

ACKNOWLEDGMENTS

THE UNIVERSITY OF MISSOURI system, the University of Missouri-Kansas City, and the UMKC Department of English were instrumental to the completion of this book. I would like to thank them respectively for awarding me a University of Missouri Research Board Grant, a UMKC Faculty Research Grant, and a one-semester research leave. I am also grateful to The Ohio State University for their assistance during the early stages of this project. I thank Ohio State's Department of English for granting me both the Estrich and the Departmental Dissertation fellowships, the Department of Women's Studies for supporting my work with the Gee Award for Research on Women, the College of Humanities for providing a summer grant, and the Graduate School Alumni Association for its research award.

I respectfully acknowledge the Mistress and Fellows, Girton College, Cambridge, for allowing me to reprint portions of Emily Davies's letters held in their archives; the Harry Ransom Research Center at the University of Texas, Austin, for granting permission to use Mary Elizabeth Braddon's letters from the Robert Lee Wolff collection; the staff at the Cincinnati Public Library, for making available their copies of *Victoria Magazine;* and the Ohio State University libraries, for the use of their copies of *Harper's Magazine, Cornhill Magazine,* and *Belgravia Magazine.* I am particularly grateful to Elva Griffith at the OSU Rare Books Room, Lucy Shelton Caswell at the OSU Cartoon Research Library, and Robert Ray at UMKC Special Collections for assisting with the illustrations for this book.

Portions of chapter 2 appeared in the Spring 2000 *Victorian Periodicals Review* as "Clearing Away the 'Briars and Brambles'": The

Education and Professionalization of the *Cornhill Magazine*'s Women Readers, 1860–65." I thank William Scheuerle for granting permission to reprint this article in revised form here. I appreciate the generosity of The Ohio State University Press for permitting me to reprint portions of chapter 1 as "Literary Piracy, Nationalism, and Women Readers in *Harper's New Monthly Magazine*, 1850–1855," in *American Periodicals* 14, no. 1 (Spring 2004); to publish a revised version of chapter 3 as "'Henceforward I Refuse to Bow the Knee to Their Narrow Rule': Mary Elizabeth Braddon's *Belgravia Magazine*, Women Readers, and Literary Valuation," in *Nineteenth-Century Contexts* 26, no. 2 (June 2004); and to reprint selections from chapters 2 and 3 as "'I Should No More Think of Dictating . . . What Kinds of Books She Should Read': Images of Women Readers in Victorian Family Literary Magazines," in *Reading Women: Literary Figures and Cultural Icons from the Victorian Age to the Present,* edited by Jennifer Phegley and Janet Badia (University of Toronto Press, forthcoming 2005). I am also obliged to those at The Ohio State University Press who so enthusiastically and efficiently ushered this project through the publication process, particularly Heather Lee Miller and Eugene O'Connor.

I wish to express my sincere gratitude to Marlene Longenecker, Andrea Lunsford, Clare Simmons, and Susan Williams, who challenged, questioned, and encouraged me as I began this project. Janet Badia, Susan Bernstein, Andrea Broomfield, Jennifer Cognard-Black, Joan Dean, Beth Dolan, Miriam Forman-Brunell, Jane Greer, Linda Hughes, Lisa Kiser, Sally Mitchell, Deborah Maltby, Jim Phelan, and Barbara Ryan also deserve thanks for their helpful and supportive responses to my work. The UMKC Interdisciplinary Faculty Forum, the Ohio State University First Draft Group, the Research Society for Victorian Periodicals, and the Interdisciplinary Nineteenth-Century Studies Association also offered stimulating discussions of this project. I thank the members of the VICTORIA and SHARP list-servs as well for generously answering my questions.

Finally, I thank my family and loved ones, who keep me grounded in the real world but encourage me to reach for the stars.

INTRODUCTION

The Scene of Women's Reading:
Mid-Nineteenth-Century Culture, Professional Critics,
and Family Literary Magazines

NINETEENTH-CENTURY BRITISH and American critics claimed that women readers were dangerous.[1] Scholars have acknowledged that the mid-nineteenth-century critical anxiety about women readers was a cultural phenomenon that was largely the result of the mass production and mass marketing of print culture—exemplified by the availability of a wide variety of inexpensive magazines—and the consolidation of middle-class power that gave women the leisure time to devote themselves to reading. As literacy rates rose, printing technologies improved, taxes on newspapers were revoked in England, and the publishing industry was centralized in the United States, periodicals began to dominate nineteenth-century print culture. The development of this unruly mass of periodical literature gave critics a forum in which to make their living as well as a subject around which they could build their reputations. The primary critical response to the unprecedented abundance of literary material was to initiate a new discourse that called for the regulation of women's reading in order to ensure the morality of the primary literacy educators of the family, the literary taste of the middle class, and the preservation of the nation's culture.

Scholars typically base this conception of the nineteenth-century woman reader on the analysis of elite literary journals run and read by highly educated Victorian men, whose discourse about the dangers of women's reading is very similar to contemporary discussions about the dangers of children's exposure to violent video games or television shows. While this image of women's reading was certainly prevalent in nineteenth-century elite culture, it was not the only image of women readers presented to the public. In *Educating the Proper Woman Reader* I reevaluate prevailing assumptions about the relationship between nineteenth-century women readers and literary critics by examining how four important family literary magazines—the American *Harper's New Monthly Magazine* and the British magazines the *Cornhill, Belgravia,* and *Victoria*—defended women from the highly publicized accusation that they were uncritical readers whose reading practices threatened the sanctity of the family and the cultural reputation of the nation. Contrary to most scholarly discussions of the condescending and even destructive attitude of critics toward women readers in the nineteenth century, I argue that family literary magazines empowered women to make their own decisions about what and how to read. Despite the dominant attitude toward women as dangerous readers, this genre of magazine led the way for women to participate in professional critical discourse as both consumers and producers of literary culture. Family literary magazines attempted to change the landscape of the debate surrounding women readers by combating the portrayal of improper reading as a particularly female malady and instead depicting women as intellectually competent readers.

John Ruskin's emphatic warning to parents to "keep the modern magazine and novel out of your girl's way" ("Sesame and Lilies" 66) illustrates the typical anxiety nineteenth-century critics expressed about the dangerous combination of periodical literature and female readers. Such warnings were precipitated by the booming magazine industry, which touched nearly every British and American citizen. During Queen Victoria's reign, there were as many as 50,000 magazines published in Great Britain alone (North 4). By the mid-1800s, there were more than one thousand journals devoted solely to literary subjects (Thompson 3). In the United States 2,500 magazines were issued between 1850 and 1865, despite the hampering effects of the economic panic of 1857 and the Civil War (Mott 4). The development of periodical literature had such an impact that critic George Saintsbury declared in 1896, "Perhaps there is no single feature of . . . the nineteenth century, not even the enormous popularisation and multiplication of the novel, which is so distinctive and characteristic as the development in it of periodical literature. . . . [I]t is quite certain that, had . . . reprints [from magazines] not taken place, more than half the most valuable books of the age . . . would never have appeared as books at all" (166). As a result of the overwhelming abundance of inexpensive magazines and the novels they contained, critics on both sides of the

2

Atlantic took it as their mission to direct readers to choose the proper texts and read in the "right" ways. The eminent Victorian Frederic Harrison justified the need for critics like himself to guide readers by declaring that he "could almost reckon the printing press as amongst the scourge of mankind" because its immense productivity encouraged people to "act as if every book were as good as any other" (5, 10). He argued that critics were necessary to teach "the art of right reading," which "is as long and difficult to learn as the art of right living" (11).

James Machor describes the role nineteenth-century critics like Ruskin, Saintsbury, and Harrison created for themselves as that of "literary philanthropists" who benevolently bestowed their wisdom upon less educated literary consumers (65). Women readers were the most frequent beneficiaries of this "philanthropic" effort, though it was not always so benevolent. Condescending critics tended to define themselves as professionals and experts at the expense of women by initiating a discourse that pathologized women's reading practices. Whereas masculine middle-class reading was defined as professional and critical, feminine middle-class reading was seen as amateurish and careless. Moreover, periodical and novel reading, often considered mindless, were characterized as primarily feminine pursuits. The regulatory function of critics was justified by the characterization of women as the most susceptible victims of the "disease of reading," which was believed to be a threat to the sanctity of the family and to the social order of the nation.[2] As a result, many of the attempts to preserve literary culture and professionalize literary criticism were waged in the press as efforts to protect the woman reader from the rampant forces of production-line culture, which were assumed to be corrupting to her, her family, and the nation.

The profession of literary criticism was built upon the notion that the work of critics served national interests by cultivating a healthy cultural atmosphere that would preserve (or, in the case of the United States, build) the nation's strength. As Susan Bernstein contends, nineteenth-century attitudes toward women readers were influenced in England by national imperial anxieties and articulated in anthropological terms as women's reading came to be seen as "either evidence of the threat of a degenerating . . . civilization or a symptom of . . . the encroachment of the so-called 'lower' orders with their forms of entertainment into legitimate, sanctioned culture" ("Dirty Reading" 215). In the United States these national anxieties were more focused on the status and reputation of a young nation seeking to legitimize its cultural productions in the face of well-established and well-respected British

and European exports. One example of the nationalistic pathologiza-
tion of women readers in England can be seen in an article called "Vice
of Reading," featured in *Temple Bar* (September 1874). This article
depicts reading as an addiction "just as real, just as imminent, and we
fear yet more deadly, since far more insidious" than dram drinking, tea
drinking, or tobacco smoking (251). The habit of reading is described
as an excuse for idleness and a "stumbling-block in the way of education" that will enfeeble the mind, make "flabby the fibre" of the body,
and undermine the "vigour of nations" (ibid.). Such a feminized
rhetoric of the dangers of reading highlights the inseparability of anxieties about reading, women, and national cultural supremacy. *Temple
Bar* even goes so far as to declare the invention of croquet the savior of
many women who have, as a result, avoided contributing to the "dete-
rioration of the human species" through improper reading practices
(256–57). Moving women into a more social, group-regulated activity
such as croquet (even if it was an outdoor "sport" that took women out
of the parlor and into the company of men) was seen as a remedy to
the private and unregulated spaces in which solitary and "insidious"
reading could occur.[3] In order to stave off the feminization of British
culture, *Temple Bar* surprisingly suggests that women take on more vigorous, masculine activities and abandon the dangerous vice of reading.

Though the specific dangers of reading were often only vaguely
alluded to, they were frequently associated with women behaving in
ways unbecoming to a proper wife and mother. In other words, critics
amplified fears that what women read (especially if it happened to be
sensational or scandalous) and how they read (particularly if it was
quickly and uncritically) would infect them with (at best) romanticized
expectations that would leave them dissatisfied about their lives and (at
worst) with immoral thoughts that could lead to immoral behavior. An
article on "Novel-Reading," printed in the American magazine
Putnam's, illustrates the connection between fears about women's reading and fears about their proper roles.[4] The article opens with the scene
of a mother's dutiful regulation of her daughter's reading practices:
" 'Pray put away that book,' 'I wish you were not so fond of novels,' and
the like phrases of displeasure and reproach, are familiar to the lips of
many mothers, to the ears of many daughters" (September 1857, 384).
While a supposedly real mother who is quoted in the article admits that
she enjoys nothing better than a good novel, she maintains that "such
books are decidedly dangerous for young girls. They exert a bad influence on growing minds, especially on feminine minds, by nature
inclined to an overbalance on the side of feeling. They excite the imag-

ination, arouse morbid emotions and aspirations, and so render them unfit for homely duties and aims of common life, and cause them to feel unsatisfied with its realities'" (ibid.). By putting such speeches into the mouths of mothers, *Putnam's* cleverly enlists women to justify the need for their own regulation in order to keep them fit for their roles as wives and mothers. Here mothers serve a contradictory role: They are asked to monitor the reading of those under their care, but they are also required to submit to the regulatory powers of the critics who will teach them how to do so.

Although much of the discourse surrounding the corruptibility of the woman reader was at odds with the popular idea of woman as moral agent, Machor points out that "reviewers were unable to see—or perhaps unwilling to admit—that their ideas about female readers rested on incompatible conceptions of womanhood in the culture at large" (68). Likewise, in *Women's Worlds: Ideology, Femininity, and the Woman's Magazine,* Ros Ballaster, Margaret Beetham, Elizabeth Frazer, and Sandra Hebron argue that "the definition of the female reader of magazines is a contradictory process in which women's importance is both confirmed and strictly delimited, through which the 'feminine' is both repressed and returns irrepressible" (77). Thus, middle-class women readers were central to many commentaries on proper reading practices precisely because of their revered status as the protectors of morality, a status that coincided with an intense anxiety about the potential failure of individual women to live up to their idealized reputations by reading improperly. Whether critics' regulatory attempts were the charitable acts they characterized them as or cynical acts of patriarchal dominance through which reviewers marginalized and disempowered women in what Machor identifies as "an ultimately phallocentric system of reading" that women were supposedly incapable of joining (74), it is clear that women readers became the contested ground on which literary culture was defined and the profession of literary criticism was established.

By studying the influential genre of the family literary magazine in the context of critical discourse on women's reading, I reveal an alternative to the relationship between women readers and nineteenth-century magazines outlined earlier. While focusing on the ways in which the negative idea of the woman reader served as a major defining force behind the divisions between high and low culture, the definitions of literary forms such as realism and sensationalism, and the development of the literary canon, this book illustrates how some critics and magazines created a distinct image of women readers that has not yet been

5

uncovered. The fact is, women readers were crucial to the establishment of family literary magazines, which targeted women as the primary consumers of literature and the disseminators of culture within the home. The untapped audience of middle-class women was excluded from other serious magazines that addressed literary and cultural issues. Largely because they included women, family literary magazines stood apart from and outsold the weighty political and critical quarterly reviews, which had been the primary venue for respectable literary opinions in Great Britain since the eighteenth century. With a drop in demand for the old quarterlies (such as the *Edinburgh Review* and the *Quarterly Review*), literary reviewing became the province of review-oriented weeklies like the *Athenaeum* and *The Saturday Review*, conducted by university men. The concomitant push toward making the university the center of literary authority spawned specialty journals such as the *Reader* and the *Academy,* which offered to fulfill Matthew Arnold's call for an English counterpart to the French Academy to monitor the nation's cultural activity and ensure its high quality (Kent xx). However, these new journals were aimed at a more highly educated male audience than the family magazines, and, as such, they increased what Margaret Shaw calls the "stratification of literacy" along class and gender lines, "which ultimately solidified and privileged the construction of a new 'man' of letters and his forms of literate behavior" (196). As the professionalization of this man of letters took hold, critics such as Frederic Harrison declared their concern about directing the public's reading practices. In "The Choice of Books" featured in the *Fortnightly Review* in April 1879, Harrison claims that "Systematic reading is but little in favour even amongst studious men, in a true sense it is hardly possible for women. A comprehensive course of home study, and a guide to books, fit for the highest education of women, is yet a blank page remaining to be filled" (4). While the elite literary reviews focused on what John Morley of the *Fortnightly Review* called the "momentous task of forming national opinion" by providing education, guidance, and the resolution of doubt for male audiences (quoted in Houghton, "Periodical Literature" 7–9), the family literary magazine had already begun to supplant these periodicals by establishing itself as one solution to the educational void that existed for women readers.

To do so, family literary magazines did not condescend to women readers; instead, they replaced the predominantly unhealthy discourse of women's reading with an alternative, healthy discourse. While this approach had its roots in marketing, it was also justified in terms of protecting middle-class values and preserving the cultural health of the nation. In *The Reading Lesson* Patrick Brantlinger rightly points out that critical opposition to novels and novel reading in the Victorian period as "a widespread reaction to one of the earliest forms of modern, commodified mass culture, is familiar, well-charted territory" (2); however, he goes on to chart the less familiar criticisms of novel reading within novels that he claims are a defining feature of the genre itself. I hope to map another less familiar territory: the *defense* of novel and magazine reading within magazines themselves, which I argue is a defining feature of the family literary magazine. Against the well-founded critical background of protests against gendered reading practices outlined by scholars, *Educating the Proper Woman Reader* explores a specific kind of response to common critiques of women readers that has been largely ignored. I hope to show that the unique response of family literary magazines to women readers placed them firmly in the center of the nineteenth-century literary marketplace as participants in a cultural debate rather than as subjects to be debated. I maintain that these magazines defended women readers against critics for both commercial and cultural purposes that ultimately created greater personal and professional opportunities for women.

By resisting the professionalization of literary criticism at the expense of women readers, family literary magazines also contributed to a better environment for women writers than other "serious" magazines. While women contributed to and sometimes edited other types of magazines, this genre was particularly welcoming to women.[5] Taking the *Cornhill* as an example, Janice Harris claims that women writers contributed about 20 percent of its contents between 1860 and 1900, with women writers rising as high as 60 to 70 percent in certain issues during the 1860s and 1870s–the heyday of the genre (385).[6] Harris compares these figures to Walter Houghton's estimate that only 14 percent of the writers included in the thirty-five journals indexed in his *Wellesley Guide to Victorian Periodicals* were women.[7] This increase seems to indicate that the family literary magazine's inclusion of women readers may have led to a more favorable environment for women writers. Harris claims that the greater number of women writers was largely the result of the attention these magazines paid to "topics of interest to women" as well as the assumption that "women–and men–were interested in more and different topics than either the exclusively 'women's' publications or the major reviews had covered" (392). As a result, women writers felt invited to contribute serious articles as well as fiction and poetry to family literary magazines. By the 1880s, when the genre was declining, the number of women writers also began to decline.

In *Edging Women Out,* Gaye Tuchman and Nina Fortin posit that by the 1880s male critics and authors had "actively redefined the nature of a good novel and a great author," effectively "edging women out" of the profession in which they had thrived during the 1860s and 1870s (8). Tuchman and Fortin surveyed the archives of Macmillan Publishing—a company that also launched its own family literary magazine bearing the house name—from 1867 to 1917. They found that 62 percent of fiction manuscripts were submitted by women at the beginning of this period, whereas only 48 percent of them were submitted by women by the end of the period (60). While Tuchman and Fortin do not consider the effects that novel serialization or contributions to magazines may have had on these figures, they identify a trend that corresponds to the rise and fall of the family literary magazine. I contend that while this periodical genre dominated, women were more successful as professional writers. As novel serialization in magazines waned, the reign of the three-volume novel and the circulating library collapsed, and the single-volume novel emerged, male writers began to resume control of the literary marketplace.

Although Ellen Miller Casey and Marysa Demoor complicate this narrative somewhat, they do not refute it. Miller Casey read 11,000 fiction reviews printed in the *Athenaeum,* the preeminent British review, between 1860 and 1900. She agrees that the number of novels by women decreased during that period but maintains that there was a "genuine though grudging acceptance of women novelists as the equal of men" at the end of the century (152). She also qualifies the concept of "edging women out" by denying a "smooth" and "unidirectional" rate of change in the number of women's novels reviewed, though she concedes that between 1885 and 1890 there was a dramatic drop in the number of women novelists discussed (153–54). Likewise, Demoor's study of women reviewers who wrote for the *Athenaeum* indicates that the journal itself experienced a sharp decrease in the number of women contributors by the turn of the century, when critics' credentials increasingly included academic degrees (146). Although these scholars present a complex assessment of women's relationship to the London literary marketplace, they all agree that women writers were more successful during the 1860s and 1870s than later in the century. What I find most interesting about this is that these years coincide with the predominance of the family literary magazine, a genre welcoming to women readers, writers, and editors alike. This was, I believe, the result of the confluence of a period and a genre friendly to women, a moment in history forgotten or repressed by Virginia Woolf when she notoriously claimed that there was no legitimate history of women's literature to record. This book aims to bring this forgotten or repressed moment in literary history to the surface. While my primary focus is on the empowering discourse about women's reading that has been overlooked, I also show how women readers were sometimes able to transform themselves into writers and critics as a result of their rising status as readers in family literary magazines.

The Periodical Form as Literary and Scholarly Subject

While most nineteenth-century critics avoided condemning all fiction and magazine reading, their general distaste for the periodical form and its biggest star, the serialized novel, pervaded the profession of literary criticism well into the twentieth century. As a result, the field of periodical literature has, until recently, remained largely unexplored by scholars. According to Laurel Brake, Victorian periodicals have been a "subjugated" form

> not only in their own period where they were prime and highly visible quiddities in a struggle between literature and journalism, but also in the twentieth-century construct of "literature" which is predicated on their defeat, devaluation and invisibility. . . . In the desire to establish English as an academic subject, it was attempted to sever links between literature and journalism, and to obscure their intimate material involvement and intertextuality in the period. (*Subjugated Knowledges* xi–xiv)

The nineteenth-century impulse toward the professionalization of literary criticism as a way of regulating cultural production and consumption marginalized not only women readers but also periodical literature and serialized novels. Many twentieth-century scholars who dismissed magazine publications took their cues from nineteenth-century critics who began to standardize the canon of books deemed worthy of literary study based on criteria that either excluded periodical literature altogether or divorced supposedly more literary works from their original periodical contexts. In *Sesame and Lilies,* for example, John Ruskin makes the distinction between "books of the hour" and "books of all time." Books of the hour, he argues, should not even properly be called books as they are "merely letters or newspapers in good print," whereas books of all time are works of art that express truth (7–9). Ruskin draws a barrier between periodical literature and art, developing a definition of high culture that necessarily excludes popular newspaper and magazine sources. However, his formula breaks down when one considers that the majority of "classic" Victorian novels were originally serialized within the pages of magazines or issued in monthly parts.

During the nineteenth century, magazines were generally believed to encourage skimming, skipping, and leisurely enjoyment–supposedly corrupting methods of reading assumed to be opposed to professional and critical ways of reading. The reliance of family literary magazines on fiction serials coupled with the fear of magazines themselves increased their potential for critical dismissal. Why were serials so objectionable? Jennifer Hayward argues that the serialized novel's commercial status and responsiveness to readers have been equated with "femininity and immaturity" as well as "pernicious social influences" since the nineteenth century (7).[8] Like fears about women readers, Victorian critical distaste for both the serial and the periodical was also linked to the critic's anxiety about his own status. The advent of part-issue publication, originating with Charles Dickens's *The Pickwick Papers* in the 1830s, forced critics to act not as experts but as everyday readers, reading and responding as a novel was in process. Hayward notes that this was distasteful primarily because it undermined the professional status critics were just beginning to establish, making them equal participants in the reading community rather than revered experts (24). As a result of the loss of some of their regulatory power over serials, critics often depicted "the serial phenomenon" in terms of "familiar, disparaging models of addiction and industrial production" (27). The profession of criticism was thus simultaneously threatened and sustained by women readers, periodicals, and serial novels.

By the 1860s part-issue serialization began to give way to magazine serialization. This move was in large part due to the advent of family literary magazines, which provided publishers with a consistent outlet and advertising vehicle for their wares and the public with a cheap and varied source of reading material. Norman Feltes acknowledges that serials in magazines were particularly marked by their status as "branded goods" (69). As texts that drummed up sales for particular magazines, which were often used as advertising vehicles for their publishing houses, magazine serials were even more distasteful than part-issue publications. Not only were readers forced to consume literature bit by bit in monthly portions that invoked suspense and invited reader interaction, they were now assaulted with an additional, overwhelming array of highly commercialized reading material. For many of the same reasons, the critical distaste for serials persists today as they have transitioned into television and other digital media.

Ironically, the very divisions between high and low culture that critics formulated in the pages of nineteenth-century magazines often discouraged twentieth-century literary scholars from exploring the "low" and "ephemeral" form of the periodical. A fetishization of the book led critics to ignore the fact that serialized novels in magazines dominated the Victorian literary arena. Furthermore, a disciplinary emphasis on individuality and solitary authorship encouraged literary scholars to neglect the highly communal and eclectic form of the periodical. Even today, many scholars of periodicals feel the need to justify their work by organizing it around canonical literary figures or focusing on periodicals only as they enrich our understanding of already revered writers. Furthermore, despite Lyn Pykett's call for critics to make the transition from thinking of periodicals as mirrors that reflect society to understanding them as active shapers of culture, magazines are still often used as tools to study other subjects, and their own specific agendas and anonymous articles are given short shrift ("Reading the Periodical Press" 102). Few studies take into account magazines as genres or treat them as collaborative and corporate forms that are worthy of study in their own right.[9] This book seeks to remedy some of the neglect periodicals have received as a genre by examining family literary magazines as a class of coherent texts with recognizable traits, paying attention to particular authors and editors only as they are relevant to advancing the agenda and character of the periodicals themselves. This approach draws attention to the actual experiences of nineteenth-century readers and allows us to better understand the ways in which literature and journalism intersected.

By focusing on *Harper's*, the *Cornhill, Belgravia,* and *Victoria,* I am asserting both that each periodical conforms to the generic qualities of the family literary magazine and that each one also has a particular character and agenda that was often guided by the editor and that inevitably influenced contributors. Mark Parker points out that although periodicals seem to offer an unparalleled openness of form that would invite a myriad of writing approaches and reading responses, they also provided writers and readers with a highly determinate set of expectations that shaped contributions and responses (15). Likewise,

Linda Hughes argues that periodicals are a form in which "random dis-order . . . coexists with order" and that "can be said to affirm pluralism at the local level, conformity at the global level" (119, 121). Within the pages of periodicals, editors, contributors, and readers interact to cre-ate a seemingly chaotic and open form that maintains a logical coher-ence. This coherence determines the periodical's genre as well as its distinct character and agenda, which is larger than the sum of its parts and permeates even the seemingly disparate and discrete sections of the collection of works in any given issue. As a result, works included in periodicals are not merely extensions of their author's intentions or related to the context of the magazine in a secondary way, as is some-times assumed. Instead, these works gain deeper meaning when exam-ined within the periodical because that context gives them their mean-ing. In this study my primary interest is in the meaning the periodical context lends to images of women readers within the pages of these magazines during their first five years of publication, a time when each periodical was developing its own coherent character and agenda.

Educating the Proper Woman Reader would not be possible without the gradually but steadily increasing interest in periodicals and their readers that reaches back to the scholarship of Richard Altick, William Charvat, and others who in the mid-twentieth century paved the way for studies focusing on the effects of the publishing industry on author-ship and readership. Their work, along with the rise of interdiscipli-nary, feminist, new historicist, and cultural studies approaches to liter-ature, has spawned a major critical movement in recent years that includes both periodical studies and book history. The formation of the Research Society for Victorian Periodicals in 1969 and of both the Research Society for American Periodicals and the Society for the History of Authorship, Reading, and Publishing in 1991 have hastened the development of bibliographic resources that established a map of nineteenth-century periodical literature upon which scholars could begin to chart their own courses of study.[10] The leadership of these organizations and the development of important scholarly tools have resulted in a booming field of research that is highlighted by the num-ber of recent books that have made readership, print culture, and peri-odicals acceptable subjects of literary-historical scholarship.

Despite the recent excellent work in the field, there are still gaps in our understanding of the function of women readers in periodical cul-ture. In *Reviewing Sex: Gender and the Reception of Victorian Novels,* Nicola Diane Thompson calls for a serious, full-length investigation of the role women readers played in the development of critical standards in literary magazines (5). Likewise, Ballaster and her colleagues note that though the connection between women readers and literary magazines was crucial to the development of the nineteenth-century periodical press, no study has been devoted to examining this relationship (76). In addition, as Kate Flint points out, though "'woman as reader' is a fashionable topic in feminist criticism . . . most of the current debate has either focused on the practice of women reading today, or has looked at the construction of the woman reader . . . divorced from a fuller socio-historical context" (16). This book seeks to return the concept of the woman reader to the neglected social, historical, and literary context of periodical literature that broadens and enriches our understanding of both her symbolic function in Victorian society and her practical impact on literary debates.

The Family Literary Magazine as a Genre

When I use the term "family literary magazine," I am referring to that class of magazines typically called shilling monthlies in England, including *Macmillan's* (1859), *Temple Bar* (1860), *St. James's* (1861), *The Argosy* (1865), *Tinsley's* (1867), and *St. Paul's* (1867). Instead of using the more commonly recognized label, I have coined the term "family literary magazine" because, in my estimation, it more accurately describes the attributes of these magazines than the simple designation of their price implies. In *Sensation Fiction and Victorian Family Magazines*, Deborah Wynne uses the term "family magazine" to refer to similar kinds of middle-class fiction magazines. I prefer the addition of the term "literary" to emphasize the cultural pretensions of these magazines as well as their function as a forum for serialized novels. I also expand the British context to include inexpensive American monthlies like *Harper's* and *Putnam's,* which I see as two of the earliest examples of the genre. A decade after *Harper's* showed how successful it could be for a publishing house to begin a general literary magazine as an advertisement for its publications and an outlet for its authors, this magazine genre exploded in London, where nearly every major publishing house began its own magazine. As a result of my study of *Harper's,* I have decided to exclude weekly magazines such as Charles Dickens's *All the Year Round,* which Wynne includes in her category of family magazines. I see the weeklies as halfway between the penny papers aimed at the working classes and the middle-brow, family literary magazines that are my focus. My analysis of *Harper's* transformation of elements borrowed from Dickens's weekly *Household Words,* the predecessor to and model for *All the Year Round,* has contributed to my understanding of the family literary magazine as distinct from even Dickens's literary weeklies. While literary weeklies were certainly closely related to the monthlies and were often geared toward the same broadly defined, middle-class audience, the monthlies usually looked less like newspapers and were of a higher quality, often including lavish illustrations and full-page text layouts rather than the newspaper-style columns and lack of illustrations that characterized Dickens's magazines.

So, what did this new magazine genre look like, and how did readers approach the multifarious collection of cultural artifacts contained within its pages? Richard Ohmann's fictionalized account of an American woman's response to her favorite periodical suggests one answer to this question. In his study of turn-of-the-century American magazines, Ohmann sets the scene of periodical reading for a middle-class woman who desires to be culturally educated as well as entertained by her magazine. Though this scene of reading takes place decades after the heyday of the family literary magazine, it dramatizes the effects these magazines may have had on their more commercially oriented, late-century successors and their readers. Ohmann writes:

> When the morning mail arrives, on a muggy autumn day in 1895, Mrs. Johnson . . . comes down from the sewing room and . . . picks up the October issue of *Munsey's Magazine.* . . . [She consults her] favorite departments: "The World of Music," "Literary Chat," "In the Public Eye" . . . and, with more of a sense of duty than of pleasure, "Artists and Their Work." She especially looks forward to the hour she will spend tonight with the final installment of Robert McDonald's "A Princess and a Woman" (dashing Americans now caught up in a Carpathian intrigue). And during the month, she will return to the magazine for other fiction, including a new serial. . . . She will carefully read the article on the Strauss family . . . duly noting that "Americans hold Strauss and his music in great esteem." . . . This kind of information helps her find her bearings in a cultural landscape that she knows mainly through magazines and those friends who belong to it by birth and education. (1–2)

This illustration is interesting for its emphasis on the prominent role magazines played in women's intellectual development even at the end of the nineteenth century. In addition to providing entertainment, family literary magazines were a primary source of the formation of women's identities as readers: These magazines self-consciously packaged themselves as tools to help women become culturally literate, to become better literacy instructors for their families, and to become proper middle-class citizens.

The new genre of the family literary magazine was distinctly unlike women's magazines such as the *Englishwoman's Domestic Magazine* or *Good Housekeeping*.[11] Whereas domestic magazines articulated women's proper roles as housewives by providing articles on decorating, cooking, and household management, family literary magazines produced an image of the proper woman reader as a symbol of national health and vitality. Instead of teaching women to be proper consumers of products as domestic magazines did, family magazines taught women to become proper readers and to represent themselves as tasteful, middle-class citizens without engaging in the alarming rhetoric of feminine corruption and cultural decline. While women's magazines wanted to cure women's bodies with products and advice, family literary magazines wanted to cure the nation's cultural anxiety by presenting positive images of women readers.

Family literary magazines were thus a hybrid genre—appealing to women not solely through domesticity but also through literary values that the proper woman reader could use to advance the cultural status of her nation. As Mary Poovey argues, the idea of the proper woman "was critical to the image of the English national character, which hoped to legitimize both England's sense of moral superiority and the imperial ambitions this superiority underwrote" (9). Poovey contends that the Victorian ideal of womanhood—to which the ideal of the proper woman reader was intimately connected—served to depoliticize class differences by focusing on moral and psychological differences among classes and by subsuming all individuals into a representative Englishman or Englishwoman (ibid.). Although women's proper moral and domestic behavior was implicit in the family magazines, the spotlight was on their countrywomen's literary taste and cultural sensibility as a means of justifying the cultural superiority of the nation. Indeed, the act of reading was promoted in such magazines as a means of nation building as readers interacted with, internalized, and embodied the national cultural values that emerged from their reading.

As embodiments of national cultural taste, family literary magazines also followed in the footsteps of Mudie's Select Circulating Library, which characterized itself as a surrogate parent who would

15

choose proper reading material for the family, thus easing the worry of actual parents, who could rest assured that whatever their family members were reading from Mudie's would be moral and wholesome.[12] Family literary magazines marketed themselves as miniature select libraries that contained material appropriate for the entire family that was still stimulating for male readers. However, these magazines did not merely dictate what was appropriate reading material; instead, they encouraged readers to use the magazine's contents to develop their own abilities to choose good literature. It was not only the contents of family literary magazines that were important, but also their physical presence as decorative objects in the home. Barbara Quinn Schmidt contends that bound volumes of these magazines, seen as guaranteed repositories of suitability and good taste, were prominently displayed as signs of social status in middle-class households ("Novelists" 142). Women who purchased such magazines signified their individual literary taste, their family status, and the cultural superiority of the nation. It is no coincidence that many of these magazines, including the *Cornhill, Temple Bar, Belgravia, St. James's,* and *St. Paul's,* took the names of particular areas of London. In England and America—where magazines like *Harper's* and *Putnam's* were among the first to seek truly national rather than regional audiences—the family literary magazine became a geographical signifier of the nation's capital of culture. These magazines confidently placed the responsibility for the dissemination of that culture on the shoulders of the nation's women.

Since the publicly acceptable rationale for women's education was to prepare them to teach their children properly, these magazines took on an instructive—but not condescending—persona aimed at women who were learning to be upwardly mobile and culturally literate, middle-class subjects. Part of the great appeal of the family literary magazine was its ability to simultaneously address men and women and upper- and lower-middle-class readers by speaking instructively to those who needed it and confidingly to those who didn't. In other words, the features of these magazines reinforced the middle-class behavior and values of those who belonged to that class and tutored those who were attempting to move into it by speaking authoritatively on middle-class culture with a few nods and winks to those who already knew the ropes. The editors of family literary magazines addressed their readers as a part of this already genteel and educated audience while simultaneously emphasizing the need for readers to become genteel through the magazine's cultural instruction.

Understanding the educational mission of the family literary magazine is crucial to understanding the genre's relationship to women readers, which focuses on increasing women's cultural knowledge and improving their readerly reputations. I examine several articles featured in the *Cornhill* as case studies of the family literary magazine's progressive attitude toward cultural instruction because it is precisely this attitude on which the magazines built to advance the cause of women readers. In the *Cornhill,* William Thackeray compares the cultural role of the family literary magazine to that of a connoisseur who watches over the reader's shoulder, educating the reader "to admire rightly" because an "uninstructed person in a museum or at a concert may pass without recognizing a picture or a passage of music, which the connoisseur by his side may show him is a masterpiece of harmony, or a wonder of artistic skill" ("Nil Nisi Bonum," February 1860, 133). Thackeray and other editors of family literary magazines shaped their periodicals as interpreters of culture, but they also intended them to be important instruments in the spread of culture. This goal is stated in a *Cornhill* article on "The National Gallery" (March 1860), in which the magazine introduces its own economical plan for a gallery renovation that would present the nation's best art in the most attractive manner and, more importantly, make it accessible to the greatest number of people, thereby promoting "a taste for art throughout the kingdom" (355). In this case the family literary magazine becomes a strong advocate for cultural experiences that are beyond its pages and that extend its own project of bringing culture to the vast range of the middle classes, particularly to women. Likewise, in articles such as "Amateur Music" (July 1863), the *Cornhill* advocates the "cultivation of music as a recreation" for all classes. This article argues that musical enrichment would allow the nation's culture to thrive by "striking its roots down lower in the social scale" and thus enabling "its topmost branches" to become "widened and strengthened" (93). The *Cornhill,* an exemplar for the genre, not only disseminated culture, but also interpreted it and, in its view, strengthened it by including new audiences.

However, there are some indications of the genre's ambivalence toward the spread of culture to the masses. In "The Opera 1833–1863" (September 1863), for example, the *Cornhill* acknowledged that some loss of prestige and distinction given to the cultural elite would inevitably occur once access to culture was widened. Still, the magazine maintained that glory to the nation as a capitol of culture and the knowledge and appreciation of music (or any other form of cultural enrichment) provided benefits that outweighed the costs (295). In accordance with this view, *Harper's* featured articles on American architecture and landscapes as well as monthly reports on current cultural events; *Belgravia* ran a series on parks and monuments of London; and *Victoria* included essays on art exhibits, theaters, and other "public entertainments." The family literary magazines in this study reveal their awareness of the arguments against a widespread cultural education but nevertheless support such a mission, especially as it applied to the improvement of women and the middle classes. Family literary magazines not only advocated improved cultural knowledge for a wide audience, they also unabashedly promoted themselves as the perfect educational handbooks for those who desired to obtain that knowledge in an accessible way.

As cultural experiences were made available to a wider (female) audience, these magazines also helped to manufacture middle-class taste. In the *Cornhill,* the vast array of articles on taste, when taken in their context alongside numerous explorations of the British military, parliament, and the strength of the nation, become nationalistic arguments to improve British culture as a means of maintaining the nation's position as the greatest country in the world. Articles on etiquette, homes, furniture, fashion, and makeup repeatedly emphasize simplicity and understated elegance as a way to combat the ostentatious display of status, replacing vulgar consumerism with economy and simplicity, which are established as the sober and realistic standards of middle-class taste. Prominent among such articles is Richard Doyle's series "Bird's-Eye View of Society" (April 1861–October 1862). Doyle's humorous commentaries and their accompanying foldout illustrations are "intended chiefly for the information of country cousins, intelligent foreigners, and other remote persons; also young ladies and gentlemen growing up, and not yet out" (April 1861, 497). These miniature guidebooks expostulate on parties, balls, charity bazaars, art shows, seaside escapades, horse races, and music concerts, reminding readers of proper and improper behavior and attire for such public events. According to Andrew Blake, the *Cornhill* "celebrated the promotion of the middle class into new influence, and welcomed changes in behavior that accompanied this" (96). Doyle's "Bird's-Eye" views and family literary magazines generally anticipated and encouraged behavior that would benefit both the middle classes and women. To this end *Harper's* linked its cultural and educational commentary to a sense of middle-class nationalism that would be enacted by women; *Belgravia* featured numerous articles on fashion, health, and beauty to ease the assimilation of the upwardly mobile woman and maintain the civility of the middle class; and *Victoria* offered alternative ways for middle-class women to acceptably enter and participate in the male-dominated public sphere for the benefit of the nation. Thus, family literary magazines attempted to initiate newcomers as they constructed rules for maintaining a middle-class lifestyle that would be beneficial to women readers and the nation.

By presenting themselves as proper purveyors of culture, family literary magazines defied many reviewers in the cultural elite who saw periodicals as initiators of the downfall of the nation's literature. To counter this negative press, the *Cornhill* linked its own status to important periodicals of the past. In "The Four Georges" Thackeray claims that reading magazines such as the *Spectator* and the *Tatler* is the best way to learn about the culture of the eighteenth century: "In the company of that charming guide, we may go to the opera, the comedy, the puppet show, the auction, even the cockpit" to relive the past (July 1860, 18). If eighteenth-century magazines are so filled with historical fruits, why shouldn't those of the current century also be considered valuable, Thackeray implicitly asks. Another *Cornhill* article, titled "Journalism," goes beyond arguing that magazines are valuable historical artifacts to proclaim their status as a part of contemporary literature: "Journalism will, no doubt, occupy the first or one of the first places in any future literary history of the present times" (July 1862, 52). Likewise, "A Memorial of Thackeray's School Days" provides readers with a chronicle of the importance of periodicals to that great writer's education, describing how he and his friends pooled their spending money to subscribe to magazines such as *Blackwood's,* the *New Monthly Magazine,* and the *London Magazine:*

> It is uncertain what college tutors or schoolmasters may think of magazine reading for their pupils; to the set of whom I am now speaking my belief is that it was most advantageous, and that it proved to be a very strong stimulus of literary curiosity and ambition. The constantly fresh monthly and weekly supply of short articles seemed to bring home the fact of literary production, and made it appear, in some degree, within reach. (January 1865, 126)

Thus, the *Cornhill* presented itself as more than an educator of cultural values; it promoted itself as the inspiration for (as well as the instrument of) great cultural productions. *Harper's* and *Victoria,* with their unabashed reprints of articles from other magazines, and

Belgravia, with its strident defense of the value of newspapers and periodicals, also contributed to the elevation of periodical literature as a whole and of the family literary magazine in particular as a vital literary resource for the nation.

Just as important and intimately linked to its cultural value was the family literary magazine's defense of women readers. All of the magazines in this study repeatedly positioned themselves in opposition to the elite reviews, most notably the *Saturday Review,* which had a reputation for being dismissive toward women readers. For example, in "The Sharpshooters of the Press" (February 1863), the *Cornhill* goes so far as to blame some male journalists' belief in the innate inferiority of women on their personal shortcomings: "They cannot escape their fate—though it is such a hard one—to be unsuccessful with women, and to write as if they were so" (242). The author goes on to argue that such journalists "question the reality of women's virtue, arraign their motives, ridicule their tastes, and dictate to them in what mode or under what condition they shall be allowed to employ or amuse themselves, and at what season, and in what fashion they shall perform certain feminine affairs" as a way of controlling and belittling them (241). Though *Belgravia* and *Victoria* make the most overt and consistent attempts to support women readers by attacking other magazines and their prominent reviewers, family literary magazines are generally serious about defending women as intellectually capable members of its reading public by offering positive images of intellectual women readers in their featured poetry, fiction, nonfiction, and illustrations. Even though these magazines asserted that women should be empowered to read a wide variety of texts and trusted that women's reading could be critical and productive, they diverged in their views of what would be obtained by women's reading as well as in the degree to which they accepted the independence of women to read without regulation or supervision.

In chapter 1, I examine the transatlantic cross-fertilization of the family literary magazine by looking at the ways in which the American *Harper's Magazine* first formed itself out of "pirated" scraps from British periodicals and then maintained transatlantic relationships that established the family literary magazine as a viable commodity in both America and England. This chapter discusses *Harper's* suggestion that American women readers use the literature it reprinted from British periodicals to teach their families higher standards of literary taste that would allow them to play a role in establishing a nation capable of producing its own literature. I contend that *Harper's* promoted the British realist novel as a high cultural text suitable for middle-class women readers, who would instruct their families in proper literary taste and thereby lay the groundwork for the development of a new generation of writers able to create a distinctly American literature. The magazine thus, surprisingly, used British literature to forge a patriotic American message. *Harper's* made clear the relevance of the domestic realm to the success of public culture and allowed women to play a vital role in the development of America's identity by passing knowledge on to their children.

Beginning with an examination of one of the most popular magazines of the nineteenth century allows me to place the genre of the family literary magazine within a transnational context that not only increases its significance as a literary form but also illustrates that transatlantic literary relationships were more reciprocal than it is often assumed. This chapter also reveals the roots of the magazine genre in the nationalistic goals of the growing middle classes, who were struggling to construct a coherent identity through literary culture. Indeed, as Frank Luther Mott claims, *Harper's* "immediately and profoundly" affected "the whole course of development of the American magazine" (3). My study of *Harper's* shows that it affected the course of the development of the British magazine just as profoundly. The connections among national identity, literary culture, and women readers established in *Harper's* are central to the genre of the family literary magazine in both America and England.

Chapter 2 illustrates the ways in which the *Cornhill,* the most reputable and critically revered of the family literary magazines, inherited *Harper's* agenda by consistently depicting women as domestic readers who were guided in their reading choices by the magazine itself and who read for the benefit of their families. However, the *Cornhill* went beyond *Harper's* more traditional arguments urging women to pass on their intellectual abilities to the next generation. I argue that the magazine advocated women's formal education—and, to a lesser degree, women's movement into the professions—as a means of assisting the development of the newly defined "professional gentleman," who was emerging as the leader of the British nation. In the context provided by the *Cornhill,* a woman who learned to read properly would participate in both self-improvement and nation building as she learned to follow particular codes of conduct that would ensure the cultural dominance of the middle class. If middle-class women were allowed to be educated or to work to support themselves, the magazine suggested, middle-class men would be free to distinguish themselves in their professions, consolidate their wealth, and increase the power of the class and the nation before entering into a costly and attention-diverting marriage. Thus, for the *Cornhill,* women's reading was vital to the dominance of the middle classes. The *Cornhill* is crucial to any examination of the family literary magazine because it set the standard upon which the genre was modeled throughout the 1860s, when it emerged as a powerful force in London's literary marketplace.

In chapter 3, I discuss the ways in which *Belgravia Magazine* worked to counteract negative images of women readers by providing them with the autonomy to both enjoy and learn from what many critics saw as a scandalous fictional form, the sensation novel. This magazine built itself on the foundation laid by the *Cornhill,* but sought to radicalize the *Cornhill*'s message by introducing pleasure as an important consideration in deciding what to read as well as by insisting that women's reading be considered separately from the ways it could benefit the family. Editor Mary Elizabeth Braddon not only defied critics who disparaged women readers and the form of the sensation novel, she also overtly encouraged women to choose their own books and read for their own reasons. *Belgravia* worked to transform attitudes toward women readers and popular literature first by imagining the woman reader as active, independent, and informed and second by redefining the genre of the sensation novel as realistic, artistic, and instructive. I maintain that while Braddon may not have been the best spokesperson for legitimizing women's independence as readers of sensation novels due to her own personal and professional scandals, her voice was important because it promoted women's independence as readers and broke through the predominantly moralistic critical discourse to claim that reading could be personally fulfilling for women without being dangerous. *Belgravia* marks a notable milestone in the development of the family literary magazine because it was one of the few and the most notorious periodicals edited by a woman. *Belgravia* provided a strong defense of women readers and revolutionized the parameters of reading, allowing women to partake of the private pleasure that the other family literary magazines sought to transform into a public duty performed on behalf of one's class and nation.

Finally, chapter 4 delineates *Victoria Magazine*'s establishment of a feminist tradition of literary criticism that promoted women's reading by encouraging them to become writers and critics who could contribute to the creation and definition as well as the consumption of literary culture. This magazine realized the progressive ideal of the woman reader that the other family literary magazines only imagined.

Victoria established a real community of intellectual women readers who became editors, printers, and contributors to a family literary magazine that overtly promoted a feminist agenda. Together, Emily Faithfull, Emily Davies, and the working women at Victoria Press produced a politically motivated literary magazine that both envisioned and created alternative roles for middle-class women. Using Queen Victoria as a model of women's ability to be powerful public figures and proper wives and mothers, the magazine urged women to enter public culture by reading and writing in ways that allowed them to participate in the most important issues of the day. *Victoria* is a significant family literary magazine because it pushed a nascent feminist social agenda more boldly than any of the other magazines while demonstrating the results of that agenda in its pages. From developing a feminist criticism to hiring women writers to printing the magazine at a woman-run press, this periodical engaged women in the process of producing a literary culture amenable to their vision of a society in which they were equal partners with men in guiding the progress of the middle class.

Belgravia and *Victoria* made more radical statements regarding the relationship of women to literary (and not so literary) texts, but *Harper's* and the *Cornhill* each had a more dominant voice in the period and serve as a more typical gauge of the alternative public image of the much-maligned woman reader. Though *Harper's* provided an influential model for the genre that was developed by the *Cornhill* and its competitors, the *Cornhill* was the most prestigious of these periodicals. The *Cornhill* did not suffer the intense criticism that *Harper's* faced from its competitors for reprinting much of its contents from British magazines (a practice that had also established Harper and Brothers as a mainstay of American publishing). The *Cornhill's* prestige was linked to the fact that it was issued by the respectable Smith, Elder, and Company, edited by the revered William Thackeray, and featured novels written by critically acclaimed authors such as George Eliot, Elizabeth Gaskell, and Anthony Trollope. *Belgravia,* on the other hand, was issued by the maverick publisher John Maxwell and managed by Braddon, whose reputation as the "queen of the sensation novel" and illicit relationship with Maxwell garnered critical disrespect. Braddon's magazine also showcased her own sensational novels as well as stories by other, lessknown writers that did little to improve the magazine's image. Likewise, *Victoria's* lack of "quality" literary material and its position within the protofeminist Langham Place Circle detracted from its power and prestige among the general population. Thus, the publishers, editors, and contributors determined the reputation of each magazine and had a

23

profound effect on its construction of the proper woman reader. While the more marginalized *Belgravia* and *Victoria* were positioned to take risks in transforming images of women readers by appealing to women's personal pleasure and social self-interest, the more reputable *Harper's* and *Cornhill* took progressive, but safe, routes to promote and recruit women readers. In providing analyses of these four magazines, I explore a class of underread and uncategorized literary periodicals that shed new light on the dynamics of gender and reading. Analyzing the methods these magazines use to defend women readers is my primary goal in the chapters that follow. However, I also explain how the family literary magazine's concept of the woman reader is linked to its definitions of high and low culture. As a result, a brief introductory discussion of these categories—as they manifested themselves in the magazines in terms of realism, sensationalism, and sentimentalism—is necessary.

Realism and Cultural Authority in Family Literary Magazines

As documents that claimed cultural authority, family literary magazines could not avoid participating in the broader critical discussions of what constituted high culture. While it is often assumed that the important literary debates about high and low culture were taking place in high-brow journals, family literary magazines participated in defining the same critical terms under discussion in the elite reviews in which criticism was being professionalized. These cultural debates were focused on the definition of realism, which varied from one critic—and one magazine—to the next. Generally speaking, the term was applied to domestic novels about middle-class families that were considered to have an appropriately moral message, that achieved an acceptable level of verisimilitude, and that focused on character development over plot. Often, however, realism was conceptualized as more "ideal" than "real." Realist works were expected to paint a picture of life that seemed "true" in its details but that required its main characters to serve as moral role models for middle-class audiences. In *The Realistic Imagination,* George Levine argues that such a conception of realism allowed nineteenth-century authors—and the critics who touted realism as equivalent to high culture—to claim "special authority" for themselves. Levine claims that:

Realists take upon themselves a special role as mediator, and assume self-consciously a moral burden that takes a special form: their responsibility is to a reality that increasingly seems "unnamable" . . . [and] to an audience that requires to be weaned or freed from the misnaming literatures past and current. The quest for the world beyond words is deeply moral, suggesting the need to reorganize experience and reinvest it with value for a new audience reading from a new base of economic power. (9–12)

The slippery nature of realism is, in part, a result of its function as both a descriptive term to define a genre of fiction and a signifier of the author's and critic's own professional power to shape middle-class values. Definitions of realism were reliant not only on the aesthetic and moral elements of a work of fiction, but also on its constructions of the emerging middle-class subject.

The authority that realism signaled was played out in gendered terms as well. Men were more likely to be designated as realist writers, while women were relegated to lower cultural forms. Even women writers who focused on representing detailed depictions of domestic life were often categorized as practitioners of "detailism." The excessive use of detail was cited by many critics as a sign of women's inability to do anything other than copy in minute detail what they saw around them. As Lyn Pykett argues in *The Improper Feminine,* the predominance of a "gendered critical discourse" perpetuated two main ways of viewing women's writing either as "a world of surfaces and sympathy–or as a riot of detail and promiscuous emotion" (27). Women who attempted to conform to the high form of realism were often dismissed for their superficiality, while women who wrote sensational or sentimental fiction were seen to be lost in details of a more bodily and disruptive kind. Although realism was defined in relation to what was usually conceived of as its opposite, growing out of what Alison Byerly calls realism's "impulse to contradict" (4), the forms that were defined in opposition to realism were often discussed as exaggerations of realistic techniques that encouraged excessive emotions and/or immoral behavior.[13]

Pamela K. Gilbert contends that delineating genres such as realism, sensationalism, and sentimentalism is equivalent to endorsing "a set of reading instructions" that "critics, publishers, authors, and readers will enforce" as they read, thereby ignoring certain qualities of a work in order to classify it (59). While both sensational and sentimental fiction incorporated realistic traits, works containing sensational and sentimental elements were delimited by their genre's position as realism's low cultural opposite. Even though accepted realist writers could incorporate sensational or sentimental techniques, those who were designated as sensationalists or sentimentalists had a harder time escaping their generic confines. Within the logic of the typical nineteenth-century review, then, the following qualities were constructed and perpetuated as inherent to high and low cultural forms:

High Culture	Low Culture
Masculine	Feminine
Realistic	Sensational or sentimental
Idealistic	Hyperrealistic ("detailism")
Cerebral	Physical
Artistic	Market driven
Represents proper female characters	Represents aggressive and criminal or suffering heroines
Emphasizes character over plot	Emphasizes plot over character
Emphasizes the moral strength of the middle classes	Blurs class distinctions

While these qualities are broadly generalized, they suggest what Nancy Glazener argues: that defining realism against sensationalism and sentimentalism is at bottom misogynist, male dominated, and embroiled "in class hierarchy and the consolidation of white bourgeois cultural privilege" (146).[14]

Indeed, defining realism seems just as ideological and politically charged today as it was 150 years ago. In *Narrating Reality,* Harry Shaw provides an overview of twentieth-century critical discussions of realism that forgo praising the form for its moral and artistic authority, but employ it "as a scapegoat genre that helps [critics] affirm values they find antithetical to the values they impute to it" (11). According to Shaw, realism has been disparaged for the same reason it was praised in the nineteenth century—because it "supposedly attempts to make the world of the bourgeoisie seem 'natural' and 'full,'" representing the world in a totalizing way that refuses to admit that it offers only one *version* of reality (9–10). On the other hand, it has been championed for "its *refusal* to totalize" (11). Shaw indicts critics such as Georg Lukács, Roland Barthes, Terry Eagleton, Michel Foucault, and Mikhail Bakhtin for ignoring the experiences of actual readers as they define realism to suit their own political purposes. Like the family literary magazines that championed the power of readers over nineteenth-century critics, Shaw complains that twentieth-century critics have followed the tradition of the previous century by dismissing readers as "chumps" who are overcome by some sort of "mass hypnosis" and cannot make appropriate reading choices on their own (33–34). In the nineteenth century, realism was a socially and politically driven category used to signify a moral and educated readership that had critically shunned dangerous, low cultural forms; in the twentieth century it became a socially and politically driven category used to signify the complacency of the unthinking masses captivated by a false and lulling sense of reality. In each case, realism has been crucial to defining how culture works in society. Shaw's goal is uncannily similar to that of family literary magazines: Both defend the supposedly unknowing reader against the supposedly knowing critic by questioning the efficacy of the divisions between high and low cultural forms.

Family literary magazines embraced women readers and both high and low cultural forms. Instead of presenting women as objects for critics to protect and guide, family literary magazines imagined them as subjects who were initiated into critical discussions in which they became full participants. These magazines generally asserted that reading low cultural forms was entertaining and harmless even as they asked their readers to prove that they were savvy enough to know the difference between entertaining and edifying literature. In his lecture "On English Prose Fiction as a Rational Amusement," Anthony Trollope—who edited the family literary magazine *St. Paul's*—articulates the common attitude toward high and low culture in family literary magazines. He contends that "a novel is bound to be both sensational and realistic. And I think that if a novel fail in either particular it is, so far, a failure in Art. . . . Truth let there be;–truth of description, truth of character, human truth as to men and women, if there be such truth I do not know that a novel can be too sensational" (123–24). Trollope recognizes the critical binaries between realistic and sensational novels but attempts to destroy what he characterizes as false divisions that obscure the ability of both novels and magazines to teach "lessons of life . . . from the first page to the last," especially if they deal with "the false and the forward, as well as with the good and gracious" (110). The significance of these ideals to family literary magazines becomes even clearer when combined with Trollope's support for the same kind of integrated audiences family magazines promoted. Trollope argues that "he who condemns the reading of novels for his daughter, should condemn it for his son;

27

and that he who condemns it for his children should condemn it for himself" (107). He thereby refutes the focus on women as highly corruptible readers whose cultural consumption should be regulated more stringently. In his refusal to blindly uphold cultural divisions and to use women as a rationale for the profession of literary criticism, Trollope espouses the philosophy of the magazines in this study.

While family literary magazines followed elite reviewers by setting up common critical binaries, they did not uphold them in practice. Rather, the critical oppositions served as a means to articulate cultural authority while the magazines actually conveyed that the divisions between the high and the low, the masculine and the feminine, were more permeable, blurred, and mutually constitutive. In other words, family literary magazines engaged with the terminology of the binary critical system while subtly refuting it. These binaries collapsed as family literary magazines instigated genre trouble by inviting women readers to judge literature for themselves, thus denying this as the sole right of critics. At the same time "Victorians were struggling to name and classify, to define and enclose" the world (Bernstein, "Ape Anxiety" 267), family literary magazines resisted strict classifications, definitions, and enclosures.

My analysis of *Harper's* illustrates how the false binary between realism and sentimentalism, upheld by its editors in an effort to teach literary taste to its readers, is blurred by the magazine's concomitant attempts to convince the public that it was a nationalist periodical. The magazine's desire to increase its patriotic profile and appeal to women readers led to its inclusion of many sentimental tales by American writers. The collapse of the high/low cultural boundaries *Harper's* theoretically endorsed culminated in the magazine's focus on Charles Dickens—a writer who represents the intermingling of reason and fancy, realism and sentimentality, the high and the low—as the ultimate exemplar of a respectable literary culture. I argue that the dual narrators of Dickens's *Bleak House* duplicate the competing editorial voices within *Harper's* itself that simultaneously maintained and blurred the high/low cultural boundaries. The sentimental female voice of Esther Summerson thus parallels *Harper's* nationalistic and feminine appeals to its readers while the "objective" observations of the omniscient narrator coincide with the authoritative voice of *Harper's* editors, who advocated realism as a literary model for Americans to follow.

Similarly, the *Cornhill* set up a false opposition between fact and fiction that paralleled the opposition between high and low culture. However, in practice, the opposition was collapsed. With William

Thackeray as its driving editorial force, the magazine recommended an educational diet of reading that stressed the need for "nourishing facts" to balance out its "fictional sweets." However, the *Cornhill*'s promotion of realist novels as educational tools that would allow readers to arrive at some new understanding of "fact," or real life as it is lived, and of factual articles that held their readers' interest by including fictional elements such as dream sequences and dialogues made it difficult to distinguish between the two forms. The *Cornhill*'s theoretical elevation of fact/realism is further complicated by its contention that sensation novels, while highly "unreal," were valuable sources of entertainment as long as readers could distinguish between the two opposing forms. In other words, the *Cornhill* proposed simple distinctions between high and low culture that it argued were not ultimately as important as the informed choices made by readers who understood the differences between the cultural forms but did not allow their reading practices to be dominated by those differences.

In *Belgravia Magazine,* Mary Elizabeth Braddon engaged with the same critical binaries as she attempted to debunk them, interacting with and confounding the dominant critical discourse that constructed the sensation novel as the opposite of the realist novel. Braddon's magazine counteracted the rampant fear of sensation fiction as a sign of an infectious, mass-produced low culture dispersed primarily through railway newsstands. Instead of presenting sensationalism as a threat to the nation and to high literary culture, *Belgravia* allied it with a high cultural tradition descending from writers like Sophocles and Shakespeare. In fact, Braddon claimed that sensationalism was a new form of realism that was ultimately more artistic and more effective than the idealized domestic narratives that critics typically praised. *Belgravia* overtly attempted to overturn the cultural boundaries that other family literary magazines questioned more subtly.

Finally, in Emily Faithfull's *Victoria Magazine,* the strict separation between the high and the low was reinstated in order to establish an authoritative, feminist critical voice. In other words, the magazine's protofeminist critics, led by Emily Davies, fell in line with elite critics (despite expressing overt disdain for their dismissal of women writers) in order to legitimize their own promotion of women authors and their redefinition of realism to include a focus on positive portrayals of female characters that served as role models for the emerging "new woman." Despite *Victoria*'s sometimes elitist critical stance, which more boldly attacked sensation fiction than did other magazines of the genre, the magazine's poor financial situation led to the inclusion of sensation tales much like those it rejected in its criticism. However, I argue that *Victoria* purposely published what its editors saw as a tamed or domesticated sensationalism that adhered to its feminist and high cultural values. Thus, *Victoria,* like the other family literary magazines, used realism as a means of establishing its literary authority, while advocating the legitimacy of low cultural forms that adhered to its feminist literary values.

Family literary magazines succeeded in establishing the authority of middle-brow culture and in empowering women readers to participate in important literary debates that would determine the standards of culture for years to come. These magazines were active and powerful defenders of women readers in the nineteenth-century press, though their voices may not have been the dominant ones. Women may have been "edged out" by the professionalization of literary criticism, the corporatization of the publishing industry, and the establishment of English as an academic discipline, but family literary magazines contributed significantly to creating a social climate in which women's formal education was on its way to becoming standard for middle-class women by the turn of the century. Though these magazines were not overtly political in nature, they participated in a wide public debate that affected the intellectual lives of women for years to come. Because of magazines like *Harper's,* the *Cornhill, Belgravia,* and *Victoria,* women's growing intellectual abilities and independent reading practices became less controversial and more acceptable as an inevitable part of societal progress. As Kelly J. Mays declares, while "reading may have been forever lost as an art in the nineteenth century, it had been simultaneously gained as both a discipline and a profession" (185). Those who defined the discipline and the profession were often preoccupied with the effects of literary culture on women. The family literary magazines featured in the following chapters are crucial for their documentation of an alternative relationship between literary authorities and women readers.

—→⟹ 1 ⟸←—

PIRACY AND THE PATRIOTIC
WOMAN READER

Making British Literature American in
Harper's New Monthly Magazine, 1850–1855

DURING THE EARLY NINETEENTH century, most books sold in the United States were foreign imports or copies. At an 1834 book trade sale, for example, of the 114 fiction books printed in America, 95 were English reprints (Exman, *Brothers Harper* 50). A reliance on British literature was facilitated by the lack of an international copyright law and what Laurel Brake has called "a vestigial, high cultural value attached to the ejected imperial power" (106). However, America's nascent publishing industry was also shaped by what Meredith McGill refers to in *American Literature and the Culture of Reprinting* as a "Jacksonian resistance to centralized development" that kept the nation's book production system dispersed (109). This decentralization compounded and reinforced the young nation's lack of a strong literary identity and led to its reliance on imports from Great Britain for literary sustenance. British novels easily filled the bill for this decentralized system of publishers who struggled to survive by printing what was well known and had a ready audience of consumers. American magazines were no exception: They took the culture of reprinting even further by adapting a wide variety of British publications for their own purposes. Despite a growing sense of literary nationalism that was emerging at mid-century, McGill contends that reprinting was the cultural norm for most of the century and was even considered to be proof of an enlightened democracy because it produced affordable books for the general public and avoided monopolistic publishing practices. In fact, opponents of an international copyright agreement defined the manufacturing and dissemination of texts as America's primary cultural role, not the creation of original literature (95). *Harper's New Monthly Magazine* is the quintessential example of a literary endeavor that sought to adapt British literature to the establishment of a healthy and egalitarian publishing empire in the United States.[1]

That *Harper's* was strongly influenced by British literature is evident to anyone who skims its pages, which are brimming with articles copied directly from British periodicals and with novels written by British authors. *Harper's* popularized novel serialization in America in a monthly format at the same time Dickens's weekly magazine *Household Words* was successfully serializing novels for middle-class families in England. Dickens's magazine served as an important model and a valuable resource for literary material that was copied directly into *Harper's* pages. However, *Harper's* altered Dickens's weekly magazine formula by adding lavish illustrations, increasing the amount of material, calling attention to its own cultural superiority, and appealing more overtly to the pride of middle-class readers who would be able to express their class status by purchasing the magazine. While Dickens changed the reputation of weeklies by including high-quality fiction in *Household Words* and later in *All the Year Round,* his magazines still appeared to be more like cheap newspapers with narrow columns of print and no illustrations. Thus, *Harper's* essentially became the first family literary magazine by building on, borrowing from, and transforming British literary sources. McGill suggests that "the transnational status of reprinted texts makes it difficult for us to assimilate them into national literary narratives." As a result, critics have tended to "sift through" relics of a reprint culture looking "for signs of an original, national difference," rather than assessing "the ways in which foreign literature is repackaged and redeployed" (2–3). For McGill, it is crucial to see the predominance of reprinting in America as a culture rather than a barrier to culture. In this chapter I keep this in mind as I examine how *Harper's* successfully repackaged and redeployed British literature for a nationalistic purpose, thereby participating in the nation's transformation from a culture of reprinting to a culture of authorial originality and nationality.

While *Harper's* mimicked the survival techniques that many American publishing houses used in the eighteenth and early-nineteenth centuries, its preoccupation with creating a national literary identity out of "pirated" scraps of British periodicals signals a transition from national dependence on British culture to a more patriotic devotion to elevating the status of American literature during the 1850s.[2] As literary nationalism rose, so did more centralized and nationalized systems of publication. Harper and Brothers was one of the first national publishers, and *Harper's* was intended to be a national–and not just a regional–magazine. Through what seems an unlikely appeal for a publication famous for its literary piracy, *Harper's* editors forged a patriotic message addressed primarily to women readers. While the magazine valued British novelists such as Edward Bulwer-Lytton, Charles Dickens, and William Thackeray over American writers, its focus on British authors was rhetorically constructed as nationalistic. The editors theorized that by providing the public with these examples of "excellent," high cultural texts, the magazine would raise the standards of American readers and in turn raise the quality of American literature. Thus, *Harper's* urged its women readers to nurture the next generation of native readers with the British literary models it provided so that they would eventually have the skills to both recognize and create a distinctly tasteful American literary culture.

My argument coincides with McGill's claim that "Reprint publishers frequently acknowledged nationalist aims, using foreign texts to refract an image of the nation as a whole that was seemingly impossible to produce by domestic means alone" (20–21). Foreign texts, McGill claims, offered neutrality during a time of sectional division and thereby became indispensable to creating a unified national identity (24). However, while McGill sees *Harper's* as a prime example of reprint culture and its rival *Putnam's* as a magazine devoted to the sensibility of nationalism, I argue that *Harper's* was actually able to straddle these two modes to produce a new periodical format that was not merely eclectic and cosmopolitan, but focused and nationalistic.[3] In the midst of developing its patriotic message based on the cultural logic of reprinting, which treated reprinted British works as reconstituted American texts, *Harper's* managed to adapt British material into a new genre of magazine that would travel back across the Atlantic to become a model for the most popular periodical format in 1860s England, the family literary magazine. Examining *Harper's* within the context of the emergence of a new magazine genre thus complicates the standard notion of transatlantic exchange that assumes a one-way flow of ideas from Britain to America rather than a reciprocal trade.[4] My study of the first five years of *Harper's* shows that while it borrowed from and even revered British culture, it also influenced the development of that culture. In *Atlantic Double-Cross*, Robert Weisbuch argues that the widely accepted idea that Americans had no real culture typically elicited an "aggressive, parodic response" to British literature from American writers (15). *Harper's,* in contrast, called for the reverence of British models as a means of helping Americans produce something new without engaging in aggressive competition with their counterparts across the Atlantic. Surprisingly, this precarious project did produce something new, an influential magazine genre.

In England, *Harper's* was familiar to the most prominent authors of the period, whose works were serialized in its pages. It was also known by major publishers who saw *Harper's* as a successful example of how to use an in-house magazine as an advertising forum for a company's publications. *Harper's* became increasingly influential in London publishing circles with its astounding success in America, and its parent company's development of successful publication deals with British writers such as Wilkie Collins, Dinah Mulock Craik, George Eliot, and Charles Reade. The model relationship between publisher and magazine set forth by Harper and Brothers led the way for the development of a healthy trade in family literary magazines in London a decade after *Harper's* had proven itself as a profitable endeavor that was publicly embraced as an authoritative cultural arbiter. The overwhelming success of *Harper's* and of family literary magazines that followed it eventually led Harper and Brothers to launch a successful British version of the famous magazine in 1880, which shared most of its contents with the American version.[5] The invasion of *Harper's* onto British soil led the London *Bookseller* to voice its fear that the success of Harper and Brothers would put an American company at the head of England's publishing industry (Exman, *House of Harper* 160–61). While this anxiety proved groundless, it was *Harper's* emphasis on transatlantic connections that prompted its unprecedented success in America and that facilitated the migration of the family literary magazine to England. Those transatlantic connections and the magazine's promotion of them therefore warrant a closer examination than they have yet received.

In order to understand how *Harper's* achieved such powerful transatlantic influence, it is necessary to trace its origins and its rise to dominance at home, where it was the most successful magazine in America between 1850 and 1855. Published at the beginning of the American industrial age, *Harper's* rose to prominence in part by featuring some of the earliest electroplate images in the nation and being produced at one of the country's first steam-powered presses, located at Harper and Brothers headquarters in New York (Allen 5–11). The magazine's editorial staff also brought status to the endeavor. From 1850 to 1856 *Harper's* was officially edited by the reputable journalist Henry J.

Raymond, who also founded the *New York Daily Times* in September 1851. However, one of the Harper brothers, Fletcher Harper, oversaw the magazine until about 1875 (Mott 391). As a result of the collaborative nature of the magazine's editorial control, compounded in this case by the fact that the "Editor's Easy Chair," the "Editor's Drawer," and the monthly "Literary Notices" were all conducted by different subeditors (including "Easy Chair" penmen Donald G. Mitchell and George W. Curtis, "Editor's Drawer" writer Lewis Gaylord Clark, and "Literary Notice" editor George R. Ripley), I often refer to *Harper's* as having a collective voice that reflects its distinct and emerging character and goals rather than the opinions or decisions of one particular leader. As John Gray Laird Dowgray puts it, "There was no real editor," and the problem of "actual responsibility for the contents" is a difficult one to solve (39, 36). While my personification of this magazine—and others mentioned in this book—serves as a convenience that may elide the agency of the editors and writers, it coincides with my view that every periodical has a distinct character that results from a combination of editor, contributor, and reader influence. Furthermore, I like the way this construction of a magazine's agency stresses the collaborative nature of periodicals, in which no single author, originator, editor, or publisher can be identified as having sole responsibility for what emerges as its agenda.[6]

In any case, Fletcher Harper did initially guide *Harper's* format as a middle-class, family literary magazine by cultivating a nonpartisan tone, avoiding political controversy, and emphasizing nationalism over sectionalism on the eve of the Civil War. He defined the noncontroversial periodical as "a popular educator of the general public" that would serve the nation's citizenry while also turning a profit (Perkins 167). To further ensure the broad appeal of the magazine, *Harper's* subscriptions were sold at an affordable, three-dollar yearly subscription rate, or for twenty-five cents an issue. All of these factors helped raise the magazine's circulation from its first run of 7,500 copies in June 1850 to 50,000 copies six months later. Between 1850 and 1865 the magazine's sales averaged an astounding 110,000 copies per issue, prompting *Harper's* competitor *Putnam's* to proclaim that "Probably no magazine in the world was ever so popular or so profitable" ("Harper's Monthly and Weekly," 293). However, the key component to the magazine's success was neither its cost nor its apolitical tone, but its focus on selling British literature to women readers as a patriotic reading endeavor.

Laurel Brake contends that *Harper's* "'transatlantic connection' was first and last economic and commercial" (104). While this is certainly true, *Harper's* elaborately justified the literature that made it into a money-making machine. The magazine not only benefited from the convenience and profitability of publishing British works that had proven their success across the Atlantic, but also canonized them by defining British realist novels, particularly those by Dickens and Thackeray, as examples of high cultural realism appropriate for women readers. For *Harper's,* realism was defined as a particularly British literary form that pointed out the vital impact women could have on public culture while maintaining their traditional domestic roles. Realism was seen as a genre that would effectively teach women to participate in and improve public culture by passing proper taste on to their children, who represented America's literate and literary future. Touting British realism allowed *Harper's* editors to establish themselves as vital public servants worthy of respect. Realism, then, was also equated with the professionalization of literature as a field of study. Nancy Glazener argues that

> The construction of realism as a non-addictive variety of fiction was probably the most important means by which realism was fitted to be an object of connoisseurship. The emotional discipline that differentiated men's cultural consumption from women's also differentiated the cultural consumption of privileged groups from that of people casually lumped together as "lower." Mirroring the imaginative embourgeoisement of realist readers was the professionalization of realist authors, which was supposed to guarantee that they provided healthy, public-spirited, non-addictive works of fiction. (95)

Harper's editors used the category of realism in precisely these ways, legitimizing the magazine and its choice of featured British novelists, ironically, through a discourse emphasizing the national benefits of realism. The taste for realism encouraged by *Harper's* represented sophistication and self-control for readers and professional respect for authors; both of these traits translated into advantages for the development of American literature.

This already complex explanation of *Harper's* construction of the national benefits of British realism is further complicated by the magazine's relationship to American sentimentalism. From its inception *Harper's* struggled to appeal to a wide range of readers, to make a healthy profit, to promote high culture, and to sustain a good reputation within literary circles. The endeavor to unite these contradictory goals among a diverse editorial staff helps to explain the frequently competing voices that emerge within the magazine. The voices motivated by both profit and a strict sense of literary standards exhorted readers to improve their literary taste by reading British realist novels that were defined as gentlemanly, high cultural texts and to indulge sparingly in sentimental American tales that were overtly criticized as feminine embodiments of low culture. British realism and American sentimentalism were repeatedly constructed as gendered opposites in the editorial commentaries, which rendered invisible the female British and male American writers included in the magazine. Though the magazine overtly judged national literatures by the gendered categories of high and low culture, *Harper's* actually included many sentimental stories and articles. In fact, several recent critics characterize *Harper's* tone as overwhelmingly sentimental (see Lea Bertani Vozar Newman, Sheila Post-Lauria, and Laurie Robertson-Lorant). I argue that despite its rhetoric of high culture and its equation of good literature with British realism, in practice *Harper's* supported a melding of the forms of realism and sentimentalism rather than a strict division between the two literary modes. In fact, the magazine's defense of Dickens as the most important realist novelist was predicated on his ability to provide Americans with a guide for the creation of an effective national literature that would not completely eschew sentimentality, but would show writers how to transform an American tradition of sentimentality into a higher cultural form.

A "Good Foreign Magazine": Literary Piracy and the British Origins of Taste

At a time when some American magazines were going to great expense to create a unique American literary identity in what many of the best writers saw as a culturally barren nation, *Harper's* continued to fill its pages with selections from British magazines at virtually no cost. *Harper's* planned to use what others labeled its piratical practices "to place within the reach of the great mass of the American people the unbounded treasures of the periodical literature of the present day" to be sold "at so low a rate . . . that it shall make its way into the hands or the family circle of every intelligent citizen of the United States" ("Advertisement" to Volume I). In this way, *Harper's* participated in and profited from the democratization of print culture that served as the initial nationalistic impulse of the magazine. However, there was another impetus to focus on British fiction: Harper and Brothers had made its fortune publishing inexpensive copies of British novels. The company's successful "Harper's Household Editions," advertised as "uniform, compact, legible, handsome, and cheap," had made the company a brand name associated with the most famous and popular British novelists (*The Archives of Harper and Brothers* B3). The extension of the company's book-publishing skills into the world of magazine publishing was facilitated by building on its popular association with British fiction. During its first five years, all of *Harper's* major serials were British novels later published as "household editions." The company was therefore able to profit twice on works it first serialized and then sold in volume form. By 1855 *Harper's* had showcased three of England's premiere novelists by serializing Edward Bulwer-Lytton's *My Novel, or Varieties in English Life* (October 1850–February 1853), Charles Dickens's *Bleak House* (April 1852–October 1853), and William Thackeray's *The Newcomes* (November 1853–October 1855).

The tone was set for *Harper's* focus on British works when in the introductory note to the first issue the editors declared their intention to "transfer to its pages as rapidly as they may be issued all the continuous tales of Dickens, Bulwer, Croly, Lever, Warren, and other distinguished contributors to British periodicals," which "enlist and absorb much of the literary talent, the native genius, the scholarly accomplishment of the present age" ("A Word at the Start" 2, 1). The editors cite *Blackwood's, Dublin University Magazine,* and the *Edinburgh Review* as sources they will use to provide readers with the "wealth and freshness of the literature of the nineteenth century . . . embodied in the pages of periodicals" (1). While *Harper's* avoided expressing political views that were central to the periodicals it mentioned, it focused on a major cultural issue debated in those magazines: literary taste. Pulling from a wide array of British periodical resources (including magazines like the *Lady's Companion,* which had a much more overtly domestic focus), *Harper's* forged a new magazine form intended to appeal to the entire family and to balance entertainment with cultural improvement.

The first issue of *Harper's* included only British writers and, although the authors were rarely identified, almost all of the selections unabashedly advertised that they were reprinted by citing their British periodical sources beneath their titles. The contents of *Harper's* premiere issue represented material from a cross-section of British magazines, but the most frequently cited source was Dickens's *Household Words*.[7] Dickens's magazine is lavishly praised in "A Word at the Start":

"Dickens has just established a weekly journal of his own, through which he is giving to the world some of the most exquisite and delightful creations that ever came from his magic pen" (1). Eight articles from *Household Words* were copied in *Harper's* first issue alone. During its first year, items from *Household Words* dominated the magazine, with the July 1850 issue including the highest number of selections from the magazine, at fourteen.[8] Furthermore, in August 1850 the "Monthly Record of Current Events" admitted its dependence on Dickens's *Household Narrative*–a supplement to the magazine that reported current news items–by stating that "The English literary intelligence of the month is summed up in the Household Narrative, from which mainly we copy" (422). The importance of Dickens to the establishment of *Harper's* is apparent. What deserves further investigation, and what I address in greater detail later in this chapter, is what Dickens symbolized to Americans and how his work came to embody the magazine's nationalist project.

Throughout its first year, *Harper's* reveals its rootedness in the culture of reprinting by shamelessly advertising where its articles were copied from and even articulating antinationalist literary arguments that created a rationale for its role as a cultural disseminator rather than a cultural originator. For example, its reprint of *Dublin University Magazine's* "American Literature" (June 1850) proclaims that America's excessive "Liberty, equality, and fraternity" are not "so favorable to the cultivation of elegant tastes as might be imagined" (37). According to the article, America's loose class structure and preoccupation with money as a class marker decreased the likelihood that the nation would cultivate its own tasteful literature. The novel, in particular, was seen as a genre strongly connected to the British nation and its class system. As Nina Baym points out, the message was "if the novel depended profoundly on the class structure for its effects, then American novels could not, or ought not to be, written" (241–43). *Harper's* goal, then, was both to fill a void in American life and to facilitate the democratization of print culture by making these novels more accessible to Americans than they were to the British. *Harper's* thus cast its piratical practices as beneficial to readers in a nation in which a native literature was going to be difficult to develop.

One point in the *Dublin University Magazine* article does not coincide with *Harper's* agenda. The article insists that since there was no clear cultural elite to regulate knowledge in America, the nation's literature would inevitably suffer from market value running rampant over aesthetic value. However, *Harper's* did not necessarily see these values as opposed. The fusion of market value and aesthetic value was central to the magazine's mission and its transatlantic character, as well as to its expression of critical authority. By melding these seemingly opposing forces, *Harper's* attempted to establish itself as the nation's primary regulator as well as popularizer of literature.

Rival magazine publishers responded angrily to *Harper's* privileging of British works and vociferously attacked what they characterized as its blatant piracies not because they did not follow similar policies in their own magazines but because they had not been as diligent in the practice or as overwhelmingly successful. John Jay, who had gained exclusive rights to reprint *Blackwood's* in America, advised another publisher in 1851 that "in consequence of the fatal rivalry of eclectic magazines such as *Harper's*," which provided "choice selections from all the British miscellanies," single magazine reprints were no longer viable (quoted in Barnes 44). In addition to such rivalries, reprinting was becoming distasteful as a matter of principle due to the belief that the reliance on British writers was primarily responsible for preventing American authors from making a living and America from creating its own literature.

Amid the climate of growing American literary nationalism, *Harper's* British character was an easy target for criticism from magazines that were financially strapped by their payments to American writers. The magazines that were breaking away from the culture of reprinting failed to generate the profits *Harper's* produced not only because they sold fewer copies, but also because their expenses were much higher. As a result of the extravagance and success of its practices, *Harper's* was universally reviled as unpatriotic by the American publishing community. In March 1851 one of its competitors, *Graham's*, described it as "a good foreign magazine" and predicted that even "The veriest worshipper of the dust of Europe will tire of the dead level of silly praise of John Bull upon every page." *Graham's* goes on to argue that America is fast catching up with its mother country: "John is a stout fellow–drinks his ale, and eats his roast beef with great *gusto*–but he hasn't *quite* all the brains of the family. . . . [H]e forgets young Johnathan has whipped him twice in war–is his master at mechanics, and is not *altogether* a dolt at letters" ("Graham versus Reprints" 280). Equating *Harper's* literary selections with an excessive reverence of Anglo-European traditions and outlining the past successes and current potential of the United States helped spark a sense of outrage among the American literati that began to transform a literary climate in which foreign books were acceptable and even necessary into one in which native authors were privileged. *Graham's,* which claimed to have paid as much as $1,500 an issue for its original contributions by American writers, was losing its hold on the public largely because of the success of *Harper's* cheap reprints. *Graham's* attacks on *Harper's* proved to be futile, however. The magazine was failing to compete even as it struggled to sustain a national literary culture. *Graham's,* which had been around since 1841, was pushed out of the market in 1858 after a last ditch attempt to woo *Harper's* readers by doubling its length to include reprints from British magazines (Wrobel 158).

In a similar scenario, the *American (Whig) Review,* a journal founded on the principle of improving American literature, publicly blamed *Harper's* for shirking its national duty and keeping American writers in poverty. In "A Letter to the Proprietors of Harper's Magazine" (July 1852), the *Review* angrily protested that the magazine's practices were not only unfair to American as well as British writers, but also immoral:

> As a scheme for making money, I cannot too highly commend your enterprise. It is a manifest improvement on the shopkeeper's maxim of buying in the cheapest market and selling in the dearest, for you do not buy in the market at all. . . . You prove your right to the enviable title of sharp businessman, but you also show yourselves utterly destitute of regard for the literary talent of your own countrymen. . . . To regard this as a fair business competition, would require a species of moral training to which I could not wish myself or any honorable citizen subjected. (15, 18)

As with *Graham's,* the popularity of *Harper's* quickly helped push the ethically and patriotically motivated *American (Whig) Review* to its demise in 1852.

However, *Harper's* defended its piratical practices on the grounds that they provided literary models that would serve a nationalistic end despite the fact that reprinting—now cast in the outlaw garb of the term "piracy"—was beginning to be seen as unpatriotic, unethical, and even criminal. While this philosophy was sustained throughout the magazine's first five years, increasing pressure from the literary community pushed *Harper's* to alter its image. Due largely to a changing culture of ethics surrounding copyright issues and reprinting, *Harper's* blatant piracies declined. After its first year, the magazine eliminated credit lines for its reprinted articles and instated a policy of payment and attribution, especially to major authors like Dickens, who was paid generously for *Bleak House.*[9] The magazine's shifting strategy can be seen in the "Editor's Easy Chair" for January 1852. This column, written just three months before the serialization of *Bleak House* began, includes a comment on the American publishing industry's failure to properly remunerate Dickens for his writing: "We could honor Mr. Dickens with such adulation, and such attention as he never found at home; but when it came to the point of any definite action for the protection of his rights as an author we said to Mr. Dickens, with our hearts in his books, but with our hands away from our pockets, 'We are our own law-makers and must pay you only in–honor!'" (255). With *Harper's* unpaid reprints from *Household Words* silently swept under the rug, the magazine may already have been negotiating its agreement with Dickens, for which it now hoped to be recognized as a prime mover on the copyright issue that Dickens toured America to promote in 1842.[10] However, the magazine also underwent more overt changes in its format and appearance in response to the antinationalist charges it faced.

"A Strictly National Work": The Americanization of Harper's

Though the American reading public was more amenable to *Harper's* rhetorical and editorial shifts than the professional literary community, the magazine quickly adapted its editorial practices in response to growing criticism from that small but loud constituency. The Americanization of *Harper's* was marked by a shift in the advertisements for the magazine placed at the front of each bound volume. While *Harper's* continued to privilege British serial novels, its ads increasingly focused on the national character of the magazine. By the second volume (December 1850–May 1851), *Harper's* opening advertisement tones down its British identity and claims that "in addition to the choicest productions of the English press, the magazine will be enriched with such original matter as in [the editor's] opinion will enhance its utility and attractiveness." It was announced that the magazine would include "original" American works if they matched (or exceeded) the quality of the rest of the magazine, implying that American works that could compete with British works existed, but also indicating that they were not easy to find. With the publication of volume three (June–November 1851), the editors made a more definitive claim for American cultural production, stating that "the best talent of the country has been engaged in writing and illustrating original articles for *Harper's* pages." Furthermore, they declared that the magazine would now regularly include "one or more original articles upon some topic of historical or national interest, written by some able and popular writer." By the fourth volume (December 1851–May 1852), many more American writers and topics were incorporated, and the opening advertisement boldly declared that "the most gifted and popular authors of the country write constantly" for *Harper's*. This public-relations campaign helped to alter *Harper's* image as a "foreign magazine," but the nationalistic claims were nonetheless exaggerated. Despite *Harper's* contention in the advertisement to volume two that it intended to be "a strictly national work" filled with "patriotism," Bulwer-Lytton, Dickens, and Thackeray continued to dominate the early years of the magazine, holding the coveted position of featured serial novelists.

Harper's did, however, make some changes that coincided with its advertising claims. For example, in the first issue, the "Monthly Record of Current Events," overseen by Henry J. Raymond, is described as "a digest of all *Foreign Events,* incidents, and opinions that may seem to have either interest or value for the great body of American readers" (emphasis added; June 1850, 122). Only a month later Raymond informs readers that "THE DOMESTIC EVENTS of the month (which in accordance with requests from many quarters, this Magazine will hereafter regularly record) have not been numerous or very important" (July 1850, 275). While acquiescing to demands for the inclusion of American news, *Harper's* still implied that the country's events were insignificant (even though the news report included the invasion of Cuba and a congressional debate on slavery). By *Harper's* second volume, the "Monthly Record" was organized nationally, with American news listed first, followed by reports on British and European events. Similarly, the series "Leaves from Punch," which began in January 1851 and featured humorous material copied from the famous British magazine, was changed in June 1852 to the less derivative title of "Comicalities, Original and Selected" and began to feature more original pieces by American artists (Dowgray 73).

Harper's also responded to criticism by increasingly incorporating features on American landscapes and governmental institutions into its pages. This move is, in part, consonant with McGill's contention that "Nationalist manifestos customarily began with a condemnation of American subservience to British literary models, and finished with a call for a literature commensurate with the majesty of American scenery and the ideals of republican institutions. Throughout, the emphasis was on independence and self-sufficiency figured as the reciprocity of art, land, and nation" (192). While *Harper's* did not condemn subservience to British literary models and in fact argued that America would benefit from those models, the magazine began to strategically place essays on American history and scenery on its front pages. Articles such as Benson J. Lossing's "Our National Anniversary" (July 1851), which featured illustrations of John Adams, Thomas Jefferson, and Benjamin Franklin and included a facsimile of the signatures as they appear on the Declaration of Independence, honored American thinkers and institutions without treading into issues of high and low culture. Similarly, *Harper's* began to focus on America's landscapes and architecture as aesthetically pleasing national treasures in articles such as "Sketch of Washington City" (December 1852), "The Landscape of the South" (May 1853), "Monticello" (July 1853), and "Arlington House" (September 1853). By volume seven (June–November 1853), the editors confirmed the success of their strategy by claiming in the advertisement that "No feature of the Magazine has met with more general approval than the series of illustrated articles upon American scenery and History." This emphasis on American themes in nonfiction allowed *Harper's* to appear more nationalistic while continuing to argue that America would benefit from following British literary models.

Harper's, in fact, began to include more and more American writers, though their contributions were typically anonymous. The most prominent authors whose names were featured in the magazine tended to contribute nonfiction works that avoided American themes. The Abbott brothers were the most popular writers of this class. John Abbott was famous for writing the longest-running serial in *Harper's* history, *Napoleon Bonaparte* (September 1851–February 1855), which gave readers an anti-British view of the French leader by emphasizing his honorable qualities. Jacob Abbott wrote exotic travel narratives such as the serial *Memoirs of the Holy Land,* introducing Americans to exciting and remote places. Despite–or possibly because of–their avoidance of fiction and of American topics, Jacob Abbott opened fourteen and John Abbott opened four of the first forty-two issues of the magazine. Not only were these American brothers honored with bylines and opening positions within the magazine, but they also fared quite well monetarily.[11]

The magazine's creation of several new editorial departments–the "Editor's Drawer," the "Editor's Easy Chair," and the "Editor's Table"–was one of the most visible and lasting signs of *Harper's* attempt at Americanization. The "Editor's Easy Chair" featured the notable critics

Donald G. Mitchell and George W. Curtis. However, the editorial commentaries of these distinctive American voices reflected the principles of the magazine more than the values of the writers themselves.[12] *Harper's* American critics continued to champion British novels over American ones. When the magazine did support American literature, it was often in Lewis Gaylord Clark's "Literary Notices" section, which reprinted positive British reviews of American works as proof of their literary value. Ironically, the practice of citing British sources as a confirmation of the worth of American books became more and more common as the magazine decreased its reprinting and increased its nationalist profile. Thus, while the magazine characterized itself as patriotic and attempted to appear more "American" than it was when it was launched in 1850, it was still open to charges like the one made by its rival *Putnam's*. In March 1857, several years after *Harper's* had undergone its transformation, *Putnam's* gave itself credit for what it characterized as its rival's superficial facelift:

> [T]he first immediate effect of *Putnam* was to nationalize *Harper*. That magazine ceased to be a second table of the English periodicals, and became gradually more and more American. But it was American in subject rather than American in treatment. Its spirit was still timid and hesitating. Every month it made its courtly bow; and, with bent head and unimpeachable toilet, whispered smoothly, "No offense, I hope." ("Harper's Monthly and Weekly" 294)

By characterizing *Harper's* as not only piratical, but also too eager to please the public, *Putnam's* summarized the magazine's lasting reputation within nineteenth-century critical circles. But, as far as the reading public was concerned, *Harper's* formula worked regardless of the nationality of its writers.

Despite its efforts to change, *Harper's* spent decades shedding its reputation as a pirate periodical. On November 12, 1870, *Punchinello*—itself an American derivative of *Punch*—printed a cartoon satirizing *Harper's* piracies, indicating that twenty years later the magazine's early publishing practices were still fresh enough in people's minds to make them laugh (Figure 1). The cartoon's caption explains that it depicts the "piratical rover, 'Harpy,' springing a trap upon the good ship 'Author' in a favorable trade wind" (105). An issue of *Harper's* that is held to the deck with a miniature sword peeks out from under the pile of bodies. These casualties of the magazine's bloody editorial practices are concealed from the waving crowd of onlookers by Fletcher Harper, who

FIGURE 1. "The Literary Pirates." *Punchinello* (November 12, 1870): 105.

appears to be yelling orders to editorial columnist George W. Curtis. Curtis stands on a barrel labeled the "Easy Chair" (the title of his editorial column) playing violin music, which, according to the accompanying poem "The Harpy," is a seductive siren song that lulls the magazine's readers into complaisance (104). Amid the chaos Fletcher's sword remains hidden from the public, who can see only the welcoming authors, who appear waving and reading to them from the ship's deck. Both *Harper's* publishing practices and its seduction of readers remained notorious, though the magazine had been dramatically altered by the time this cartoon was printed.

"The Vestal Virgins . . . on the Altar of the Fine Arts": *Appeals to Women Readers*

While *Harper's* engaged first with the culture of reprinting and then experimented with literary nationalism, ultimately uniting the two, the magazine never strayed from one unifying mission: the initiation of common readers into the culturally informed middle class. *Harper's,* like the American publishing system, was characterized by a democratic view of its relationship to readers. The magazine created what Ronald Zboray calls "a fictive people," an audience that is invented as it is described. This audience was encouraged to participate in the pursuit of socioeconomic mobility through "self-culture," a strict program of reading that would not necessarily provide economic improvement but an improvement of the heart and mind, joining the masses with the educated middle class in a precarious marriage of sensibility and taste (129–30). The editors proclaimed the magazine's superior ability to transform the common reader into the educated reader by stating that they had "no doubt" they could "present a Monthly Compendium of the periodical productions of the day which no one who has the slightest relish for miscellaneous reading, or the slightest desire to keep himself informed of the progress and results of the literary genius of his own age, would willingly be without" ("A Word at the Start" 2). However, while the magazine was constructed as the embodiment of democracy, its message was hierarchical and authoritative. *Harper's* defined itself as a magazine *for* the literate but undereducated masses, but not *of* them; it was a sort of anthology of the best literature of the day chosen by experts who would guide readers toward high cultural literacy. As Nancy Glazener puts it, both *Harper's* and its high cultural contemporaries like the *Atlantic Monthly* fulfilled the "need to secure a wider audience for high culture who could testify to the worthiness of its controllers' leadership by submitting to their rules of access and standards of valuation, and the need to signal that not just anyone was in the position to understand that culture and enjoy it properly" (35). While the magazine claimed to empower readers, it also endowed itself with the cultural power to compel them to buy the magazine in order to signal their literary taste.

The magazine's call for more literate and, especially, tasteful Americans (for more *Harper's* readers) is exemplified in a statement on America's participation in England's Great Exhibition in the December 1851 "Editor's Easy Chair." According to *Harper's*, the greatest display of the attainments of civilization was not a success for the United States:

> [I]t is quite certain that on the score of *taste,* we have made a bad show in the palace. It was in bad taste to claim more room than we could fill; it was in bad taste to decorate our comparatively small show, with insignia and lettering so glaring and pretentious; it was in bad taste not to wear a little of the modesty, which conscious strength ought certainly to give. (132)

Harper's suggests that Americans would do best to take a lesson in sub-tlety from their forebears before attempting to boldly create a new style that could embarrass the young nation. The bad taste exemplified by the gaudy ornamentation of the American exhibit—which corresponds with the magazine's critique of the excessive emotionalism of American sentimental literature—emphasizes the need for British influence to tame and therefore cultivate the growth of American aesthetic sensibil-ities. *Harper's* took as its broader mission the improvement of American taste by studying British examples, and women readers—as guardians of the cultural life of the family and nurturers who would ultimately raise the level of public culture by influencing the private lives of potential-ly powerful public figures—became the primary targets for the maga-zine's lessons in literary influence.

In keeping with the common conception of women as both the primary readers of fiction and the literacy educators of the family, *Harper's* aimed its rhetoric of taste at them.[13] By feminizing the maga-zine's readers, the editors were better able to adopt an authoritative (and sometimes condescending) tone that eliminated the need to negotiate the boundaries of taste with male readers, whose status would be closer to their own. James Machor points out that this was not an uncommon practice. He maintains that critics and editors used "a strategy of informed reading that was essentially conservationist and ultimately nar-cissistic" as they "sought to multiply their own images, as cultural incar-nations, in modified and well-controlled female replicas" (75). The gen-eral public was thus represented by the educable and educating American women readers, to whom *Harper's* devoted its literary lessons, lessons that focused on British novels as a means to create tasteful, mid-dle-class readers who would ostensibly participate in the larger project of preparing Americans to produce their own literature and establish a national literary identity that was lacking within *Harper's* pages. As a means of bolstering its authority through the empowerment of its target audience of women readers, the magazine placed importance on the pri-vate realm as a place in which future public skills would be nurtured. In other words, if women readers could gain literary taste and an appro-priate sense of national duty, they would transform the public realm by educating the literate and literary Americans of the next generation (who would hopefully continue to read *Harper's*).

The magazine's focus on women is apparent in its first issue, which showcased at least eight selections that concerned primarily women's lives, including articles about how to effectively use hard water in the household; the life of the Duchess of Orleans; the duties

FIGURE 2. "Fashions for July." *Harper's New Monthly Magazine* (July 1853): 287.

of motherhood; and the superior qualities of married (over single) men. In addition, the substantial number of pieces copied from the *Ladies' Companion* during the first year and the standard inclusion of two to three pages of fashion plates indicate that *Harper's* catered to the female members of its audience. In fact, the fashion plates not only offered tasteful clothing styles to go along with the other lessons in taste the magazine presented but also provided the magazine's rhetorical readership with images of their imaginary selves, arranged in everyday home or outdoor settings, looking back at them from *Harper's* pages.

Isabelle Lehuu's analysis of the fashion plates in *Godey's Lady's Book* is relevant in the context of *Harper's* as well. Lehuu argues that women readers of American magazines were not positioned as passive consumers, but rather as active participants in the transformation of American culture (74). In particular, she argues, fashion plates depicted women in standardized duos or quartets that became "repetitious representation[s] of almost identical ladies, like a species" constituting a "'sisterhood' of middle-class women" and a "blueprint for the formation of a group consciousness" (81–82). This consciousness was defined not only through tasteful attire but also through domestic activities such as reading that would strengthen the family and the nation. In fact, several of *Harper's* fashion plates depict women with books in their hands, indicating the power of print even while focusing on the fashionable, middle-class body (Figure 2).

The books depicted in *Harper's* fashion plates serve as a reminder that the power of women within the magazine was not confined to fashions or even household duties. Indeed, *Harper's* women readers were expected to improve their minds so that they could effectively fulfill their roles as middle-class wives, mothers, and disseminators of cultural knowledge. Therefore, the editors announced that they would "seek to combine entertainment with instruction, and to enforce, through channels which attract rather than repel attention, the best and most important lessons of morality and of practical life" ("Advertisement" to Volume I). The moral and the practical were united in women's roles as guardians of their family's literacy and taste. The fitness of women for the job of dispensing literary knowledge to their families is clearly established in an article on "Woman's Offices and Influence" (October 1851), written by University of Michigan Professor J. H. Agnew. Agnew claims that along with their duties to create a happy home, to soften the effects of public life on their husbands, and to maintain morality and religion within the family, women "are the vestal virgins to watch the fires on the altar of the fine arts," whose obligation it is to "Tell [their] sons and [their] sires that there are higher sources of joy. Point them away from earth's sordid gold to the brighter gems of literature. Direct their energies to the intellectual and moral advancement of their age" (555). Thus, *Harper's* insisted that women had a responsibility to maintain their family's pursuit of literary activities because their husbands could be too easily distracted by their association with the corrupting world of business.

The magazine never wavered from its insistence that women were crucial to the development of a superior literary culture and even gave this endeavor an intellectual tenor that might seem surprising. For example, "Men and Women" (June 1850), an article signed by "A Young Wife" and reprinted from *The Ladies' Companion,* reinforces *Harper's* argument that in addition to their traditional domestic duties, women should play an intellectual role within the family. It exhorts men to learn "to choose wives among the women who possess [intellectual] qualities" because "The improvement of both sexes must be simultaneous." According to the article, it is unfortunate that "A 'gentleman's horror' is still a 'blue stocking,' which unpleasing epithet is invariably bestowed upon all women who have read much, and who are able to think and act for themselves" (89). This article encourages the development of female intellect but acknowledges that men must be conditioned to accept smart women as a positive influence on their family and their country. As *Harper's* invited women to participate in and perpetuate the literary lessons it offered, it asked men to accept the vital role women could play in refiguring American cultural life, including aspects of the public realm.

It is precisely because of the editors' stated belief in women's power to transform public culture that *Harper's* was so preoccupied with creating proper women readers and controlling the literary values that would be passed on to the next generation. As Lori Merish argues in *Sentimental Materialism,* while conceptions of taste typically reinforced male authority, taste was also envisioned as "the natural property of women" (5). Women's tasteful consumption became a civic identity that justified an increasingly commercial society and in fact reinvented commodities as "forms of interiority proper to . . . domestic life" (6–7). While women were supposedly protecting men from the undue influence of commerce, what they bought—whether a magazine or a bonnet—was a crucial signifier of individual and national identity. Women's tasteful consumption of literature was therefore subject to strict controls intended to sustain the magazine's own authority as a commodity that would bring credit to the home and the nation. Whenever the feminine public's consumer desires seemed to deny the civic duty *Harper's* assigned to them, the magazine scolded its readers for participating in literary "crazes." For example, when readers—identified as women—rushed out in droves to attend Thackeray's American lecture tour, they opened themselves up for an attack on the grounds that they were participating in a distasteful literary trend. Thackeray, seen as an otherwise admirable British realist, suddenly became objectionable because of his association with unpredictable consumer impulses that the magazine sought to control. The January 1853 "Editor's Easy Chair" reflects this anxiety about women's ability to determine literary trends:

> At the date of our writing, [Thackeray] is beguiling two evenings a
> week very pleasantly, for a very large crowd of listeners, in most
> crisp and pointed talk about Humorists of a century ago in England.

51

. . . Mr. Thackeray's talk has given start to a Swift, and Congreve, and Addison furor; the booksellers are driving a thrifty trade in forgotten volumes of "Old English Essayists"; the *Spectator* has found its way again upon parlor-tables . . . Tristram Shandy even is almost forgiven his lewdness; . . . and hundreds of Lilliput literary ladies are twitching the mammoth Gulliver's whiskers. (279)

This passage seeks to quash the literary craze by calling into question the morality and taste of the eighteenth-century works that Thackeray praised. The "lewdness" of Shandy and the intimacy of the ladies with Gulliver's whiskers certainly suggest an inappropriate relationship between such literature and women readers.

The February 1853 "Easy Chair" similarly criticizes women readers for jumping on the bandwagon of popular fads:

Aside from the *Henry Esmond* and Thackeray fever of the winter, we do not know that we have any particular contagion to speak of. New York ladies are certainly literary the present season. . . . The taste for German, Hungarian, and music, has yielded to a taste for old English literature; and the number of "British Essayists," and "Addison's Works," and "Gulliver's Travels" . . . which have been done up in calf and gilt, and sold for Christmas *cadeaux,* is, we are told, most surprising; and far exceeds the number for any previous year. (419)

Harper's reasserts its control by poking fun at the crowds who blindly follow Thackeray's return to the eighteenth century and by instructing its readers to stick to the realist and moralist British works of the nineteenth century, which it promotes as the embodiment of high culture. Of course, less than a year later the magazine seemed to have jumped on the bandwagon itself as it proudly promoted its new Thackeray serial, *The Newcomes.* These self-contradictory statements point to *Harper's* obsession with both preventing the spread of disease-like fads that would threaten literary taste and maintaining its own respectability even while marketing high culture to the feminized masses. Frivolous gift books and literary fevers, signs of a literary consumer culture run amok, threatened the taste and stability that *Harper's* promoted. Even though the system of literary consumer culture allowed *Harper's* to exist as another artifact of the expanding and increasingly national publishing market, the magazine attempted to avoid becoming a symbol of crass consumerism by controlling taste and thereby creating a literary demand that only it could fill.

Interestingly, it is Thackeray's novel *The Newcomes* that provided *Harper's*'s audience with a model woman reader able to successfully fulfill both her private and public roles as educator and patron of the arts. Ethel Newcome transforms herself from a strong-minded yet directionless woman into an educated and self-sacrificing one. At the beginning of the novel, Ethel's grandmother Sophia Newcome taints the idea of women's intellectual activity by dying after she has stayed up reading alone late at night. However, Ethel makes reading a positive force for the public good. After breaking her engagement to Lord Farintosh and gracefully accepting the news that her cousin and true love, Clive, has married another woman, she not only "devoted herself entirely to the nurture and education of her brother's orphan children. She educated herself in order to teach them" (July 1855, 205). Her self-education allows her to appreciate the importance of art as she learns to see in it the "secret of all secrets," "the truth [that] may lighten . . . darkness" (August 1855, 345). Ethel continually defends and supports her cousin Clive's decision to be an artist despite the fact that her family sees this as an unworthy profession. She is regardless, too, of his own admission that he is not even a very good artist: "[M]y art, Ethel, is not only my choice and my love, but my honor too. I shall never distinguish myself in it; I may take smart likenesses, but that is all" (February 1855, 370). Ethel respects Clive for his honorable devotion to art rather than for his artistic productions.

Within the context of *Harper's* this commentary on the struggling artist and the self-educating woman reader takes on an added richness. Clive corresponds to *Harper's* conception of the American writer, who must be nurtured and provided with British literary models in order to move to a higher level. In fact, Clive only succeeds in selling his art to his friends, who buy it as an act of charity. Several of *Harper's* rival magazines argued that such acts of charity were the responsibility of American publishers and magazines and accused *Harper's* of neglecting this duty. *Harper's,* however, leaves the job of nurturing art to its women readers. Moreover, this is a job Ethel does well as she ultimately sacrifices part of her own inheritance to preserve Clive's devotion to his unprofitable work. When she discovers a letter hidden away in the book that her grandmother Sophia was reading just before she died, Ethel is spurred to action. Addressed to Sophia's lawyer, the letter expresses her intention to change her will to include Clive. Ethel thereby reads her way to rescuing her cousin and his family. Ethel finds happiness by following the path suggested by *Harper's* itself: She educates herself, passes her knowledge on to her family's youth, and ultimately saves art—or at least one struggling artist.

Realism, Sentimentalism, and Charles Dickens's "Heart-Mind": Bleak House as an Exemplar of Literary Taste

Sentimental literature was often characterized in *Harper's* as a weak and feminine form that would destroy the nation's ability to create its own high literary culture. The December 1853 "Editor's Easy Chair" laments the fact that such a practical people as Americans could also be "the most sentimental people in the world. . . . There is a kind of literature and art grown up among us, which is weak and unhealthy, and yet the most popular of all" (132). *Harper's* rejects women's sentimental fiction as a predominant trend in American literature and discourages readers from wasting their time on the "pert sentimentalism" of "alliterative ladies" like "Tabithy Toadstool" when Dickens and Thackeray "are easy to obtain, and are of an incomparable superiority" (ibid.). The magazine warns that "If you suffer yourself to be so much pleased by . . . sentimental books, you will find that you have lost your taste for the great works of literature" (ibid.). Thus, sentimental fiction was characterized not only as an inferior form, but also as a form that was dangerously appealing to women because it interfered with the development of high literary taste and would, as a result, weaken the nation's potential to produce good literature.

In theory, *Harper's* defined American sentimentalism as an inferior and addictive pleasure for women readers and an amateur and frivolous endeavor for women writers who often adopted silly pseudonyms. However, despite *Harper's* often harsh antisentimental rhetoric, in practice, the boundaries between the real and the sentimental were deliberately collapsed as the magazine contained many of its own sentimental selections and frequently used sentimental language to appeal to its readers. Highlighting the magazine's repressed sentimentality, Dowgray calls *Harper's* "a school for sentimentalism" that "also included an academy annex in English serial fiction for the revolt against sentimentalism" (114). In 1857 *Putnam's* explained *Harper's* paradoxical character by stating that it had "managed to hit the average taste of the public" as a consequence of the fact that it had "no strong expression, except of pathos or humor, because, as it wanted to sell itself to everybody, it was necessary that nobody's prejudices should be hurt. . . . In the very reasons of its success lay the impossibility of its becoming an intellectual power in the country" ("Harper's Monthly and Weekly" 293–94). While *Harper's* may indeed have struggled overmuch to satisfy the public and maximize profits, it took seriously its mission to define its own standard of taste. Despite the fact that *Harper's* safely straddled the old culture of reprinting and the new culture of literary nationalism and refused to overtly defend American sentimentalism or devote itself to American authors, it defined sentimentality and realism as symbiotic forms that could coexist successfully and even strengthen one another. Indeed, *Harper's* justified implicit acceptance of sentimentality as a means of elevating the function of literature in society. According to the December 1853 "Editor's Easy Chair," in order for sentimentalism to be valuable, it had to serve a greater purpose than providing a simple emotional outlet for readers. Just as "Marat was fond of kittens," anyone could experience an emotional response to literature and continue to be unfeeling in real life (132). Thus, sentiment had to have a function similar to that of high cultural works, which are characterized as "tenderer than sentimentality" because "tears which are drawn from an easy sensibility do not wash away much unhappiness from the world" (ibid.). *Harper's* argues that it is not tears but the recognition of literature's higher societal purpose that is vital to a healthy culture and a more humane world. Because it linked reading literature and transforming the public realm, the magazine accordingly called on women readers to teach literary values to their families. The magazine seems to propose that once readers sympathetically engaged with the world's problems represented in literature, they could effect change. However, the mechanisms for change were never fully articulated. Regardless of the vagueness of the relationship between reading and public transformation, it was clear that pure tearfulness or a love of kittens would be useless, but good literature—whether it contained sentiment or not—was constructed as that which helped to transform the public consciousness by tapping into the moral power of *Harper's* women readers.

Though *Harper's* editors trumpeted the supremacy of British realism as a cultural form and implied that Dickens was an exemplary British realist, the qualities that made Dickens a central figure in *Harper's* had at least as much to do with his sentimentality as they did with his creation of a sense of reality. While printing the work of Dickens was an obvious choice for a periodical that intended to capitalize on the success of British serial novelists, the magazine editors chose not to promote their serialization of *Bleak House* by focusing on his popularity among both readers and critics. Instead, *Harper's* translated the aesthetic qualities of Dickens's work into a particularized standard of taste that it promoted. The poem "Sonnet to Dickens, Esq.," reprinted from *The Examiner* in September 1854, points out what made Dickens so powerful within the pages of *Harper's*:

> So, unto hosts of lives thy varied powers
> Have given to heart and mind a better birth. . . .
> So doth thy pen delightfully compel
> The hardest heart to yield unto thy sway. . . .
> Thou master of most pleasant Humor-wit,
> Thine is the largest Heart-mind ever writ! (572)

The use of the term "heart-mind" to explain Dickens's talent reflects what his contemporaries saw as his expert ability to unite emotionalism and rationalism in his writing and to simultaneously appeal to the heart and the intellect by combining sentimentality and realism. So, while *Harper's* advocated British novels because of their high cultural cachet as realist works, the magazine actually emphasized the superior sentimental qualities of Dickens's work as much as the realistic qualities. Examining the specific ways in which *Harper's* praises Dickens helps to clarify what the standard of taste in the magazine really was, since it was not as simple as the editorial commentaries made it seem. Although the magazine separated realism and sentimentalism in theory, its most popular writer embodied the magazine's own melding of these two forms.

Dickens's ability to combine the sentimental and the real helped establish his reputation in America even before *Harper's* adopted his work as its model of high culture. In December 1844, two years after Dickens's rock-star-like tour of America (organized in part to raise awareness about the need for an international copyright law), the influential critic E. P. Whipple began his own successful lecture tour, during which he lauded Dickens as the greatest novelist of the century. Published in the *North American Review* in October 1849, Whipple's analysis of Dickens was reprinted in journals and newspapers all over the country (Gardner 8–10). "Novels and Novelists: Charles Dickens" summarizes the major aspects of Dickens's work that I contend made him a suitable choice for *Harper's,* including his combination of realism and sentimentalism, his mild but stirring social critiques, and his educational purpose.

Whipple begins by praising Dickens as a poet of practical life, whose "perfection of knowledge and insight" give his novels "their naturalness, their freedom of movement, and their value as lessons in human nature as well as consummate representations of actual life"

(392). He sees Dickens as a writer who accurately depicts the world while also providing a moral philosophy that educates readers. Even though Whipple argues that Dickens's genius is reliant on his depictions of "reality" and "truth," he also values the writer for his ability to move readers emotionally: "It is difficult to say whether Dickens is more successful in humor or pathos. . . . It is certain that his genius can as readily draw tears as provoke laughter. . . . One source of his pathos is the intense and purified conception of moral beauty, that beauty which comes from thoughtful brooding over the most solemn and affecting realities of life" (403–4). This is a significant statement because it shows that Whipple believed Dickens provided realistic representations that touched the hearts of his readers and, even more importantly, that Dickens attained such a high level of realism by accurately expressing sentiment. According to Whipple, morality itself derives from the experience of sympathy, which Dickens evokes through his realistic writing. Thus, for Whipple, Dickens's sentimentality—his ability to evoke intense emotional responses through the depiction of sympathetic (if not pathetic) characters—is integral to his form of realism. However, Whipple avoids using the word "sentimental" to describe Dickens, and he draws clear distinctions between the *sentimentality* of so many American writers and the *pathos* of Dickens's works, as well as between the *caricature* presented in American fiction and the ability of Dickens's novels to excel "in the exhibition of those minor traits [of character] which the eye of genius alone can detect" (402). Though Whipple, like *Harper's*, overtly disparages sentimental American writing, it is precisely Dickens's ability to meld the realistic with the sentimental that makes him a "genius." According to Whipple and *Harper's*, emotional identification with characters leads to moral understanding and to public change, both of which are at the heart of realism. This assessment of Dickens's value coincides with *Harper's* promotion of his work through a variety of editorials, literary notices, pilfered pieces from *Household Words,* and, most significantly, through the serialization of *Bleak House* in nineteen monthly issues of the magazine.

Bleak House, in particular, demonstrates Dickens's skill at combining the real and the sentimental for a moral purpose. As Mary Lenard claims, "many of Dickens's central themes and literary techniques—his use of illness and other forms of physical suffering to arouse feelings of pathos in his audience, his allusions to commonly held religious beliefs, his understanding of death, even his construction of himself as a preacher who taught his audience their social duties—all mark Dickens as a part of a feminized, sentimentalist discourse of social reform" (60).

Whether *Harper's* admitted it or not, Dickens had a lot in common with the American women writers the magazine sometimes ridiculed. Furthermore, the form and themes of the novel suited the magazine's efforts to allow private, feminine voices to influence public life with the legitimizing guidance of its own expert intellectuals who wrote editorial commentaries.

One of the most powerful ways *Bleak House* combines the real and the sentimental is in the juxtaposition of its dual narrative voices. In fact, the voices of Esther and the omniscient narrator in *Bleak House* echo the conflicting voices within *Harper's* itself. What Sylvere Monod has called Esther Summerson's "sentimentality and frequent tearfulness" parallels *Harper's* sentimental appeals to its women readers, whereas the "imperious authority" Monod notes in the omniscient narrator coincides with the authoritative voice of *Harper's* cultural arbiters, who attempted to exert control over public taste (18, 6). These voices compete within *Bleak House* and serve as contrasting bookends for the narrative, which is introduced by the "objective" omniscient narrator and concluded by the sentimental Esther.[14] The novel opens by comparing the Court of Chancery, around which the events of the plot revolve, to its surrounding environment of smoke, mud, and fog, which symbolize the pollution of the law and the court system:

> London. Michaelmas term lately over, and the Lord Chancellor sitting in Lincoln's Inn Hall. Implacable November weather. As much mud in the streets, as if the waters had but newly retired from the face of the earth. . . . Smoke lowering down from chimney-pots, making a soft black drizzle with flakes of soot in it as big as full-grown snowflakes—gone into mourning, one might imagine, for the death of the sun. . . . Fog everywhere. . . . Never can there come fog too thick, never can there come mud and mire too deep, to assort with the groping and floundering condition which this High Court of Chancery, most pestilent of hoary sinners, holds, this day, in the sight of heaven and earth. (April 1852, 649)

Just as *Harper's* critics unflinchingly draw the line between high and low cultural forms (though the magazine proceeds to violate them), the omniscient narrator of *Bleak House* passes judgment on the entire Chancery Court system with an incisive use of metaphorical language that compels the reader to submit to its own seemingly self-evident conclusion about government officials who are so deeply immersed in their own bureaucracy that they are inevitably driven to entrenchment and corruption. These portions of the novel take us into male institutions such as courtrooms and solicitor's offices, allow us to follow Detective Bucket from fact to fact until he uncovers the mysteries of the novel, and bring us into the aristocratic realm of the Dedlock family. This narrative voice provides access to professional spaces and class domains that Esther cannot have much experience with because she is a middle-class woman. The domineering editorial voices in *Harper's* likewise familiarize women readers with critical realms they may not be fully cognizant of because their intellectual experiences have been limited. Both the omniscient narrator of *Bleak House* and the seemingly all-knowing editors of *Harper's* provide a background against which women (represented by Esther's narrative voice on the one hand and *Harper's* ideal women readers on the other) can make their private wills public.

In contrast to the omniscient narrator, Esther provides access to middle-class scenes of domesticity and sympathetic depictions of the living conditions of the poor, with which women would typically be more familiar. Esther's delineation of her own sentimentality highlights her suitability not only for the private sphere but also for performing charitable acts that transgress the boundaries between the private and the public realms. As a narrator she is able to guide readers through private experiences such as her childhood as an orphan, the emotional abuse she receives at the hands of her aunt, a bout with smallpox that leaves her scarred, the nurturing relationships she has with the many downtrodden children she encounters, a covert reunion with her long lost mother, and her secret love for Allan Woodcourt. All of these events are delivered through tears, self-deprecation, and a few fainting spells as Esther self-consciously constructs herself as a sentimental heroine. She plays this role well, sometimes with a sense of irony, but always with an understanding of what is expected of her as a proper woman:

> I don't know how it is, I seem to be always writing about myself. I mean all the time to write about other people, and I try to think about myself as little as possible, and I am sure, when I find myself coming into the story again, I am really vexed and say, "Dear, dear, you tiresome little creature, I wish you wouldn't!" but it is all of no use. I hope any one who may read what I write, will understand that if these pages contain a great deal about me, I can only suppose it must be because I have really something to do with them, and can't be kept out. (June 1852, 95)

Indeed, by the end of the novel Esther has something to do with each aspect of the omniscient narrator's public tale as well as her own private one. Her story demonstrates the integral role women can play in the course of public events despite their societal limitations. Even the omniscient narrator acknowledges Esther's importance, asking the rhetorical question "what connexion can there be" among so many characters and plot lines, a question that only Esther herself can answer (September 1852, 374). As Carol Senf argues, Dickens's use of two narrators in *Bleak House* is not intended to present two mutually exclusive worlds, but rather to allow the reader to "synthesize the two narrators as he or she reads the novel" (22). While Senf concludes that the synthesis of the two narrators leads to an androgynous voice that critiques the separation of spheres, I maintain that the dual narrators showed contemporary readers something a bit more modest and practical. Without overturning the idea of separate spheres, the synthesis of the voices of the omniscient narrator and Esther Summerson, like the synthesis of the voices in *Harper's,* indicates that private, female voices could indeed have a powerful effect on the public, masculine sphere.

Despite *Harper's* strong support of Dickens, the author began to face harsh criticism for his exaggeration of both social wrongs and individual characters with the publication of *Bleak House.* In the May 1852 article "On The Genius of Charles Dickens," *The Knickerbocker* expressed the generally accepted view of Dickens in its anticipation of his new novel: "No man knows better how to . . . appeal to our best sympathies, and sustain the cause of the suffering poor. . . . [Dickens's works] shall be admired at some later day . . . because they have set forth nothing less general than the truth of nature, and appeal to all men by a common bond" (430). However, as George H. Ford points out, the increasingly harsh social criticism in *Bleak House* and Dickens's subsequent works drove a wedge into his formerly solid critical support (100). By October 1853, the last month of *Harper's* serialization of *Bleak House,* the *North American Review* had turned on Dickens. In opposition to Whipple's earlier insistence in the *Review* that it was not Dickens but rather American writers who were caricaturists, the journal proclaimed that "Mr. Dickens is, so to speak, only a caricaturist" and that "In point of literary merit . . . *Bleak House* is a falling off from its predecessors" (424). Likewise, in England, the *Athenaeum* declared that "There is progress in art to be praised in this book,—and there is progress in exaggeration to be deprecated" (108). *Bentley's* noted that "A book which, Mr. Dickens himself assures us, has had more readers than any of his former works, is, to a certain extent, independent of criticism. . . . [But], in no other work is the tendency to disagreeable exaggeration so conspicuous as this" (372). Critics on both sides of the Atlantic struggled with Dickens's protest against contemporary societal institutions as well as with exaggerated characters such as Mrs. Pardiggle and Mrs. Jellyby, whose over-the-top devotion to their socially active agendas result in the neglect and abuse of their duties as wives and mothers.

Harper's, however, vigorously responded to "sharp criticisms upon Mr. Dickens's Mrs. Jellyby" in its "Editor's Easy Chair" for June 1854: "As usual, whenever Dickens is censured, we do not agree. We believe that the satire was the result of very shrewd observation and wise consideration. . . . The Borrioboola-Gha style of philanthropy is the most fatal blow to real charity. Fictitious feeling exhales in a fancied sympathy, which not only tends to bring actual sympathy into disrepute, but dissipates the action and the charity of those who are truly, but not wisely, generous" (119–20). Dickens's characters are defended on the grounds that they are essentially real, even if they are satirical or sentimental, because they convey a moral message that expresses truth. Once again, the magazine maintains its complex aesthetic by dividing false sympathy (which could be manufactured by overly sentimental writing or an affection for kittens) from true sympathy (presumably elicited from Dickens's more "realistic" use of sentiment). For *Harper's*, Esther exhibited true sympathy because she reinforced the construction of women as private forces for public change who could do their jobs more skillfully from within the home than from weakened positions as public actors. Within this context Esther Summerson's narration of half of the novel exemplifies "real charity," whereas presumptuously public women like Mrs. Jellyby and Mrs. Pardiggle "bring actual sympathy into disrepute."

Esther's moral authority is made clear when, after observing Mrs. Jellyby's indifference to her filthy and neglected children, Esther describes the "telescopic philanthropist" as a middle-aged woman "with a curious habit of seeming to look a long way off" as if she "could see nothing nearer than Africa!" (April 1852, 663). Mrs. Jellyby is so focused on the Africans that she neglects her family, leaving them hungry, dirty, and miserable. She even neglects her own hygiene, forgetting to brush her hair and failing to properly dress herself. In reporting what she witnesses at the Jellyby household to Mr. Jarndyce, Esther indicates that she has her own priorities straight. She concludes that "it is right to begin with the obligations of home, sir; and that, perhaps, while those are overlooked and neglected, no other duties can possibly be substituted for them" (May 1852, 816). As Esther passes her first test of domesticity, Jarndyce immediately hands her the all-important keys to the household stores and allows her to assume the fairy-tale role of "Dame Durden," loved and respected head of the household.

Esther describes Mrs. Pardiggle as another one of those ladies distinguished by her "rapacious benevolence," her loud voice, and her ability to take up most of the space in a room, knocking down chairs with her skirts as she passes through (June 1852, 90). Mrs. Pardiggle is shown to be a bully who abhors Mrs. Jellyby's neglect of her children but tortures her own by forcing them to participate in her exhaustive charitable activities, which consist primarily of condescendingly preaching to the poor (ibid., 94). In contrast to Mrs. Pardiggle's alienating ministrations, Esther becomes the ideal reformer who listens to the poor, feels true compassion for their plight, and helps each sufferer she meets on an individual basis. Esther's reflection on the caricatures of Mrs. Jellyby and Mrs. Pardiggle leads her to a more acceptable balance between fulfilling her household duties and participating in the reformation of society. Like Ethel Newcome, Esther embodies the model woman reader imagined by the magazine, the reformer who works from within the private sphere to effect the public sphere but does not move from one sphere to the other as the dangerous women activists do.

The novel concludes with Esther's characteristically self-deprecating response to her husband's inquiry, "don't you know that you are prettier than you ever were?": "And I did not know that; I am not certain that I know it now. But I know that my dearest little pets are very pretty, and that my darling is very beautiful, and that my husband is very handsome, and that my guardian has the brightest and most benevolent face that ever was seen; and that they can very well do without much beauty in me—even supposing—" (October 1853, 686). Esther's seeming passivity and reluctance to admit her own powers of attraction (and of housekeeping, healing, charity, and organization) contrast with the authoritative statements the omniscient narrator makes. Yet, her subjective tale overpowers the omniscient narrator's critique of societal institutions. Esther's domestic narrative counteracts the omniscient narrative of poverty and legal tyranny and defeats the bleak world with a new Bleak House that is not so bleak after all. The sentimental domestic form thus "wins" the battle of the competing narratives, but remains dependant on the objective, realist form to legitimize the relevance of the private sphere to the public realm. In other words, a reader's belief in the "truth" of Esther's private narrative is reliant on the factuality and confirmation of the omniscient public nar-rative. It is only the power of Esther's private voice, however, that effectively transforms the public realm. Likewise, the "critical authori-ty" of *Harper's* editors is useful only insofar as it interacts with the pri-vate voices of the magazine's women readers, who are given the mis-sion to transmit the cultural literacy the magazine supplies to their fam-ilies for the good of the nation (and, of course, of Harper and Brothers' bottom line).

"Assuredly No British Offshoot": The Serial Showdown between Melville and Dickens

Recognizing *Harper's* origins in an American culture of reprinting and its implicit support of sentimental realism helps to explain the Harper brothers' neglect of one of their most promising American writers, Herman Melville. Although they had already agreed to publish Melville's *Moby-Dick* and may have potentially increased profits from the novel by first serializing it in their magazine, Harper and Brothers chose not to do so. Instead, *Harper's* featured only a brief excerpt from *Moby-Dick,* "The Town-Ho's Story," in October 1851, one month before the novel's publication. Though Harper and Brothers used "The Town-Ho's Story" to advertise the book, duly noting its forth-coming publication by Harper and Brothers as well as Bentley's in London (658), it might seem surprising that such a financially savvy publishing house would forgo the opportunity to publish more excerpts from the book or to serialize it in its entirety before publish-ing it in volume form in order to maximize profits. Though *Harper's* may have urged its women readers to follow Ethel Newcome's exam-ple by saving the nation's art and supporting the next generation of American writers, the magazine was not in the business of saving struggling American writers itself, particularly writers like Melville who did not conform to its sentimental-realist style.

The only step the company took was to continue publicizing the book within the magazine by printing reviews and advertisements for it. The "Literary Notices" section for December 1851 opens with an original review by George Ripley, one of *Harper's* most prominent "lit-erary guides," who wrote many of the notices and edited that section of the magazine (Hetherington 213). Ripley praises the novel for sur-passing "the former productions of this highly successful author" and constructing "a romance, a tragedy, and a natural history, not without numerous suggestions on psychology, ethics, and theology," which illustrate "the mystery of human life" (137). Though Ripley contends that "the genius of the author for moral analysis is scarcely surpassed by his wizard power of description," Harper and Brothers had not been convinced that Melville's work was worthy of a prominent place in their magazine. The "Literary Notices" for January and April 1852 include reprints of favorable British reviews of the book from the *London Atlas* and the *London Leader,* respectively. The *London Atlas* declares the novel to be Melville's "greatest effort," revealing "finer and more highly soaring imaginative powers" filled with "thoroughly original veins of philosophic speculation" (277). The pronouncement featured in the *London Leader,* which Hugh Hetherington claims was made by G.H. Lewes (195), further confirms the originality and power of Melville's work:

> Want of originality has long been the just and standing reproach to American literature; the best of its writers were but second-hand Englishmen. Of late some have given evidence of originality; not *absolute* originality, but such genuine outcoming of the American intellect as can be safely called national. Edgar Poe, Nathaniel Hawthorne, and Herman Melville are assuredly no British offshoots. ... [It is] significant that these writers have a wild and mystic love of the super-sensual, peculiarly their own. To move a horror skillfully, with something of the earnest faith in the Unseen, and with weird imagery to shape these phantasms so vividly that the most incredulous mind is hushed, absorbed—to do this American literature is without rival. (711)[15]

While *Moby-Dick* is famous for its many negative reviews, this evidence suggests that on both sides of the Atlantic Melville was considered by some to be a very important American writer.[16] However, Harper and Brothers determined that Melville's "wizard powers of description," "highly soaring imaginative powers," "philosophic speculation," "mystic love of the super-sensual," and "weird imagery" were unsuitable for its best-selling periodical.

I do not mean to suggest that the Harper brothers' relationship to Melville's *Moby-Dick* fully explains *Harper's* neglect of American novels, but merely highlight the fact that while Harper and Brothers had easy access to Melville's work, they deliberately chose not to feature it in their magazine despite its potential popularity as a descendant of Melville's well-received works *Typee* and *Omoo*. The fact that Melville owed the company $700 preceding the publication of the book could have served as an even greater motivation to do everything possible to make money off of the writer's new book. However, the Harpers' refusal to lend Melville money on expectation of his earnings indicates that their confidence in the novel's profitability was low.[17] Furthermore, it seems that they may have made the right decision, considering that the novel did not follow in the footsteps of Melville's more popular novels. Instead, it sold only about 3,800 copies over a year and a half and earned less than any of Melville's previous works (Robertson-Lorant 295–96).

In addition to other possible motivations, Harper and Brothers may have determined that Melville's novel would not be profitable for the magazine because it would not interest its target audience or fulfill its particular standard of taste. It may well have been the case, as William Charvat suggests, that "the chief consumers of fiction in America," namely women, "settled the fate of *Moby-Dick*" since they "could not have failed to notice that . . . there was no place for women, or that there was unlikely to be one in a book about whaling" (242). Furthermore, Melville's novel certainly did not meet *Harper's* standard of sentimental realism in the way that *Bleak House* did. However, instead of providing a more comprehensive analysis of the ways in which Melville's novel was unfit for *Harper's,* I hope to show how a Dickens-Melville rivalry played out in ways that may provide more productive insights into *Harper's* character and agenda. In order to do so, I examine the connections (and disconnections) between Melville's "Bartleby, the Scrivener" and Dickens's *Bleak House,* the novel sitting in the place of honor while Melville subscribed to the magazine and wrote what would be his first published short story.

A number of critics have interpreted "Bartleby," which Melville published in *Harper's* more patriotic rival *Putnam's,* as both an imitation and a refutation of Dickens's novel.[18] The story came out in November 1853, one month after *Bleak House* had concluded its serial run in *Harper's*. The connection between the two works was noticed as early as June 1856, when Boston's *Daily Evening Traveler* commented that "Bartleby" was "equal to anything from the pen of Dickens, whose writings it closely resembles, both as to the character of the sketch and the peculiarity of the style" (quoted in Foley 241). However, despite their similar characters (law copyists Nemo and Bartleby), themes (the law, bureaucracy, and inaction), and Meville's Dickensian use of names (Ginger Nut, Nippers, and Turkey), the works diverge in their primary messages.

As I have shown, Dickens's novel criticizes societal institutions but offers hope for the nation through the influence of the domestic realm as the problems caused by the Court of Chancery are resolved by the triumphs of private relationships, especially those involving Esther Summerson. In contrast, Melville's story displays a Wall Street business world so devoid of the domestic that Bartleby's private life takes place in a public law office in which "walls" exist everywhere but fail to provide the space necessary for domestic nurturing. Even Bartleby's coworkers Nippers and Turkey bring their private bodily ills into the office, and Ginger Nut seems reliant on the crumbs of food he eats there. Furthermore, while *Bleak House* ends (re)productively with the birth of a promising new generation of humane, middle-class subjects produced by Esther, who is the domestic and moral center of the novel, "Bartleby" concludes with death as the only resolution for the inaction and alienation of the business world. Within the context of *Harper's*, Dickens's ability to balance the private and the public and to reveal the power of the domestic realm over the corrupting forces of public life was likely to be more appealing than Melville's more pessimistic, masculine approach. Dickens's emphasis on the power of the feminine, the sentimental, and the domestic corresponded with *Harper's* focus on women readers as guardians of the nation's cultural life, which was seen as necessary to temper the corrupting influence of the public sphere.

Robert Weisbuch posits that Melville's story was meant as "an all-out attack" on what he saw as Dickens's superficial analysis and easy solutions to social problems. According to Weisbuch, Melville wanted to expose Dickens's "cowardly refusal" to "dig for disturbing, obscure truth" by showing that he could delve more deeply into epistemological questions in the space of a few pages than Dickens could in his entire sprawling novel (39–41). Melville may also have wanted to prove that English realism was limited and limiting because it failed to provide satisfying answers to the deeper questions that interested him.[19] Instead, British realism offered neatly packaged appeasement and happy endings. The figure of the "copyist" in "Bartleby" may have been intended to parallel the realist writer who in an attempt to imitate life failed to create an artistic vision that moved readers to action. Bartleby's preference not to copy also parallels Melville's refusal (or failure) to write a novel that followed British models or that suited *Harper's*.

However, Melville did attempt to please *Harper's* editors with *Israel Potter*, a serialized novel that *Harper's* rejected before *Putnam's* published it in 1854. The story about a revolutionary-war hero may have seemed perfect for a magazine that intended to boost its nationalistic profile, but, regardless of Melville's attempt to conform to the magazine's agenda, the Harpers once again denied Melville a prominent place in their magazine.[20] Melville did, in fact, succeed in getting seven stories accepted for publication in *Harper's* between 1853 and 1856, including "Cock-a-Doodle-Doo!" (December 1853), "The Paradise of Bachelors and the Tartarus of Maids" (April 1855), and "Jimmy Rose" (November 1855). Interestingly, Laurie Robertson-Lorant, Lea Bertani Vozar Newman, and Sheila Post-Lauria characterize Melville's stories in *Harper's* as his most sentimental works, an assessment that suggests Melville made a concerted effort to shape his submissions to suit the style of the magazine. Even more significantly, Post-Lauria claims that, although Melville's stories published in *Harper's* "treat social issues through sentimental rhetoric that is suggestive, the author's stories for *Putnam's* criticize sentimental views that soften social and political realities" (166). This contrast in Melville's literary styles indicates that *Harper's* neglect of *Moby-Dick* and *Israel Potter* probably inspired Melville to make a concerted effort to adapt to the demands of the editors, which led to the acceptance of a series of more marketable short stories in *Harper's*. However, despite Melville's efforts to fit in, his contributions were printed anonymously in the magazine, whereas Dickens's name was scattered liberally throughout its pages.

Considering Melville's laborious efforts to publish in *Harper's,* his diatribe against copying seems to be not only an attack on Dickens or on the magazine that rejected him as a serial novelist, but also a protest against the entire enterprise of Harper and Brothers, a company founded on selling cheap copies of British literature to the masses. In fact, "Bartleby" comes to appear very much like a nationalist literary manifesto intended to hasten the demise of the culture of reprinting. Bartleby's previous work in a Dead Letter Office–and the narrator's contention in the concluding lines of the story that "On errands of life these letters speed to death" (*Putnam's Monthly Magazine,* December 1853, 615)–takes on new significance as a critique of fiction whose only purpose is to approximate life but instead results in perpetuating the status quo, acceptance, inaction, and even the metaphorical death of a nation that happily consumes foreign literature without attending to its own artistic development.

Though Melville eventually adapted his style to suit *Harper's,* in "Bartleby" he rebelled against this concession of his artistic integrity by condemning the sentimental valuation of feeling over action that he saw, perhaps incorrectly, as the magazine's focus. In "Bartleby," sentimentality prevents the narrator from facing the fact that his employee is the monstrous creation of a soulless industrial society and allows him to escape recognition of the part he has played in sustaining that world. Perhaps Melville hoped *Harper's* editors would recognize their relation to the narrator of his story. However, regardless of whether "Bartleby" was written as an explicit critique of the serialization of *Bleak House* in *Harper's* or of *Harper's* agenda itself, Melville's work defies the magazine's publishing practices. Melville's denial in "Bartleby" of the healing effects of the domestic realm and of the superiority of the realist writer clearly struck a blow to the heart of *Harper's* identity, an identity that continued to be exemplified by Dickens, regardless of Melville's publication of a series of stories in the magazine.

In his introduction to *Bleak House* (which was not printed in *Harper's*), Dickens presents a defense of himself that we can imagine as a response to Melville's critique of the novel.[21] He explains himself as a writer whose intent is to explore the fanciful within the limits of reality. Dickens claims that he has "purposely dwelt on the romantic side of familiar things" (*Bleak House* 43). However, despite his appeal to the fancy, Dickens intended his novels to "present only incidents that might occur" (ibid.). This desire to record reality faithfully is apparent in the introduction, when Dickens defends his negative portrayal of Chancery Court cases and his use of spontaneous combustion in the novel by citing documented sources as evidence that the events in the novel could actually occur. Dickens's combination of fact and fancy, reality and sentimentality, fit perfectly within a periodical that emphasized the connections between such disparate concepts as piracy and nationalism or the private and public realms. Just as *Harper's* conferred upon British literature the ability to inspire better American literary productions, it conferred upon women the power to transform the nation from the privacy of their own homes.

Jean Ferguson Carr argues that, like Dickens's magazine *Household Words*, *Bleak House* makes "use of a feminine guise, privileging the intimate, private, and authoritative powers usually associated with women over the social, public, and authoritative powers usually associated with men. But [Dickens] was also disrupting the conventional wisdom that sharply divided the domestic and public spheres [by insisting] on the interpenetration of these realms" (163). So, while *Bleak House* and *Harper's* have in common the incorporation of the feminine, they interweave this "household narrative" with a public and authoritative one. Together these competing voices made clear the relevance of the domestic realm to the success of public culture and began to allow women to make sociopolitical claims that were integral to the nation's identity. Like Esther Summerson, *Harper's* women readers held the household keys–but these keys opened more than the household stores. They opened opportunities for women readers to play a role in establishing a truly national literature if they would only transmit *Harper's* literary lessons to the next generation of American writers.

2

THE EDUCATION AND PROFESSIONALIZATION OF THE WOMAN READER

Consolidating Middle-Class Power in the Cornhill Magazine, 1860–1864

THE GENRE OF THE family literary magazine—commonly referred to as the shilling monthly—emerged in England during the 1860s with great fanfare. With a premiere issue that sold nearly 110,000 copies, the *Cornhill Magazine* was the most popular and influential of these literary magazines.[1] Nicola Diane Thompson claims that this was "a particularly vibrant period for the literary periodical" during which "over one thousand journals" related to literature were published (3). Many of these magazines hoped to ride the coattails of the new literary phenomenon begun by *Harper's* a decade earlier in America and perfected in England by the *Cornhill*. Barbara Quinn Schmidt points out that "Most [British] publishing houses brought out a magazine during the 1860s and 1870s if they did not already have one," and, despite the fact that not all of them could rake in high profits, they were considered a good investment. The proprietor of *Tinsley's Magazine* was losing £25 a month but still vowed that there was no cheaper means of advertising a publisher's name and products ("Novelists" 143). As *Harper's* had already proven, the family literary magazine was a profitable business venture that could be marketed to readers hungry for prepackaged literary goods that were affordable and that signified their membership in or aspiration to join the ranks of the culturally competent middle class.

The *Cornhill* marked a new era in periodical publishing that signaled the decline of the old British quarterly reviews. The monthly literary format aimed at the entire family also stood apart from and

70

outsold the newer elite organs of criticism such as the *Saturday Review*. As Merle Mowray Bevington notes, the "masculine world" of the *Saturday Review* "confined women to a secondary role" and "assumed as a fact that women were inferior to men" (116). The *Saturday Review* was generally condescending not only to women readers, but also to the culture of novel reading perpetuated by family magazines like the *Cornhill*.[2] Despite the *Saturday*'s condescension, however, the fact that the *Cornhill* was intended to reach a mixed audience in part accounts for its initial, overwhelming success. *Cornhill* contributor Elizabeth Gaskell commented on women's lack of access to most magazines of the day when she thanked George Smith for sending a supply of books and magazines directly to her: "With a struggle and a fight I can see all Quarterlies 3 months after they are published; till then they lie on the Portico table, for gentlemen to see. I think I will go in for Women's Rights" (August 4, 1859. Chapple and Pollard 567). The *Cornhill* opposed the negative image of women readers presented in the critical reviews by emphasizing the positive effects of women's reading practices that would make them not only better wives and mothers, but ultimately also better middle-class citizens. Thus, for Gaskell and others, the *Cornhill* provided a satisfying alternative delivered directly to the ladies, who were invited to imagine themselves as part of a serious reading audience.

The popularity of the *Cornhill Magazine* is usually attributed to its emphasis on entertainment over education and to its avoidance of controversial issues considered inappropriate for women readers. Schmidt describes magazines of the *Cornhill* genre as designed for the "comfortable, ill-educated middle-class who read for entertainment and easy instruction" in order to provide "superficial treatment of current topics in a pleasing manner with some attempt at education" ("Novelists" 143). Other critics have described the *Cornhill* as a magazine that strictly avoided offending "the ladies and their daughters" by omitting "political and religious controversy" (P. Smith 29). William Thackeray, the *Cornhill*'s editor from January 1860 until May 1862, says as much in his prospectus for the magazine: "There are points on which agreement is impossible, and on these we need not touch. At our social table we shall suppose the ladies and children always present; we shall not set rival politicians by the ears" (reprinted in G. Smith 7). Likewise, Mark W. Turner agrees that

> The absence of overtly male subjects such as politics and religion, which were constructed as the domain of the great quarterlies, in

effect privileged women readers, and women's reading regulated *Cornhill* contributions, in so far that anything deemed unsuitable for women would not be published. . . . *Cornhill*'s version of reality constructed female readers and female reading, and the content of each issue was regulated according to these constructions. . . . *Cornhill*, the most successful of the new monthlies, participated in creating a periodical literature that was gendered female. ("Gendered Issues" 229)

These typical accounts of the *Cornhill* as a magazine that was primarily lightweight, entertaining, and traditionally moralistic equate the feminization of the magazine's audience with the elimination of all controversial issues and the lack of a serious agenda. However, despite Thackeray's concern for the sensitivities of "the ladies," the magazine did not completely ignore controversial topics and indeed made an effort to cover the important issues of the day as a part of its educational purpose.[3]

I contend that the *Cornhill* went beyond offering lightweight entertainment for its female readers to provide a more open forum for women, maintaining not only that women were educable, but also that they should be educated for the good of the middle-class family and the British nation. In fact, the *Cornhill* advocated women's formal education—and, to a lesser degree, women's movement into the professions—as a means of assisting the development of the newly defined "professional gentleman" who was emerging as the leader of the British nation. To keep potential wives occupied while upwardly mobile gentlemen established themselves financially, the *Cornhill* considered the benefits of educated and even professional women. Thus, the *Cornhill*'s proper woman reader would be intellectually engaged in order to support and strengthen her class and her nation. For women readers of the *Cornhill*, as for women readers of *Harper's*, the act of reading itself was depicted as a nationalistic exercise. In contrast to *Harper's*, though, the *Cornhill* urged women to physically move into the dangerous public realm and out of the safe world of private influence in order to lighten the burden of men's financial responsibility for them. However, the magazine did not venture into the risky territory of delineating exactly what role the educated, public, or professional woman might eventually play in society beyond easing the pressures felt by middle-class men. Instead, the *Cornhill* maintained its popularity and widespread accessibility by stopping short of articulating how the public and intellectual woman it imagined would fit into society.

"The Literary Event of the Year": The Cornhill Takes Off

The *Cornhill*'s bold message concerning women readers seems particularly unusual for a periodical that achieved such a wide circulation. However, the magazine's message was defined by its promotion of all things middling: middle-brow culture, middle-class power, and a middle-of-the-road political stance. In order to understand how the *Cornhill* effectively appealed to these "middles," it is useful to see how the magazine evolved into a literary phenomenon in such a short period of time. George Smith of Smith, Elder, and Company launched the first issue of the *Cornhill Magazine* for January 1860 after determining that:

> The existing magazines were few, and when not high-priced were narrow in literary range, and it seemed to me that a shilling magazine which contained, in addition to other first-class literary matter, a serial novel by Thackeray must command a large sale. Thackeray's name was one to conjure with, and according to the plan, as it shaped itself in my mind, the public would have a serial novel by Thackeray, and a good deal else worth reading, for the price they had been accustomed to pay for the monthly numbers of his novels alone. (G. Smith 4–5)

The choice of Thackeray as editor was crucial. He agreed to take the position for an astounding £1,000 per year, an amount that was doubled after the magazine's initial stunning success.[4] As an established writer with an international reputation, he would guarantee that the magazine would command both respected contributors and a wide audience.

Thackeray and Smith paid close attention to choosing a name and cover design for the magazine that would make a positive first impression on readers and bolster the magazine's status as a symbol of middle-class taste. The name "Cornhill" came from the London street where the publishing house of Smith, Elder was located. While the magazine was synonymous with London culture, it also portrayed a romanticized pastoral image that would be attractive to busy Londoners caught up in the hustle and bustle of the city. Inspired by the association of "Cornhill" with wheat and the harvest, Leonard Huxley describes the "pleasing" cover design as an arrangement of "four medallions boldly printed in black on the familiar orange ground" surrounding the simplicity and vigor of "the ploughman, the sower, the reaper, and the thresher, representative of the seasons of the year" ("Chronicles" 368).[5] The cover was ornate and easily recognizable, and Thackeray maintained that it reflected the "jollity and abundance" of the name *Cornhill* (Eddy 14). The first issue of the magazine—with its impressive cover, its distinctive title, and its high-quality production value—appeared just in time for Christmas in December 1859.[6]

The combination of respected publisher Smith and editor-novelist Thackeray was enough to make the magazine the talk of the town. Smith notes that "When the first number appeared . . . it was the literary event of the year. Along Cornhill nothing was to be seen but people carrying bundles of the orange-coloured magazine. Of the first number some 120,000 were sold, a number then without precedent in English serial literature" (G. Smith 9). The *Cornhill*'s popularity was confirmed by the enthusiastic praise of other magazines and newspapers, whose comments were included in an advertisement for the magazine printed, ironically, in the magazine that would become its biggest detractor, the *Saturday Review.* In this ad Smith, Elder touts its newest publication with a long list of quotations from periodicals including the *Illustrated Times,* which calls it "a marvel of elegance and cheapness"; the *Sunday Times,* which claims that "It is almost impossible to imagine any further developments, either in quality or quantity, of the periodical literature of this country"; and the *Lady's Newspaper,* which declares that "If the editor can continue as he has begun, he will soon distance all competition, and reign supreme in the world of literature" (January 7, 1860, 32).[7] The *Cornhill* was an immediate and smashing success, a fact that even its competitors recognized. The only difficulty was sustaining its popularity amid a steadily growing crowd of similar periodicals.

Smith's strategy for outdoing the magazine's competitors was to pay contributors, particularly well-known novelists, outlandish sums of money. According to his own glowing account, "No pains and no cost were spared to make the new magazine the best periodical yet known to English literature" (G. Smith 7). Smith, who was nicknamed "the prince of publishers" for his generosity toward writers, offered Anthony Trollope £1,000 to write *Framley Parsonage* (January–April 1861). This was the greatest payment ever offered to Trollope until Smith paid him £3,200 for *The Small House at Allington* (September–April 1864). As Smith recalls: "Trollope came to see me and naturally asked what was my scale of payment. I replied that we had no fixed scale for such works as his; would he mind telling me what was the largest sum he had ever received for a novel? When he mentioned £500, I offered him double the amount" (quoted in Huxley, *Smith Elder* 97). After witnessing the success of Wilkie Collins's *The Woman in White,* Smith offered him

£5,000 for his next book, which, after a two-year delay, turned out to be *Armadale* (November 1864–June 1866). Collins wrote that "No living novelist (except Dickens) has had such an offer as this for one book" (quoted in Glynn 143). Doubling this sum, Smith proposed a £10,000 salary for George Eliot's *Romola* (January 1862–August 1863). Because Eliot refused to write her novel in the specified number of monthly parts, however, the fee was reduced to £7,000. Nevertheless, this amount was still astounding to Eliot's regular publisher, John Blackwood, who humbly wrote:

> Hearing of the wild sums that were being offered to writers of a much inferior mark to you, I thought it highly probable that offers would be made to you, and I can readily imagine that you are to receive such a price as I could not make remunerative by any machinery that I could resort to. Rest assured that I feel satisfied of the extreme reluctance with which you decide upon leaving your old friend for any other publisher, however great the pecuniary consideration might be, and it would destroy my pleasure in business if I knew any friend was publishing with me when he thought he could do better for himself by going elsewhere. (May 20, 1862. Haight, 35–36)

For the August 1862 issue of the magazine alone, Smith paid nearly £2,000 to contributors, and for the first four years the total cost of paying writers and artists ran close to £37,000.

Smith declares in his memoirs that "Expenditure on this scale for literary work alone was, up to this time, unprecedented in magazine literature" (quoted in Huxley, *Smith Elder* 100). However, far from throwing money away, Smith spent it productively by choosing novelists who would generate the excitement of readers as well as the respect of critics. While the *Cornhill*'s featured novels did not always increase the magazine's readership as dramatically as Smith hoped, they allowed the magazine to advertise itself as a signifier of middle-class taste and helped maintain its success as the most eminent magazine of its kind, regardless of slowly declining circulation figures, well into its first decade of publication.[8] Smith's strategy to consolidate his resources to pay "big name" novelists established the character of the *Cornhill*, but the magazine's serial fiction was only one part of its focus. Under Thackeray's leadership, the *Cornhill* also endeavored to provide high-quality nonfiction articles that would support its educational agenda, an agenda that was inextricably linked to women readers.

"Getting Out of Novel-Spinning and Back into the World": The Educational Agenda of the Cornhill

Thackeray hoped to make the *Cornhill* educational by balancing novel reading with the contemplation of serious articles on science, law, history, biography, literature, culture, art, and social institutions. He proclaimed his intent to balance fact and fiction for general educational purposes in his public introduction to the *Cornhill*, "A Letter from the Editor to a Friend and Contributor." In this letter he declares that "fiction of course must form a part, but only a part" of the magazine; "We want, on the other hand, as much reality as possible (reprinted in G. Smith 6–7). In the first installment of his editorial *Roundabout Papers* (January 1860), Thackeray proposes that the *Cornhill* serve as an educational tool, in part to assist women readers who want to participate in conversations about the major issues of the day. Just as importantly, he dispels the notion that novels should be read primarily by women and factual articles primarily by men: "Novels are sweets. All people with healthy literary appetites love them—almost all women;—a vast number of clever, hard-headed men. . . . Judges, bishops, chancellors, mathematicians are notorious novel-readers; as well as young boys and sweet girls, and their kind, tender mothers" ("On a Lazy, Idle Boy" 127). Thackeray urges audience members of both sexes to read the entire magazine in order to ensure a balanced diet of reading. He argues that both will get sick if they have too many sweets; therefore, they must "mainly nourish themselves on roast" (128). Thackeray's desire to provide "nourishment" is also exemplified in a letter in which he asks Trollope to contribute something other than a novel because "One of our chief objects in this magazine is the getting out of novel-spinning, and back into the world" (Harden 908). Richard Tiemersma's page count suggesting that the amount of fiction steadily increased after Thackeray's editorship, rising from less than half to almost 80 percent of the *Cornhill*'s contents (59), indicates the seriousness of Thackeray's agenda to balance factual and fictional modes in the magazine. Within the context of the magazine, Thackeray conceived of fact as a high cultural mode and fiction as a low cultural mode. This division parallels *Harper's* conception of British literature as high culture and American literature as low culture. Thackeray's emphasis on "fact" in the *Cornhill* was intended to improve the status of women readers, just as *Harper's* emphasis on British realism was supposed to allow women to participate in the creation of a more respectable nationa literature for the

United States. However, while *Harper's* had clear financial motivations for its endorsement of British novelists, Thackeray may have had some very personal motivations for his emphasis on nonfiction.

First, Thackeray's own fiction serials for the *Cornhill*, including *Lovel the Widower* and *The Adventures of Philip*, were not as well received as his factual *Roundabout Papers*. That Thackeray's fiction paled in comparison with Trollope's may have solidified his increasing interest in nonfiction. As Richard Oram claims, "Despite his elation over the success of the *Cornhill* . . . Thackeray was troubled by spells of depression and the feeling that he was 'written out' " (157). Whatever his motivations were, Thackeray's emphasis on fact over fiction created an atmosphere in which women readers were taken more seriously than in other magazine forums. Extending an invitation to women to read serious articles, even if they were often presented in an entertaining manner, made a powerful statement. As Barbara Sicherman points out, during the nineteenth century, reading "was the key to education, employment, and empowerment" for women ("Reading and Ambition" 75). The *Cornhill* ultimately gained the allegiance of its women readers by offering them access to educational and empowering information.

G. H. Lewes (who sporadically served as editor of the *Cornhill* after Thackeray's resignation) carried on Thackeray's message about the value of educational reading for women, but rather than focusing on the health of the readers themselves, he shifted his attention to the cultural health of the nation. In "Publishers before the Age of Printing" (January 1864), Lewes seems to provide a straightforward account of the important role books played in the cultural lives of Romans. However, it becomes clear that Lewes is writing more than a history lesson; he is arguing for a greater reverence for books and reading, particularly for women, in Victorian England. He points to women's reading practices as a vital indicator of a nation's level of cultural development and implies that England should not merely emulate the fallen civilization, but also surpass and outlast it. Lewes explains that although Roman women did not have Mudie's Circulating Library, they did have extensive collections of books in their homes as well as free public libraries, which gave them better access to books, even in an age before the existence of the printing press. Thus, he concludes, "Stockings would have been as blue then as now only stockings had not been invented" (28). While he pokes fun at intellectual women by playfully referring to "bluestockings" and by stating that Roman "women were as well read in the current literature as our idle ladies who subscribe to Mudie's," he reassures male readers that intellectual women are not a new and dangerous breed, but the byproduct of any advanced culture (ibid.). Lewes's message is clear: Women readers—all readers for that matter—should be encouraged to take full advantage of the vast resources available to them as a result of the dominance of print culture. Accordingly, Lewes urges a revival of the "fashion" for books that he identifies in Roman times and calls on his readers to construct their own libraries as monuments to their nation's superior culture (29). Presumably, the *Cornhill* itself would make a suitable start to such a collection of literary treasures for women.

Both Thackeray and Lewes focused on the contents of the *Cornhill* as the starting point for the development of women's minds. While Lewes attempted to ease anxieties about "bluestockings" and to urge Victorian men to understand the importance of intellectual women to the greatness of civilization, Thackeray emphasized the crucial role nonfiction should play in women's reading. Both of these concepts guided the *Cornhill*'s agenda and encouraged readers to draw distinctions between intellectually nourishing facts and emotionally gratifying fiction. However, just as *Harper's* collapsed the divisions it had set up between realism and sentimentalism, the *Cornhill* collapsed the divisions between fact and fiction that Thackeray set forth to guide the magazine's contents. By describing its own realistic novels as "factual fiction" and using fictional techniques such as dream sequences and dialogues within its factual articles, the magazine employed fact and fiction in dialogical ways. Within the pages of the magazine realist fiction was promoted for its educational qualities, and factual articles were made palatable by the incorporation of fictional elements that would entertain as well as instruct readers.

Realistic fictional characters and partially fictionalized representations of factual subjects were supposed to work together to serve as models of proper behavior for readers, though the line between the two was sometimes difficult to determine. By presenting characters that easily extended beyond the bounds of their novelistic settings to merge with real life, the magazine provided what Sicherman characterizes as "a common language and a medium of social exchange that helped women define themselves and formulate responses to the wider world. . . . [And] the continuum between fiction and reality gave considerable play to the imagination. Reading [novels] provided both the occasion for self-creation and the narrative form from which [women] might reconstruct themselves" ("Sense and Sensibility" 209–10). For example, Lord Lufton and Lucy Robarts, characters from Anthony Trollope's *Framley Parsonage,* became exemplars of "true love" in a factual article on "Falling in Love" by James Campbell Reddie (January 1861). Andrew Blake points out that "There could be no better example of the place of fiction in the literary culture of the time than this direct and casually assumed use of fictional characters as examples of morally correct behavior in an article exhorting good marital practice" (91). However, while this article uses fictional characters to provide concrete examples of real courtship practices, it also acknowledges that factual accounts of the nature of love are a necessary supplement to the evidence offered by the fictional world. Reddie's article does this by foregrounding the imagined reader's desertion of Trollope's novel to find the "real truth" in a nonfiction article:

> And now, you dark and merry-eyed young lady, who have professed so great an interest in that dear Lucy Robarts, how can you leave the reading of those chapters in which we look to find that poor Lord Lufton has wooed once more and won? Quite so: you deferred that till you had more time, and thought you would but glance at what this paper said about—Exactly! and perhaps you also felt it might touch yourself more closely than a mere story of true lovers. (41)

In a very conversational style intended to engage women readers, Reddie suggests that fact and fiction work in tandem to educate the magazine's audience about love, life, and society. Thus, readers were alerted to the fact that they should draw on both fact and fiction in order to have a full understanding of any subject. Even in matters of the heart, which the novel as a genre expertly explored, readers were encouraged to stay grounded in fact.

In *Trollope and the Magazines,* Mark W. Turner claims that the "real world" constructed within the *Cornhill's* pages was "defined and regulated by a type of censorship" that excluded controversial subjects and thus presented a distorted view of reality (11). However, I think what is more significant than the magazine's possible exclusion of certain subjects that could present an unrealistic view of the world is the way in which the subjects it did address combined factual and fictional approaches that challenged readers to decipher the relationship between the two forms of representation. The complex relationship between fact and fiction (and, ultimately, between high and low culture) is at the heart of the *Cornhill's* educational editorial policy, a policy that pervaded the magazine regardless of how directly or indirectly it engaged with political and religious issues. That Thackeray's emphasis on fact and Lewes's emphasis on women's intellectual prowess left a lasting legacy is attested to by the magazine's reputation for providing intellectually engaging material to its middle-class readers. In his brief history of the *Cornhill,* Spencer Eddy claims that "[t]he caliber of [the *Cornhill's*] contributors and their work encouraged the support of an intelligent audience attentive to those currents—political, historical, social, scientific, literary—which shaped Victorian life in 1860, and cultured enough to find pleasure in the presentation of lucid narrative, stylized critical and familiar essays, and superior fiction" (45). With its combination of serialized fiction and serious articles, the *Cornhill* promoted women's learning, and that learning would begin first and foremost with the monthly delivery of the magazine to the middle-class home, where it would stand as a symbol of cultural knowledge and authority. As for the magazine's lasting educational value, E. T. Cook declared in 1910 that "Any collector of the *Cornhill* who treasured his or her 599 numbers in the original parts was well qualified, I dare aver, to graduate *in literis humanioribus*" (17). Moreover, as Peter Smith acknowledges in his 1963 article on the *Cornhill,* "it is now impossible . . . to find a magazine which offers the same opportunities to the intelligent non-specialist to become acquainted with current ideas, whether scientific, literary or sociological" (31). These comments stem from the *Cornhill's* promotion of the raw ability of the ultimate Victorian nonspecialist, the middle-class woman reader, to educate herself in a wide variety of fields by reading the magazine.

"We Shall Listen to Every Guest Who Has an Apt Word to Say": The Cornhill *'s Invitation to Women Readers/Writers*

It is clear that Thackeray hoped the magazine would be educational and open to women readers. Certainly, women were targeted because they constituted an untapped market that was perfect for the *Cornhill's* literary and cultural focus and central to the creation of the family literary magazine as a genre. Thackeray, however, also sent a general invitation to women readers to participate actively in the discourse of the magazine. In his initial advertisement for the *Cornhill,* he calls on "pleasant and instructed gentlemen and ladies to contribute their share to the conversation. . . . [Because] the guests, whatever their rank, age, [or] sex . . . will be glad to be addressed by well-educated gentlemen and women. . . . We shall listen to every guest who has an apt word to say" (reprinted in G. Smith 6–7). The *Cornhill*'s overt acceptance of women as a part of its primary audience and its concomitant validation of their voices created a situation in which women felt empowered to communicate personally with the editor by submitting their writing. As Janice H. Harris points out, "the very character of the magazine continually encouraged [women] to identify with key social issues of their own times" (389) and "allowed women writers to contribute material on topics reflecting their own genuine expertise and knowledge" (392).

To gain a fuller understanding of why Thackeray so openly invited women readers to contribute to the magazine, it is helpful to explore Thackeray's personal engagement with the issues of women's education and employment. His initial "open door" policy for women can be explained in part by his growing anxiety about the future of his daughters, Anne and Minnie, during his tenure as *Cornhill* editor. In fact, it was his anxiety about their financial futures that inspired him to accept the lucrative editorial position in the first place. Thackeray was particularly concerned about Anne, who he feared was "going to be a man of genius" rather than a proper wife (Ritchie 23). In her "Notes on Family History," Anne explains that just before his death her father told her he was afraid she would have "a very dismal life" when he was gone (ibid., 129). In an 1852 letter to a friend, Anne expressed the tendencies that worried her father when she stated that she would

> like a profession so much not to spend my life crochetting [*sic*] mending my clothes & reading novels—wh[ich] seems to be the employment of English ladies, unless they teach dirty little children what to read wh[ich] is well enough in its way but no work to the mind–& I don't want to write poetry and flummery–. . . Papa says in a few years we shall have 200 £ a year to live upon & as my favorite Miss Martineau says it is far nobler to earn than to save I think I should like to earn very much and become celebrated like the aforesaid Harriet who is one of the only sensible women living. (quoted in Ray, *Age of Wisdom* 205)

With no marriage prospects on the horizon for a daughter who seemed to reject the traditional occupations of middle-class women, Thackeray decided to accept and nurture Anne's intellectual ability by encouraging her not only to read but also to write for the *Cornhill*. Although he had previously discouraged Anne from her natural inclination toward writing, soon after taking the helm of the *Cornhill* he implored her to do some investigative reporting and take up her pen for an article called "Little Scholars" to be printed in his own magazine (Ritchie 124). Thackeray's change of heart corresponded with both his acknowledgement that he was nearing the end of his life and his desire to use his editorial power for the benefit of his family.[9] Micael Clarke's observation that Thackeray's views of women grew increasingly progressive late in his life (13) may well reflect what has previously remained unacknowledged: that his desire to protect his daughters from the sorrows of the struggling women writers who distressed him as an editor influenced his personal views and the agenda of the *Cornhill*. Realizing the dismal prospects for his ambitious daughter, Anne, may have inspired Thackeray with generosity toward women readers who hoped to become writers. However, when faced with the reality of their desperation, Thackeray became overwhelmed and confused about his own editorial policies and personal hopes for his daughter.

According to Harris, women writers were responsible for an average of 20 percent of the *Cornhill*'s contents between 1860 and 1900 (385). However, during Thackeray's reign, women's contributions account for only about 12.5 percent of the magazine (or 37 of 297 contributions).[10] So, while Thackeray laid the groundwork for the employment of women writers, his call for contributions from women and amateurs proved to be somewhat disingenuous. In reality, the magazine relied primarily on professional literary men like G. H. Lewes, G. A. Sala, and Fitzjames Stephen, who wrote the nonfiction articles that were so important to Thackeray. Despite his invitation to women to add "their share to the conversation," it seems that Thackeray was more committed to having women as audience members than as contributors.

Significantly, the *Cornhill*'s most barren period for women writers occurred between July 1860 and April 1861. I do not think it is a coincidence that this ten-month period during which all fiction by women was excluded corresponds with Thackeray's most vociferous protests against the alarming abundance of submissions from women in his *Roundabout Papers* "Thorns in the Cushion" (July 1860) and "On a Chalk-Mark on the Door" (April 1861).[11] In these essays Thackeray responds to the disturbing collision of his family life with his stated editorial policy by directly reprimanding women writers for sending contributions to his home and disturbing his peace during dinner. He pleads with these contributors to stop flooding him with amateur submissions. In "Thorns in the Cushion," Thackeray admits that "Last month we sang the song of glorification, and rode in the chariot of triumph . . . But now that the performance is over, my good sir, just step into my private room, and see that it is not all pleasure–this winning of success" (123). He bemoans the daily barrage of complaints, insults, unwelcome visitors, and "thorn letters" that beg with "true female logic": "'I am poor; I am good; I am ill; I work hard; I have a sick mother and hungry brothers and sisters dependent on me. You can help us if you will.' . . . Ah me! We wound where we never intended to strike; we create anger where we never meant harm; and these thoughts are the Thorns in our Cushion" (126).[12] Just one month before resuming the publication of fiction by women, Thackeray sends a final warning that "in spite of prayers, entreaties, commands, and threats, authors, and ladies especially, *will* send their communications, although they won't understand that they injure their own interests by so doing" ("On a Chalk-Mark on the Door" 504).

Yet, however frustrated Thackeray was by the flood of contributions from women, he seems to have been equally distressed about the evidence of women's inability to earn an income by other means. His parody of a thorn letter not only censures women contributors, but also sympathetically highlights women's financial dependence on men as the primary cause of their desperate persistence. His casting of the prototypical thorn-letter writer as a governess would have immediately alerted his readers to the fact that this woman's circumstances were either the result of being inadequately provided for by her father or of being unable to find a husband. The governess was a powerful cultural icon whose appearance as his thorn-letter writer conveyed a sense of despair for the failures of patriarchal society. Thackeray's moving mock letter reads as follows:

> Sir–May I hope, may I entreat, that you will favour me by perusing the enclosed lines, and that they may be found worthy of the *Cornhill Magazine?* We have known better days. Sir, I have a sick and widowed mother to maintain, and little brothers and sisters who look to me. I do my utmost as a governess to support them. I toil at night while they are at rest, and my own hand and brain are alike tired. If I could add but *a little* to our means by my pen, many of my poor invalid's wants might be supplied. . . . Heaven knows it is not for want of *will* or for want of *energy* on my part, that our little household [is] almost without bread. ("Thorns" 126)

Even as Thackeray dismisses the authoress, he draws attention to the very real social dilemma that drives her to solicit his help: Her father is dead, her mother is ill, and it is up to her to support the family though there are few opportunities for her to do so.

Thackeray was clearly disturbed by his lack of power to help economically disenfranchised women writers: "Why is this poor lady to appeal to my pity and bring her poor little ones kneeling to my bedside, and calling for bread which I can give them if I choose[?] . . . Day and night that sad voice is crying out for help. Thrice it appealed to me yesterday. Twice this morning it cried to me" (ibid.). The conflict he expresses over his rejection of these thorny pleas reveals both his understanding of the negative societal effects of limiting the professional opportunities of middle-class women and his own sense of responsibility for the fate of his daughters. Though Thackeray berated women contributors and even barred them from the magazine, he simultaneously created public sympathy for them through his vivid dramatization of their unfortunate plight. His interest in easing the plight of unmarried women did not directly result in a campaign to increase the number of women writers for the magazine (though their numbers did eventually rise to a healthy level), but it did become integrated into the magazine's support for the expansion of educational and professional opportunities as a crucial part of its agenda to consolidate middle-class cultural, social, and economic power.

"Keeping Up Appearances": Defining the Professional Gentleman and Eradicating the Redundant Woman

Thackeray's private ideology thus coincided with the *Cornhill*'s public concern for women's education and professional development, both of which were justified by the emergence of two distinctly Victorian characters: the middle-class gentleman and that frightening personage W. R. Greg referred to in 1862 as the "redundant" woman.[13] The magazine's redefinition of the gentleman to include the middle-class professional necessitated a postponement of marriage to provide the up-and-coming gentleman with more time to make himself financially secure. In turn, middle-class women needed some occupation aside from being wives and mothers, roles that would require immediate marriage. As a result of the needs of the new gentleman, the *Cornhill* argued for women's education and possible professionalization based on a three-fold rationale: (1) there was a surplus of women for whom husbands could not be found and who needed to have some means of self-subsistence; (2) educated and even professional women would be more beneficial to upwardly mobile gentlemen than women who existed only to rush them into marriage before they could afford to maintain their gentlemanly status; and (3) working women could be successful wives and mothers. As the *Cornhill* rejected the born gentleman for a self-made species, new definitions of gentility for women became necessary. Thus, the *Cornhill* went beyond endorsing what Judith Rowbotham describes as the Victorian career of being "a professional good wife and mother," which "in an age of growing professionalism" was "the 'highest' ambition for a good girl of any social class" (12). Instead, under the guidance of Smith, Thackeray, and Lewes, the magazine promoted women as professionals not only in the home, but also in the public sphere with no negative consequences for the Victorian family unit.[14]

In *The Idea of the Gentleman in the Victorian Novel,* Robin Gilmour explains that the period corresponding to the *Cornhill*'s establishment was intensely focused on redefining the gentleman because it was "the period when the spirit of middle-class reform was making its challenge felt within the aristocratic framework of English institutions." As a result, gentlemanliness was marked by "the drive for professional status and recognition, the challenge to patronage, the campaign for civil service reform, [and] the re-examination of the public schools" (92–93).[15] All of these reform movements were crucial to the *Cornhill*'s discourse about gentlemanhood, but the magazine tended to emphasize proper middle-class behavior and professionalization as the most important signifiers of the new gentleman.

Thackeray's early idea to call the *Cornhill* the *New Gentleman's Magazine* (Harden 905) highlights his preoccupation with matters that concerned the emerging category of the middle-class gentleman. George Smith was equally concerned with the idea of gentlemanliness. According to Schmidt, Smith spent his life struggling to attain the status of the new gentleman: "Like other rising middle class entrepreneurs [Smith] had to surmount the negative impression that his family's business was only a cut above the average shopkeeper. He, typically, sought status through behaving like a gentleman" ("The *Cornhill*" 54). These gentlemanly concerns of the *Cornhill*'s founders are reflected in many of its articles, including one of Thackeray's own nonfiction serials, "The Four Georges." In this series, placed as the opening feature of the magazine from July to October 1860, Thackeray explores the evolution of the gentleman. To do this, he claims that the nation's kings, whose lives he outlines as examples of the dead breed of the aristocratic and ostentatious "fine gentleman," who has "almost vanished off the face of the earth" (September 1860, 259), have been replaced with a more common, but ironically more noble, gentleman: "What is it to be a gentleman? Is it to have lofty aims, to lead a pure life, to keep your honour virgin; to have the esteem of your fellow citizens, and the love of your fireside; to bear good fortune meekly; to suffer evil with constancy; and through evil or good to maintain truth always? Show me the happy man whose life exhibits these qualities, and him we will salute as a gentleman, whatever his rank may be" (October 1860, 406). For Thackeray, the gentleman could now be identified by behavior rather than blood lines. Following Thackeray's lead, Fitzjames Stephen's "Gentlemen" (March 1862) explains that at one time gentlemen were defined as men from a few particular families, but the "new gentleman" is someone who combines a "certain" level of social rank and "certain" artistic, moral, and intellectual qualities. While he does not directly delineate what those "certain" qualities are, his main point is to emphasize that they are not innate but learned. Stephen gets more specific when he declares that "The fact that there is no essential difference between the characters of different sections of society, or, at any rate, no difference which is in favour of the higher classes, is nowhere more apparent than in respect of those qualities in which the spirit of gentlemen is supposed to display itself most fully–the qualities of generosity, self-sacrifice, and patriotism" (340). These particular gentlemanly traits are crucial to the *Cornhill's* agenda since they were put to use in the magazine's generous redefinition of acceptable roles for women, which would require some sacrifice of male dominance and would theoretically result in a patriotic end that benefited the nation by empowering the middle class as a whole.

One of the most famous and influential explorations of gentlemanliness during the period appeared in John Henry Newman's *Idea of the University* (1852). Amidst his discussion of the value of a liberal-arts education, Newman articulated another quality of gentlemanliness that was crucial to the *Cornhill's* agenda: sensitivity to the needs of others. Newman claims that "it is almost a definition of a gentleman to say he is one who never inflicts pain. . . . The true gentleman . . . carefully avoids whatever may cause a jar or jolt . . . his great concern being to make every one at their ease. . . . He may be right or wrong in his opinion, but he is too clear-headed to be unjust. . . . Nowhere shall we find greater candour, consideration, indulgence" (145–46). While Thackeray's responses to his thorn letter writers were, in fact, intended to be jarring and jolting in order to stop women from appealing to him, they were also inspired by his sensitivity to the unfortunate plight of the women writers whose desperation assailed him. A healthy dose of gentlemanly sympathy, coupled with the magazine's intention to reach an audience that included middle-class women, resulted in the magazine's exhortation to its male readers to accept and even actively promote improved educational opportunities for women, opportunities that could lead some women toward professional activities themselves. Under the guidance of the magazine's most influential leaders, the *Cornhill* argued that behaving like a gentleman included welcoming intellectual advancements for women. To make such advancements more palatable, however, the magazine insisted that the idea was not only a mark of gentlemanly empathy but also something that was in the new gentleman's own best interests. Moreover, these interests were primarily linked to economic stability, since, as Trollope put it, "A man's daily bread–his own and that of his wife and children,–must be his first consideration" ("Civil Service" 217).

Accordingly, the *Cornhill's* guidelines for gentlemanhood also called for a professional career that would match the middle-class man's proper behavior with economic advantages and a degree of social respectability. The *Cornhill's* conception of the new gentleman brought "one scale of values–the gentleman's–to bear upon another–the tradesman's" (Reader 158–59), abandoning the aristocratic equation of gentlemanliness with leisure and instead fusing gentlemanliness with work. Of course, that work had to be of a particular kind that required education and training to legitimate the professional's expertise. Trollope's "Civil Service as a Profession" (February 1861) suggests that one way to become a new professional gentleman was to obtain a government post by excelling in competitive exams intended to ensure quality work: "[T]here is no profession by which a man can earn his bread in these realms, admitting of brighter honesty, a nobler purpose, or of an action more manly or independent" (215). Government work would also serve to bring the middle classes into visible positions of power that would strengthen their control over the nation's affairs. Trollope maintains that it is unnecessary to raise the money required to enter the church or the law because government work carries an acceptable living wage and is an honorable and fulfilling profession that allows the new gentleman to serve the needs of the nation.

However, the rise of the middle class into the gentlemanly professions had costs that the *Cornhill* recognized and addressed. Despite Trollope's optimistic view of government work, those who wished to enter other professions such as medicine or the law had to accept the

economic and social sacrifices of training. The work of professionalization resulted in prolonging men's educations and therefore in postpon-
ing economic stability. The precarious economic status of many middle-class men rendered early marriage impractical. As a result, the
average age of marriage for middle-class men between 1840 and 1870
was thirty, and about 20 percent of men postponed marriage until after
their thirty-third year (Jalland 132). Further complicating expectations
for marriage, the female population in England began to outgrow the
male population. Census figures from 1851 recorded 104.2 females to
every 100 males. In addition, between 1851 and 1901 the number of
unmarried women over the age of twenty more than doubled, increasing from 1,444,556 to 2,941,733 (Katz 5). While the population of men
decreased due to the higher survival rate among female babies, higher
rates of male emigration to the colonies, and the deaths of men who
served in the armed forces, Susan Katz argues that there was also an
increasing "tendency among men to marry . . . late in life to insure
greater prosperity for their brides" (6). Thus, the emergence of professionalization along with other population shifts combined to create the
problem of "surplus women" that received so much attention in the
newspapers and periodicals of the 1850s and 1860s. Katz claims that:

> Even if the numbers were exaggerated or misleading and the furor
> out of proportion to the problem, the conspicuousness of women of
> the middle classes and the alarm their situation caused can also be
> imputed to the ambiguous social position of the unmarried Victorian
> woman, which often made her appear to be a misfit. . . . Cultivated
> for the marriage market, deprived of substantive education or voca-
> tional training, and sheltered from financial concerns, the ordinary
> middle-class woman of the nineteenth century was insufficiently
> equipped to fend for herself in the public sphere. . . . [T]hey existed,
> therefore, in an undefined social stratum—a no man's land that
> wavered somewhere between gentility and poverty. (7–8)

In order to create a role for these women that would not place a burden on the dwindling male population, to strengthen the middle class
as a whole, and to express the proper amount of gentlemanly sympathy for the plight of middle-class women, the *Cornhill* advocated later
marriages for its newly defined gentlemen and educational and professional opportunities for its single women.

The *Cornhill*'s advocacy of later marriages is suggested most clearly in Stephen's "Keeping Up Appearances" (September 1861), an article that points out that maintaining gentlemanly status and marrying are often incompatible (305). Stephen argues that many middle-class men are forced to forfeit their social rank when they marry and that a more acceptable decision for all concerned would be to stay single and keep up gentlemanly appearances, thus preventing miserable matches with low standards of living: "A married man must be prepared to meet [his family's] expenses on a constantly increasing scale, or to cut them down at the expense of converting his wife into a drudge, and allowing his children to grow up in unwholesome and dirty habits" (310). Stephen maintains that financial considerations are a vital component of marriage for *both* women and men. As a result he urges middle-class gentlemen to postpone marriage until they are able to comfortably support the lifestyle that a respectable family required (including a decent salary and an adequate number of servants):

> Unless a woman has extraordinary health and vigor, her husband will enjoy very little of her society if she is always looking after the children or the dinner; and if both he and she are forced to spend a great deal of time and thought in contriving ways to make their income cover expenses, their minds will be very apt to assume a petty cast, and to be fixed for the most part on small and somewhat sordid though important objects. The obscure difficulties and struggles of such a mode of life are, in plain truth, great enemies both to refinement and to high aims in life. (309–10)

According to Stephen, this situation results in more than a simple loss of "appearances." It also brings about an irreversible loss in class status, which is significant to society at large because "A nation is nothing more than an aggregate of individuals, and it will be vigorous, independent, energetic and successful, in exact proportion to the number of individuals contained in it to whom such epithets can be properly applied" (314). Stephen's call to postpone marriage leaves middle-class women with little choice but to live off of their families for longer periods or to find an alternative means of supporting themselves. Thus Stephen lays the groundwork for the middle-class acceptance of work for women until they can find well-established husbands—or in case those husbands never materialize. By mapping out the pitfalls of marrying before one has achieved financial stability, the *Cornhill* urged men to postpone marriage until they were professionally and financially secure and afforded women the freedom to interest themselves in endeavors other than marriage in order to energize the nation.

Despite its primary focus on increasing the power of middle-class men, the *Cornhill* also attempted to secure the economic independence of women within marriage, perhaps as a means of enticing the educated and/or professional woman back into the home once her gentleman was ready to be married. In "Marriage Settlements" (December 1863), Stephen emphasizes the productivity and practicality of French women who were able to maintain their own identities and finances upon marriage. He suggests that English women should have the same rights and opportunities. The *Cornhill*'s plea for reform in the marriage laws was ridiculed as excessively sentimental by Stephen's former colleagues at the *Saturday Review,* and Stephen wrote a spirited response, defending both himself and English women, in the July 1864 article "Sentimentalism." Here the author maintains that his claims about marriage are based on genuinely poor laws, not on sentimentality: "We are called sentimental for objecting to the common law by which women, upon marriage, lose their personalities" (67). Stephen suggests, then, not just that he is not sentimental, but also that sentiment can be the mark of the compassionate and forward-looking gentleman. While *Harper's* incorporated sentimentality as a means of increasing women's sensitivity to culture so that they would be empowered as private agents of public change, the *Cornhill* used the idea of gentlemanly sentiment to urge men to change their own attitudes toward women's roles, allowing women greater access to the public sphere.

"Reading Books That I Had Never Heard Of, and Talking about Them Too": Intellectual Women in the Domestic Realm

The *Cornhill* softened its rhetoric of gentlemanly sympathy for the expansion of women's educational opportunities by emphasizing the ways such opportunities could enhance women's traditional roles. While the *Cornhill*'s message implied a transformation of middle-class values, the magazine's discussions of reading advocated women's development of intellectual abilities that would improve their performance as proper wives and mothers. As with *Harper's,* the most obvious way to accomplish this goal was to teach literary taste. The most famous of the *Cornhill*'s commentaries on literary taste, Matthew

Arnold's "Literary Influence of Academies" (August 1864), can be seen as a foundation upon which the magazine builds its theory of reading, though it is a foundation that is obscured by the architecture it supports. Arnold's influential essay praises the French academy's ability to determine which literary works are worthy representations of the nation's cultural achievement and should therefore be made available to the public. Arnold uses this foreign example to impress upon his fellow citizens the cultural benefits of a formal system of literary regulation. Like Lewes, Arnold promoted the idea that a nation's literature, and thereby its reading, were lofty symbols of its power and status. However, Arnold's glorification of the academic "culture police" was embraced by the *Cornhill* only insofar as an academy of culture would loosely serve as a model for the magazine itself. The *Cornhill* would do what Arnold suggests an academy should: "set standards" and "create . . . a force of educated opinion," but it would stop short of "checking and rebuking those who fall below these standards" (Arnold 160–61).

Elizabeth Teare's discussion of Arnold's later serialization of *Culture and Anarchy* in the *Cornhill* articulates Arnold's relationship to the magazine in a way that is relevant here. She argues that while the magazine "subtly reinforced Arnold's image of an ideal English culture" and gave his work "the broadest possible appeal," the *Cornhill* "endorsed a less rigorous definition" of culture that made Arnold seem pedantic or overly didactic (119–21). In other words, the *Cornhill* complicated the Arnoldian ideal of culture by urging readers to make their own choices about literary valuation within the parameters of the magazine's offerings. The magazine was intended to guide its readers only to the point at which they would learn to properly guide themselves by internalizing the Arnoldian judge. Instead of merely choosing the proper texts for its women readers as *Harper's* tried to do, the magazine would teach them to distinguish between high and low cultural texts on their own while permitting them to consume both. Of course, this philosophy also allowed the magazine to cash in on the popularity of sensation fiction, as it did with Wilkie Collins's *Armadale*. The fact that the magazine welcomed the consumption of both high and low cultural works was significant because in the elite press the dangers of obsessively reading periodicals were second only to the dangers of reading sensation novels. In fact, Deborah Wynne points out that critics were disturbed by the *Cornhill's* inclusion of *Armadale*, which did not seem to them to suit the magazine's generally high cultural standards (148).

Through Lewes's editorial commentaries in "Our Survey of

Literature and Science," the *Cornhill* tentatively drew boundaries between entertaining or sensational fiction such as *Armadale* and serious or realistic fiction such as *Romola*. However, the *Cornhill* maintained that reading for entertainment was an acceptable practice, as long as readers were aware of its purely recreational purpose. This point is made in Lewes's defense of Mary Elizabeth Braddon's *Lady Audley's Secret*, a novel that was widely attacked for its dangerous effect on readers:

> Granting, as we must, that works of this class merely appeal to the curiosity—that they do nothing more than amuse the vacant or wearied mind, if they do *that*, it is something. They may be transitory as fireworks, and raise no loftier emotions. But a frivolous and wearied public demands amusement . . . and the public may be grateful when such amusement leaves behind it no unwholesome sympathy with crimes and criminals. . . . Its incidents are not simply violations of probability, but are without that congruity which, in a skillful romance, makes the improbable credible. ("Our Survey," January 1863, 135–36)

Lewes acknowledges the low cultural status of the novel by highlighting its lack of realism but refutes the common critical assessment that the novel is dangerous. In her discussion of Lewes's scientific articles for the *Cornhill*, Susan Bernstein argues that Lewes echoes Darwinian ideals by privileging "transmutation over fixity" and reminding "his readers that the terms of any taxonomic system are only relational, approximate ideas of resemblance" ("Ape Anxiety" 252). Similarly, Lewes assumes a taxonomy of fiction that is amenable to adaptation and that emphasizes the "unreliability of rigid lines of difference" (ibid.). This unreliability informs his refusal to reprimand women for reading sensational texts like *Lady Audley's Secret* or *Armadale*. However, Lewes does suggest that the *Cornhill* expects readers to have an awareness of the imperfectly defined categories of literature to understand that sensation novels were suitable for frivolous entertainment, whereas realist novels were more likely to provide artistic enrichment and fulfill educational purposes. While sensation fiction was proclaimed to be acceptable if approached sensibly, the *Cornhill* continued to actively promote realistic fiction for its superior values. Thackeray's preoccupation with fact, Lewes's focus on women's intellectual development, and Arnold's call for cultural regulation worked together to promote realistic fiction as the embodiment of tasteful and proper reading for women.

In a review of Trollope's *Orley Farm* in another installment of "Our Survey of Literature and Science," Lewes outlines the benefits of reading realist literature for women and their families. He claims that realism could improve women's relationships with their fathers, husbands, and children by developing their powers of sympathy. For example, Trollope's realistic presentation of "human beings, with good and evil strangely intermingled" rather than the black-and-white depiction of "angels and devils" might allow readers to gain a deeper understanding of the moral and psychological motivations of real people (November 1862, 702). To emphasize his point, Lewes focuses on one of Trollope's female characters who has "sinned where a woman of a stronger nature would have resisted temptation, but [who] nevertheless . . . is pitiable and lovable" (704). Because Trollope's fiction encourages "pity for the weakness out of which wickedness springs," Lewes demonstrates that reading realist fiction increases sympathy and thus femininity (just as Stephen argues that sympathy increases gentlemanliness) (702–3). Lewes's endorsement of Trollope's realism focuses on the ways in which it encourages the melding of women's feminine and emotional qualities that make them well suited for domesticity with their rational and intellectual abilities that allow them to serve as Arnoldian judges of literary quality. Instead of fearing the dangerous results of women's reading practices, the *Cornhill* argued that women readers could discriminate between high and low cultural texts while linking such discrimination with their feminine powers of sympathy in order to read in ways that would benefit their families.

The *Cornhill*'s illustrations of women readers that accompany its realist serials made this domestic but intellectual woman reader visible. These serials and their images also eased men's anxieties about intellectual women by cautiously subordinating women's reading activities to their domestic duties, making the former valuable only insofar as it benefited the latter. Its illustrations typically depict women's reading as a practice that occurs in a family setting overseen by men. However, despite attempting to appease men, the illustrations and novels assert the intellectual competence of women and depict men who refuse to support women's intellectual development as weak and even dangerous.

"The Blind Scholar and His Daughter" (Figure 3) is an illustration by Frederic Leighton that accompanied the premier installment of Eliot's *Romola* (July 1862–August 1863).[16] Placed in its context within the novel and the magazine, the illustration casts the woman reader as

FIGURE 3. "The Blind Scholar and His Daughter."
Cornhill Magazine (July 1862): 1.

a devoted daughter whose intellectual abilities contribute to the success of the family. Leighton's illustration depicts Romola, a fifteenth-century Italian woman, conducting academic work in the service of her father, who sits clutching a book as she stands patiently by his side reading to him. Romola stands majestically over her father with a lantern in her hand, shining light on his permanent darkness. Romola is in a position of power; however, her placid facial expression and outstretched arm, placed on the back of her father's chair, indicate that her task is a daughterly duty undertaken to assist her beloved father. In the text we learn that Romola selflessly serves her father by applying the education he has provided for her to meet his ambitions and desires rather than her own. Her father rather unappreciatively describes her as "endowed beyond the measure of women . . . filling up to the best of her power the place of a son," though he marvels at her capricious memory, which "grasps certain objects with tenacity, and lets fall all those minutiae whereon depends accuracy, the very soul of scholarship" (August 1862, 153, 149). Though she may not find the details her father values worth remembering and feels inadequate as a result, Romola takes pleasure in her intellectual activities and in her ability to further her father's academic pursuits. She is, however, equally ready to give up her scholarly role if asked.

In fact, Romola does just that to marry Tito, a mysterious wanderer who displaces her as her father's primary assistant. Though Tito distances Romola from her identity as a scholar, he does not completely displace her intellectual life. In fact, he is unable to attend to her father as consistently and devotedly as she did. In Tito's increasing absences, she continues her work: "It was not Tito's fault, Romola had continually reassured herself. . . . [I]t was in the nature of things that no one but herself could go on month after month, and year after year, fulfilling patiently all her father's monotonous exacting demands" (December 1862, 722). When Romola's father dies without having completed his scholarly goals, Tito betrays her by dividing and selling her dead father's library to make some quick cash. Even after her father's death, Romola wishes to serve him by granting his dying wish, which was that his library be donated to the community. Tito's violation of her life's mission, along with his adulterous relationship with a peasant and his shady political activities, cause Romola to seek an independent life. When she discovers that Tito has been murdered by his own father (whom he also savagely betrayed), she uses both her intellectual abilities and her innate sense of duty to serve others by seeking out Tito's mistress and children in order to take on a new role as teacher and guide for this makeshift family. Serving as a sort of father figure to this new family, she guides Tito's son toward a life that is more humane than the one his father lived. Romola's real power, then, lies in her ability to both intellectually and morally transform the next generation. Within the context of the *Cornhill,* it is vital that Romola's intellect and domesticity be compatible even if a decidedly ungentlemanly man like Tito is unable to recognize that fact.[17]

Romola sets a pattern that other *Cornhill* novels and illustrations follow and expand on: While it is clear that fathers can benefit from their daughters' intellectual engagement, the *Cornhill's* reading women have a more difficult time convincing potential husbands—even if they seem to be new gentlemen—that they will not be distracted from their wifely roles by undertaking literary endeavors. In George Du Maurier's illus-

FIGURE 4. "Cousin Phillis and Her Book."
Cornhill Magazine (December 1863): 688.

tration for Elizabeth Gaskell's November 1863–February 1864 *Cornhill* serial "Cousin Phillis," the lead character, whose reading is also encouraged by her father, is shown seated in the corner of her kitchen studying Dante's *Inferno* (Figure 4). Phillis Holman has taken time out from her domestic duties to steal a peek at her beloved book, but she still holds a kitchen utensil as she reads, indicating that she is able to shift quickly from one activity to another and that she must soon return to her "real" work.[18]

Peter Manning, Phillis's cousin, peers over her shoulder to monitor her attempts at scholarly activity. In the illustration he appears to be in a position of power over her. However, in the story when she asks him to help her translate the text, he cannot even identify the language in which the text is written, let alone translate it into English. Though Phillis assures him that she "can generally puzzle a thing out in time" and can do without his help, Peter maintains his vigil (December 1862, 689). While surveilling an intellectual activity he doesn't comprehend, Peter arrives at a new realization about Phillis: "A great tall girl in a pinafore, half a head taller than I was, reading books that I had never heard of, and talking about them too, as of far more interest than any mere personal subjects, that was the last day on which I ever thought of my dear cousin Phillis as the possible mistress of my heart and life" (ibid.).

The illustration of Phillis and Peter captures this moment of rejection; even though Phillis is depicted in a kitchen and as dutifully domestic, her books make her seem to him unfit for traditional womanly activities. Later Peter introduces his boss, Mr. Holdsworth, to Phillis as someone who can serve as a Greek and Latin tutor. While Holdsworth is initially attracted to Phillis's mind and leads her to believe he will marry her, he eventually deserts her as well. Although Romola's husband Tito more drastically dramatizes the critique of men who cannot appreciate intelligent women, Peter and Holdsworth are in the same general category of undeveloped gentlemen. Neither Peter nor Holdsworth can imagine how to fit a smart woman into his life because neither is convinced that intellectual activity coincides with domesticity or that it could serve his own interests; however, the *Cornhill* argued for the efficacy of both. These men reveal their anxieties about intellectual women, but both Romola's and Phillis's otherwise angelic demeanors cast aspersion on the unsympathetic and even cowardly gentlemen who reject them rather than on the reading women themselves.

The *Cornhill* offers a striking portrayal of the misguided male desire to regulate and control women's reading in "Bessy's Spectacles," one of Thackeray's own illustrations for his *Cornhill* serial *Lovel the Widower* (January 1860–June 1860). This picture portrays a governess named Bessy Prior standing beside her friend, Charles Batchelor, with a book dangling in front of her that she cannot read until he returns her glasses (Figure 5). Batchelor attempts to maintain authority over Bessy's reading by literally controlling her ability to see the words on the page. As we learn from Batchelor, who humorously narrates the story, he takes her glasses so that he can gaze into her beautiful blue eyes in hopes of capturing her heart. Unfortunately for Batchelor, Bessy is not so easily conquered. While Thackeray's illustration indicates that Bessy is eager to return to her book, in the text she does not have a book at all. In fact, in Thackeray's novel she is minding her

FIGURE 5. "Bessy's Spectacles."
Cornhill Magazine (February 1860): 233.

young charges as she fulfills her role as governess. So why are the children she is supposedly watching replaced with a book that she wants to read in the illustration? Though her reading is not a key element in the novel, the illustration emphasizes the importance of her interest in books as a symbol of her power, intellect, and unconventionality–she was once a stage performer, after all! Bessy's book is a sign of her unsuitability for the submissive wifely role, but not of her unsuitability for wifehood.

When Batchelor fails in his brief attempt to woo Bessy by holding her glasses hostage, he gives up on pursuing a relationship with such a strong-minded woman, much like Peter and Mr. Holdsworth give up on Phillis. The traits symbolized by the book she holds in the illustration explain both Batchelor's failure to control her and her success in controlling Lovel, the man she eventually marries. Some gossiping

FIGURE 6. "Vae Victis!" *Cornhill Magazine* (October 1864): 385.

members of Lovel's circle see Bessy as cold and calculating in her attempts to win a husband and as an inappropriate wife because of her untraditional past and her class status. However, Lovel appreciates her ability to make a living and her loyalty to her siblings, whom she supports with her earnings. Regardless of her subtle domination over him, Lovel is willing to submit to her because, as even the jealous Batchelor admits, she "has practised frugality all her life, and been a good daughter and a good sister" and "will prove a good wife . . . [and] a good mother" (May 1860, 592). Despite the fact that Lovel is a somewhat comic figure whose passivity complements his wife's activity, Bessy's triumph is a happy one for both the new gentleman and the smart woman as she rises in class status and guides her husband toward new middle-class values.

George Du Maurier's illustration for Elizabeth Gaskell's *Wives and*

Daughters (August 1864–January 1866) is unusual for the *Cornhill* in that it depicts a woman reading alone without the presence of men–almost (Figure 6). In "Vae Victis!" (or "The Woes of the Vanquished"), named for the title of the chapter the illustration accompanies, Molly Gibson is seen reading by herself in a window seat. However, she is more interested in the men who pass by outside her window than she is in the words on the page. In the novel, Gaskell describes Molly as whiling away the days in the library during a visit to the Hamley household. She reads "old English classics" and the young Osborne Hamley's poetry, which make "the summer days . . . very short to this happy girl of seventeen" (October 1864, 391). When Roger Hamley returns with news of his brother Osborne's poor performance on his university exams, Molly is displaced from the library, which Roger dominates. Molly escapes to her room to read, thus avoiding Roger and the turmoil he brings with his visit. The illustration, however, collapses the scene of Molly's reading in her room with a later one in which she watches (without a book in her hand) Roger and Squire Hamley walk the grounds outside her window. This visual combination of two separate events diverts Molly's (and the reader's) attention from her enjoyment of Osborne's poetry and her resultant crush on him to the overtly scientific brother, with whom she eventually falls in love. Not only does the illustration foreshadow future events in the novel, it also shows how Roger's return to the family banishes women from the library and distracts Molly from her own literary pursuits.

At one point, however, Molly sneaks back to the library and encounters a disturbing situation. As she quietly reads a book in the dark corner of the room, Roger and Osborne enter without seeing her and accidentally reveal that Osborne is secretly married. While Molly thus obtains forbidden knowledge in the library, she is also better able to support Roger and the Hamley family as they face the problems Osborne's deception causes. Molly's independent reading, then, is not dangerous precisely because it does not threaten the male sphere or injure her proper womanly interests even though it has the potential at first to lead her toward a romance with the less responsible but more romantic Hamley brother and later to embroil her in Osborne's sexual secrets.

Molly's reading practices are also greatly influenced by Roger's guidance. In contrast to Dr. Gibson's view that his daughter should not be too well educated, Roger directs her toward more "steady" and focused reading akin to his scientific examination of specimens under a microscope. Molly's intellectual insights, however, also influence Roger: "Sometimes her remarks had probed into his mind, and excited him to the deep thought in which he delighted" (December 1864, 703). Molly's ability to share in the knowledge of Roger's profession makes her a more suitable wife for him than Cynthia, who takes no interest in his scientific endeavors. Far from being intimidated by Molly's intellect, Roger encourages her educational improvement and is inspired by her engagement with science. Not only does Roger represent the new generation of professional gentlemen, but Roger and Molly together become the new middle-class couple suggested by the *Cornhill.* Unfortunately, we never see evidence of this as a result of Gaskell's untimely death before the novel was completed, which meant that the couple's marriage would be left unwritten. Only Gaskell's notes and Frederick Greenwood's editorial explanation printed in the *Cornhill* in place of a conclusion reveal that this reading woman triumphs in affairs of both the heart and the mind.

The physical proximity that women readers have to men in the *Cornhill*'s illustrations graphically depicts the magazine's focus on the benefits educated women could have for men, even though the male characters often express their ambivalence toward women readers in the accompanying texts. Above all, these heroines imply that, for most women, improved educational opportunities are valuable not necessarily because they provide individual fulfillment but because educated women can better serve the interests of the middle classes. In order to change the status of women, the magazine set out to change the minds of its male readers. In case not all of its readers were as progressive as Roger Hamley, the magazine provided more explicit arguments for improving women's educational opportunities in its nonfiction articles. The *Cornhill* even imagined how those opportunities might extend beyond the bounds of the home.

"What Women Are Capable Of": Creating Educational and Professional Opportunities for Women

The *Cornhill* is well known for its participation in debates over the status of middle-class boys' education, as it devoted numerous articles to a subject that coincided with its interest in the development of the new gentleman. These articles, which were aimed at improving the ability of middle-class boys to succeed in the professional world, include a series of anonymous letters from "Paterfamilias to the Editor of the *Cornhill Magazine*" written by M. J. Higgins (May 1860, December

1860, and March 1861), as well as "On Some Points of the Eton Report" (July 1864) by the same author; "Schoolmasters" by J. F. Boyes (June 1861); and "Middle-Class and Primary Education in England Past and Present" by John Sutcliffe (July 1861). These selections advocated changes in middle-class schools to coincide with improvements made to the educational system for the upper and lower classes. Fitzjames Stephen cited the lack of training for teachers and the supposed promotion of mediocrity caused by the examination system as two serious problems facing the middle classes ("Competitive Examinations," December 1861, 698). As Robin Gilmour points out, "Reform of the public schools went hand in hand with Civil Service and administrative reform" as a means of improving the training and reputation of middle-class professionals and consolidating their power (93). Gilmour argues that by the 1880s public-school reform had "solved the problem of defining gentility for the middle and upper classes, and helped to forge a new elite by exposing their children to a common, shaping ritual of education." Furthermore, middle-class civil service and school-reform movements precipitated the decreasing potency of the idea of the gentleman later in the century because it "ceased to be problematic, and no longer had to carry the freight of the middle-class challenge to aristocracy" (182–83). While the *Cornhill* has been recognized as a major force in these public debates to consolidate middle-class power, what has continued to be neglected is the *Cornhill's* attention to women's formal education and professionalization as a necessary and complementary subject for reform that, if taken seriously, would also contribute to the ascendance of middle-class gentility.

Though few actual professions had been available to women (teaching, writing, and acting among them), the opening of women's colleges such as Queen's College (1848), Bedford College (1849), the North London Collegiate School (1850), and the Ladies' College (1853) allowed women to prove that they could pass competitive examinations. According to W. J. Reader, one result of these educational advancements for women was that with the 1861 census, professionals began to be separated by sex, although the actual number of female professionals remained low (172).[19] Martha Vicinus notes that by 1901 a modest 12.1 percent of unmarried women over twenty–238,510 total women–were involved in professions, holding jobs as teachers, doctors, nurses, scientists, and government employees (28). The *Cornhill* helped make these gradual changes in women's roles more acceptable to its readers by shifting away from an emphasis on the education and professionalization of married or marriageable women in its criticism and illustrations to so-called surplus women, whose need for educational and professional training was less questionable.

This shift in emphasis is most notable in Harriet Martineau's "Middle-Class Education in England—Girls" (November 1864).[20] Like Thackeray's "thorn letter" commentaries, Martineau's article reveals the difficulties that unmarried, middle-class women faced. She argues that government funding for education should be equally divided between boys and girls since there were so many unmarried women who remained helplessly unable to take care of themselves due to inadequate educations: "[T]here must be tens of thousands of middle-class women dependent on their own industry: and it can hardly be doubtful, even to the most reluctant eyes, that the workers ought to be properly trained to the business of their lives" (554). Martineau's later article, "Nurses Wanted" (April 1865), echoes this claim and, unlike Thackeray's *Roundabout Papers,* asserts that the nation can no longer see the entrance of middle-class women into the workforce as distasteful because it is an undeniable necessity: "Any pretense of horror or disgust at women having to work, is a mere affectation in a country and time when half the women must work in order to live" (409). Rather than advocating specific job training for women, Martineau calls for a well-rounded education that would include not only basic reading, writing, and womanly "accomplishments," but also Greek, Latin, and other serious subjects, for which, she argues, girls are actually better pupils than boys (552). In other words, her ideal education for girls would be equivalent to the education received by middle-class boys because, like their male counterparts, "a considerable proportion of the girls will not marry; and these may prepare to be self-supporting" for the good of the entire middle class and the nation (563).

To deter potential detractors who might disagree with her contention that education was the best solution to the problem of "surplus women," Martineau acknowledges that a balance between serious scholarship and domestic training will produce superior wives and mothers among those who are destined for marriage. Building this argument on nationalistic grounds, Martineau reverses *Harper's* use of British literary models to improve American culture by advocating the use of American models to improve the education of women in England. Martineau implores the English nation to see the education of its girls as a patriotic responsibility. England, she proclaims, must produce women who will be at least as well informed as those "[i]n the United States," a country in which "the individual goes for more than with us; and it is felt to be desirable that the mothers of the next generation should have a large intelligence and rich culture" (ibid.). Finally, Martineau asserts the inevitability of progress for women in order to discourage resistance and glorify the potential of the English middle classes:

> [N]ot all the ignorance, the jealousy, the meanness, the prudery, or the profligate selfishness which is to be found from end to end of the middle class, can now reverse the destiny of the English girl, or retard that ennobling of the sex which is a natural consequence of its becoming wiser and more independent, while more accomplished, gracious, and companionable. The briars and brambles are cleared away from women's avenue to the temple of knowledge. Now they have only to knock, and it will be opened to them. (567)

Here Martineau reveals the ugly side of the middle classes (their jealousy, meanness, and selfishness) to argue that their generosity and gentlemanliness must triumph and allow progress for women. Deirdre David, discussing Martineau's writing in another context, suggests that her arguments are suitable to the middle-class public because she reconciles "her strong-minded sexual politics" with "her legitimating functions for the English middle class" and "engineers her feminism so that it serves the ideological aims of that same social class for whom she performs her legitimating role" (32). This approach is compatible with other *Cornhill* contributors who forged the magazine's agenda by urging the advancement of women into intellectual and professional areas as a means of supporting the new gentleman.

Articles such as R. Ashe King's "A Tête-à-Tête Social Science Discussion" (November 1864), Anne Thackeray's "Toilers and Spinsters" (March 1861), and E. S. Dixon's "A Vision of Animal Existences" (March 1862) became a part of the *Cornhill*'s central message by advancing the consolidation of middle-class power, redefining proper roles for women, and merging fact with fiction in an attempt to ease the potentially jarring nature of the magazine's cautious protofeminist rhetoric. The use of techniques such as humor, dream sequences, and fictionalized dialogues in these serious articles buffer controversial points of view about women's proper roles in society and teach without preaching. Just as the presentation of the magazine's fiction as a healthy part of one's reading diet was predicated upon its "factual" nature, the use of fiction in these factual articles made their arguments more palatable. Therefore, the magazine's use of "fact" as a signifier of the high cultural value of its fiction is complemented by the use of "fiction" as another tool to persuade resisting readers to accept the necessity of educated and professional women.

R. Ashe King's "A Tête-à-Tête Social Science Discussion," which directly follows Martineau's essay on education for girls, opens with the musings of a gentleman on the day of his ninth daughter's birth. He feels his home is so overrun by his wife and daughters that he begins to fantasize about how he might combat the alarming increase in women (both in his home and in society). While pondering this topic, the narrator drifts into a deep sleep. Thus begins an outrageous dream sequence in which he envisions a mob of "monstrously crinolined women" throwing babies at him instead of serving his dinner. When he is left starving with nine screaming babies, his friend Croaker comes to the rescue with a penknife: "[T]he fattest baby's head was thrown back. I turned away in suspense and horror, only to hear one terrible scream, which woke me" (570). Upon awakening, he is struck not so much by the horror of the dream as by the realization that he is not alone in his feeling of being surrounded by women. It is not his personal plight, but the plight of the nation: "[S]uddenly flashed upon me some hateful statistics proving the extraordinary numerical predominance of the sex. . . . For hours I lay calculating all the evils of a nation of old maids. I watched in thought the tide of women steadily and inevitably setting in; first creeping under the doors of our printing offices, then our dissecting rooms, then sweeping over the bar, and at last, submerging the pulpit" (ibid.). In a satirical dialogue with Croaker (who is obviously not a proper new gentleman), the misogynist bachelor suggests everything from human sacrifice to polygamy to reduce the female population. After initially being enticed by Croaker's ideas, the narrator comes to his senses, sympathetically considers his own daughters, and decides that a better solution is to "make women more independent—more capable of self-support . . . train them by a wider and more bracing education; strengthen their mind, enlarge their ideas, and perhaps . . . awake some power of reasoning" so that they will be better equipped to play a part in the public sphere (574). Even more importantly, while he encourages women's education and professional status, King maintains that educated and professional women would not be "a whit less eligible as wives" (576). Typical of the *Cornhill*, this article encourages increasing women's options in order to both relieve the problems of the financially strapped gentleman and express proper gentlemanly sympathy for women's needs. The article's incorporation of the misogynist dream entices and reassures its doubtful male readers who, like Croaker, "don't know what women are capable of—the depth of their character, the breadth of their mind, the strength of their intellect" (ibid.). King works to bring these readers over to his side with the satiric but pedagogical form of the dialogue in which Croaker is taught to set aside his prejudices. In a sense this becomes a conversion narrative in which the wrong-headedness of the narrator and his friend are finally corrected just as, hopefully, the resistant reader is reformed.

Anne Thackeray's "Toilers and Spinsters" also links women's education to the issue of surplus women. However, she argues that the main problem for women is a lack of financial security, not a lack of husbands. For Thackeray, the expansion of women's educational and professional opportunities is the only viable solution to the financial woes that her father recognized in his thorn letters.[21] Echoing her father's dramatization of his thorn-letter writer, she creates a fictional monologue for the old maid that coincides with a stereotypical and unflattering depiction of a gloomy, self-pitying, helpless, and broken-hearted woman who is past her prime: "Oh, alas, alas! what a sad, dull, solitary, useless, unhappy, unoccupied life is mine! I can only see a tombstone at the end of my path" (318). By countering the fictionalized image of this self-pitying and contemptible spinster with a series of rhetorical questions, Thackeray pulls the unsuspecting reader into compliance with her ultimately progressive message that single women should rely on their intellectual abilities to gain employment that could bring them both happiness and financial independence:

> What possible reason can there be to prevent unmarried, any more than married people from being happy? . . . Are unmarried people shut out from all theatres, concerts, picture-galleries, parks, and gardens? . . . May not spinsters, as well as bachelors, give their opinions on every subject? . . . publish their experiences . . . write articles in the *Saturday Review?* . . . They have been doctors, lawyers, clergy-women, squires . . . been brave as men when their courage came to be tried. . . . [T]hey have farmed land, kept accounts, opened shops, inherited fortunes, played a part in the world. . . . Then surely it is the want of money, and not of husbands, which brings them to this pass. Husbands, the statistics tell us, it is impossible to provide; money, however, is more easily obtained. (319–20)

With this more inspirational view of single-women's possibilities, Thackeray still highlights the fact that money could be made only if women were educated and employed.

To facilitate women's employment, Thackeray encourages women to attend the Ladies' Reading Room at 19 Langham Place (which provided inexpensive food, stimulating conversation, and useful reading material including free copies of the *Cornhill*), to join the Society for Promoting the Employment of Women, and to use as role models the group of working women at Emily Faithfull's Victoria Press. Thackeray praises the contributions these organizations make to finding jobs for women such as "Miss A," who was reduced to poverty by her father's business failure; "Miss F," whose husband ran off to America; and "Miss G," whose husband is ill and cannot work (323). With this alphabetical list of women, she more explicitly reveals what her father agonized about but only hinted at in his *Roundabout Papers:* that it is the failures of men that necessitate the opening of professions to women. After investigating these organizations, Thackeray surmises that "It must be less annoying and degrading to be occupied by work, however humble, than to contemplate narrower stintings and economies every day—economies that are incompatible with the very existence of cultivation and refinement" (326). Thackeray's argument is reminiscent of fellow *Cornhill* contributor Elizabeth Gaskell's claims in *Cranford*—published serially in *Household Words* from December 1851 to May 1853. The old maids of Cranford revise their conceptions of women and work to allow Miss Matty, one member of a community of old maids, to work for a living after a financial disaster. Like the women of Cranford, Thackeray develops a new definition of feminine gentility that coincides with the concept of the professional gentleman and is not compromised by work, but by changes in living standards. In fact, gentility for women, just as for men, comes to coincide with the possibility of work since, as Martineau also points out, only a very small minority of women can be considered genteel if gentility "consists in doing nothing appreciable" ("Nurses Wanted" 409).

Thackeray's acceptance of middle-class women workers lends legitimacy to them and pushes them into the mainstream, while emphasizing the positive influence of "what some good women can do with great hearts and small means, how bravely they can work for others and themselves" (321). Craftily inserting women into the public sphere, Thackeray concludes, "I seem to be wandering all about London . . . and have drifted away ever so far from the Spinsters in whose company I began my paper. But is it so? I think it is they who have been chiefly at work, and taking us along with them all this time; I think it is mostly to their kindly sympathy and honest endeavors that these places owe their existence" (331). Almost without realizing it, the reader has taken a sympathetic and even genteel turn through the public—but still feminine—life of educated and professional women.

E. S. Dixon's "A Vision of Animal Existences" explores the middle-class gentleman's acceptance of the elimination of single-women's redundancy through education and work. At first, such acceptance seems unlikely in a "sci-fi" depiction of a Darwinist future that holds only intellectual and self-sufficient women who have presumably surpassed men intellectually. Dixon's fictional dramatization of factual issues considers what happens to the educated and working woman who eventually marries an economically stable, middle-class man and concludes that such women continue to balance work and family life effectively without completely destroying their femininity or the social order. Once again, these societal changes are depicted as the unavoidable wave of the future that men must accept or else continue to fight futilely.

The narrative begins at the local zoo, where the narrator's daydream is influenced by the sight of a middle-aged woman, whose countenance he identifies as that of a professional authoress, reading a volume of Darwin as she rests on a park bench. As the man begins dreaming, the woman is transformed into "Natural Selection, Originator of Species"—the name and title printed on her calling card (313). Joined by her son "Struggle-for-Life," she begins to lecture on the evolution and classification of species, proving that she can be both a competent professional and an attentive mother. The dreamer protests against her lesson about competition among species and the triumph of brute strength. He despairs at the loss of the finer (read feminine) qualities of weakness, modesty, and self-denial (which are lacking not only in her speech, but also in *her*). She responds by proclaiming that nature cannot yield "her laws to the caprices, the blunders, and the follies of men. . . . If the whole human race were to . . . obstinately defy the laws of nature, the rising tide would relentlessly swallow the whole human race" (317). The inevitable failure of any meager male resistance to the feminine world of nature reinforces the necessity of a change in the dominant masculine worldview.

This dramatic dialogue between a weak man and a strong woman suggests that an irreversible evolutionary change in gender roles is imminent. When the narrator awakens, he turns to the real woman reader sitting next to him on the bench to ask her opinion of Darwin. In a well-reasoned manner she responds, "Here we are offered a rational and a logical explanation. . . . [I]t is conscientiously reasoned and has been patiently written. If it be not the truth, I cannot help respecting it as a sincere effort after truth" (318). In contrast to the scene of science-fiction horror presented in the role-reversing dream, the calm response to Darwin supplied by the real woman is quite comforting. Dixon, then, exaggerates the fear of the manly woman who might result from education and public work in order to promote a new gentlewoman who can improve her own and her family's position in society by participating in the important conversations of the day and even by being independent and self-supporting if it is required to preserve the status of the new gentlemen around her. Pairing the controversial topics of evolution and women's intellect, this article proposes that the educated and professional woman is an unavoidable part of the future of the English nation. Dixon makes clear that it is better for men to welcome this newly evolving generation of women than to defy it and be left behind by an unstoppable evolutionary force. The choice between Thackeray's desperate thorn-letter writer and Dixon's confident authoress seems to be a clear one. Dixon proposes that the evolution of society requires the second woman to supplant the first, and Thackeray's editorial choices, as well as the choices of his successors, reflect the same conviction.

In opposition to the growing class of specialized literary reviews that excluded women readers, the *Cornhill* combined the literary and cultural instruction of the middle classes with a more controversial agenda promoting women's education and entry into the professions. As George Eliot, Elizabeth Gaskell, and William Thackeray create intellectual women who successfully fulfill domestic roles, Harriet Martineau and Anne Thackeray provide glimpses of women engaged in professional work as nurses, writers, and printers, and R. Ashe King (comically) depicts women overtaking the fields of medicine, law, and religion, the *Cornhill* uses both fact and fiction to show that women's traditional roles must be expanded in order to maintain the strength of the middle class. However, the magazine remains equivocal about the exact ways in which women are supposed to carry out their new roles. The only clear message is that, for the cultural health of the nation and the power of the middle-class gentleman, women must be educated properly, and a proper education should begin with a subscription to the *Cornhill Magazine.*

⊷⇒ 3 ⇐⊷

(IM)PROPER READING
FOR WOMEN

Belgravia Magazine *and the Defense of the Sensation Novel, 1866–1871*

MARY ELIZABETH BRADDON'S establishment of *Belgravia: A London Magazine* in 1866 marked the concrete fulfillment of the literary goal she had tentatively suggested to Edward Bulwer-Lytton, her friend and mentor, three years earlier: "I want to serve two masters. I want to be artistic and to please *you*. I want to be sensational, & to please Mudie's subscribers. Are these two things possible, or is it the stern scriptural dictum not to be got over, 'Thou canst not serve God and Mammon.' Can the sensational be elevated by art, & redeemed from all it's [*sic*] coarseness?" (Wolff, "Devoted Disciple" 14). With the encouragement of Bulwer-Lytton and the financial backing of publisher and live-in lover John Maxwell, Braddon endeavored to answer her own question about the viability of producing both artistic and popular novels affirmatively in *Belgravia* by making it the magazine's mission to establish the popular genre of sensation fiction as worthy of critical praise. In fact, Braddon served both her artistic and financial interests and defended the critical faculties of her target audience of middleclass women readers by creating a magazine that confounded the dominant discourse against sensationalism to support the genre as proper reading for women.

Founded in 1866 as a partnership between Braddon and Maxwell, *Belgravia* was aimed at what Alvar Ellegård calls "a genteel, middleclass, lady public, of low to fair educational standard" (32).[1] What Braddon considered a rather snobbish title for her magazine was intended as "bait for the shillings" of upwardly mobile readers, who hoped to signify their arrival into the cultural elite by purchasing a magazine named for one of the most fashionable areas of London (Wolff, "Devoted Disciple" 138). While this "bait" was no doubt appealing, *Belgravia*'s most powerful attraction was its sensation fiction, which presented readers with exciting and intricate plots focusing on supposedly respectable, middle-class citizens, sometimes women, who were secretly involved in criminal activities such as bigamy, arson, forgery, and even murder. *Belgravia*'s readers were presented with an abundance of serialized sensation novels, poems, travel narratives, biographies, and essays on fashion, history, science, and the arts accompanied by lavish illustrations, all for the bargain price of a shilling. The combination of the price, Braddon's "brand" name, and the exciting sensation fiction allowed the magazine to garner a respectable average circulation of 15,000 in an increasingly crowded field of family literary magazines (Scheuerle 31–32).

However, these were not the only elements of Braddon's magazine that made it attractive to readers. Indeed, in this chapter I show how Braddon's agenda to defend both women readers and the genre of sensation fiction from the attacks of literary critics made *Belgravia* particularly appealing to readers who aspired to be intellectually independent. Like *Harper's* and the *Cornhill*, *Belgravia* was optimistic about the educability of middle-class women readers and argued that women could contribute to the maintenance of a healthy national culture. However, Braddon's magazine went well beyond its contemporaries in its assertion that women not only could but also should function as independent readers who were qualified to choose their own reading materials without the guidance of literary critics or magazine editors and without regard to the standard conceptions of high and low culture. At a time when journalists and reviewers typically depicted women as dangerous, corruptible readers in need of guidance and regulation, and defined sensation fiction as a genre that violated acceptable boundaries of morality and taste, my examination of this important but infrequently studied periodical record reveals the ways in which Braddon legitimized both her literary production and women's enjoyment of sensation novels.

An increasing number of critics—including Anne Cvetkovich, Pamela K. Gilbert, Winifred Hughes, and Lyn Pykett—have discussed Braddon's sensation novels, and a recent volume of essays on Braddon edited by Gilbert, Marlene Tromp, and Aeron Haynie explores various aspects of her fiction and her career. However, these projects have ignored the crucial role *Belgravia* played in the development of

Braddon's literary philosophy and reputation. Jennifer Carnell, in her new biography of Braddon, and Solveig C. Robinson, in her article on *Belgravia,* have begun to look at the relationship between Braddon's editorship and the critical reception of sensation fiction, while articles by Cynthia L. Bandish and Barbara Onslow explore the roles of Bohemianism and science in the magazine. However, the cultural significance of Braddon's periodical deserves more attention. Building on these valuable initial studies, I explore how Braddon created a family literary magazine that would attract a broad middle-class audience, advance her career, and keep her at the forefront of the critical controversy surrounding sensation fiction as she sought to redefine the terms of the Victorian debate over the valuation of literature and culture. I argue that as a result of her efforts, Braddon also managed to revise the genre of the family literary magazine in important ways that offered women more freedom and enjoyment in reading than either *Harper's* or the *Cornhill* allowed by rejecting the standards of critics and validating the public's taste for sensationalism. Both *Harper's* and the *Cornhill* endorsed the binary opposition between high and low culture while either blending the modes in practice (in *Harper's* case) or asserting that low culture was acceptable as long as readers consumed it properly (in the *Cornhill's* case). Instead, Braddon's version of the family literary magazine sought to invert the critical standard by putting the high in the position of the low and the low in the position of the high, thereby introducing an alternative system of classification that was more amenable to women readers and writers.[2]

M. E. Braddon: The "Name Blazoned Anon on Hoardings & Railway Stations"

The sensation novel presented critics with the most contentious literary issue of the 1860s. The controversy over this genre was a subset—albeit a dominant and domineering one—of the broader struggle to draw distinct lines of demarcation between high and low culture. The predominant thrust of the elite critics who wanted to preserve high culture is typified by Matthew Arnold's now-familiar refrain that the nation as a whole would be strengthened if citizens focused their attention solely on the most glorifying aspects of culture. This culture, as Arnold speculated in his 1864 *Cornhill* article, might best be preserved if it were controlled by a body of critics akin to the French Literary Academy.

Although no such institution was to be established in England and the *Cornhill* itself refused to fully endorse Arnold's cultural judgments, his conception of the disinterested critic whose job it was to recognize and promote "sweetness and light" endowed literary professionals with an unprecedented authority to serve not only as the guardians of culture, but also as moral educators of the public whose duty it was to teach the nation, and particularly women, what and how to read. For many members of the growing class of professional critics, sensation fiction became the defining issue of their careers, a subject on which they could safely take a stand and make their mark as crusaders whose mission it was to save the nation's culture by separating the good from the bad, the tasteful reflection of a superior civilization from the barbaric trash produced solely for profit. Sensation fiction was an easy target because it was a wildly popular and artistically dubious upstart genre dominated by women writers and supposedly consumed primarily by women readers.

Sensationalism was problematic because it violated the boundaries critics were drawing between high and low culture by combining elements of each. As Winifred Hughes declares:

> The subject matter of the sensationalists is at once outrageous and carefully documented, "wild yet domestic," extraordinary in intensity and yet confined to the experience of ordinary people operating in familiar settings. The narrative technique combines a melodramatic tendency to abstraction with the precise detail of detective fiction, an unlimited use of suspense and coincidence with an almost scientific concern for accuracy and authenticity. (16)

In its obsessive concern with "journalistic" or "photographic" details that meticulously represented scenery and physical characteristics of people and objects, the genre relied on a conception of the real that served as an implicit challenge to the core values of realism. The attempts of sensation writers to present scenes that were technically "realistic" in their presentation of an abundance of descriptive details were sneeringly labeled unrealistic or hyperreal because of their lavish excesses and their failure to combine details with characters who were role models and with story lines that taught clear moral lessons. Because the qualities of the new genre brought the conventions of realism into question, Patrick Brantlinger argues that the sensation novel initiated "a crisis in the history of literary realism" ("What Is 'Sensational'?" 27). Braddon perpetuated this crisis in *Belgravia* by sensationally constructing a topsy-turvy world in which low culture was transformed into high culture and the woman reader was constructed as more critically perceptive than the professional critic. Before examining how Braddon challenged the tenets of realism and the cultural authority of critics while peddling her wares, I would like to consider what led up to the critical power struggle that was played out in the pages of *Belgravia*.

While the three best-selling novels of the decade (and of the century) were sensational—Wilkie Collins's *The Woman in White* (1860), Ellen Price Wood's *East Lynne* (1861), and Braddon's *Lady Audley's Secret* (1862)—Braddon received the brunt of the critical uproar over the genre. Henry James was one of the first critics to crown Braddon "the founder of the sensation novel," a title that brought with it more ridicule than accolades.[3] The critical focus on Braddon was partly due to her precarious personal life, which alienated her from "polite" society. As a result of her father's adultery, financial failure, and subsequent separation from the family, Braddon embarked on an eight-year career as an actress to earn money in 1852. This was not a career choice likely to bring respect to a seventeen-year-old girl and her middle-class family. To protect her family name, she adopted the stage name Mary Seton. To further mitigate any damage to her reputation, she was diligently chaperoned by her mother. After shifting her attention to the profession of authorship in 1860 at the age of twenty-four, Braddon developed a scandalous relationship with her publisher, John Maxwell. Braddon moved in with Maxwell and his five children despite the fact that he was legally married to another woman. Maxwell was estranged from his wife, who was apparently insane and living either in an asylum or in Ireland with family members. Maxwell and Braddon proceeded to produce six children of their own, one of whom did not survive. Their socially unacceptable relationship became even more scandalous in 1864, when Maxwell leaked false news of their marriage to the press, hoping to put an end to the gossip they had aroused. However, this news only stoked the fire as counterreports issued by Maxwell's brother-in-law revealed that his first wife was indeed still living. Not until 1874 were they finally able to marry as a result of the death of Maxwell's wife. Braddon's sensational life and her sensational story lines were inextricably linked in the minds of her critics. Her violation of Victorian codes of proper femininity as an actress, writer, and mistress who was thrust into the spotlight when thousands of copies of her books began to sell was compounded when she took on the powerful public position as editor of a literary magazine. While this position gave her the possibility of reshaping her literary reputation, it also made her an even more visible target for critics.

To illustrate why Braddon's fiction was targeted, and how her early reputation was established, I briefly examine one of the first and most devastating reviews of her body of work. W. Fraser Rae's "Sensation Novelists: Miss Braddon" (September 1865), published anonymously in the *North British Review,* reveals typical attitudes toward Braddon and exposes the roots of the critical fear of sensationalism. It also illustrates Rae's desperate attempt to establish himself as precisely the kind of critic Braddon would later oppose so vigorously in *Belgravia.* Even though Rae has frequently been quoted, his response to Braddon has not been viewed in the context of her emergence as a powerful magazine editor. I want to place his comments within this context in order to lay the foundation for the highly charged series of exchanges between Braddon and her critics that played out in *Belgravia.*

Writing a year before Braddon launched her magazine, Rae set out to assess the seven novels Braddon published between 1862 and 1865 according to what he calls a "purely literary standard." However, he proceeded to carry out a moralistic attack based on his contention that "That which is in bad taste is usually bad in morals" (181). Thus, Rae contends that "the impartial critic is compelled . . . to unite with the moralist in regarding [Braddon's novels] as mischievous in their tendency and as one of the abominations of the age. Into uncontaminated minds they will instil [*sic*] false views of human conduct" by leading readers "to conclude that the chief end of man is to commit murder, and his highest merit to escape punishment; that women are born to attempt to commit murders, and to succeed in committing bigamy" (203, 202). Rae's conclusion that morality and taste were inseparable provides another reason why Braddon became the primary target of critics: As a controversial woman writer who created unsavory women characters, she was believed to lack both qualities.

Lyn Pykett argues that Braddon attracted criticism for participating in what she calls sensation's tendency to rewrite the "script of the feminine" by exploring the contradictions inherent in Victorian ideals of femininity and articulating alternatives to these restrictive ideals (*"Improper" Feminine* 5). Faced with an unstable and shifting definition of middle-class femininity, Rae–along with the majority of elite critics–focused on Braddon's sex and on her creation of women characters who transgressed gender and class boundaries. When it came to her female characters, Braddon's personal life often became a subtext that interfered with assessments of her professional work. Rae implied that a proper, middle-class woman would not create such characters: "An authoress who could make one of her sex play [such a role], is evidently acquainted with a very low type of female character, or else incapable of depicting what she knows to be true" (190). Moreover, it was not only Braddon who was linked to her immoral characters. Her readers, too, were implicitly identified with sensational heroines. As Bernstein contends, the female reader of the genre was not seen as the "thrifty housewife of domestic ideology" but as "the madame monster of the marketplace, the woman dazzled by her desires for material acquisitions and sensual pleasures" ("Dirty Reading" 217). Braddon's financial success as a novelist and her privileged but scandalous position as the mistress of a powerful publisher of popular literature fueled her image as a "monster of the marketplace" which was transferred to her readers. Thus, Braddon's fiction represented transgressive femininity, immorality, and profitability wrapped into one dangerously enticing package that was believed to pose a danger to its audience.

It is probable that critics attacked Braddon as a symbol of her genre for other reasons as well. As Andrea Broomfield argues, Victorian editors, journalists, and critics often fomented controversy in order to attract readers. Broomfield claims that critics' "antagonism was partly staged and their rhetoric exaggerated to promote themselves and to bolster certain periodicals' reputations and sales. . . . Marketing controversy for profit—a staple modern media practice—was apparently thriving in the 1860s" ("Catch Phrases"). Following Broomfield's logic, Rae and many other critics depended upon their salacious critiques of Braddon—and the genre of sensation fiction—to attract the public's interest and establish their own reputations. Attacking Braddon allowed Rae to accomplish both goals while also perpetuating an ideology of literary criticism that would increase the power of critics over popular literature as well as over women readers and writers. But, as I show in my discussion of *Belgravia*'s tactics, Braddon also relied on attacking the critics to define herself and formulate an agenda for her magazine that would sustain her own readership.

While Rae wanted to attract a wide range of readers for himself, he was apparently appalled that "the unthinking crowd . . . regarded [Braddon] as a woman of genius" (180). This "false" conception, along with Braddon's "bewitching" popularity, led Rae to make his famous statement that Braddon had "succeeded in making the literature of the Kitchen the favourite reading of the Drawing room" (204). During the 1860s a number of *Punch* cartoons humorously illustrated critics' anxieties about the power of fiction to dissolve class and gender boundaries by, for example, depicting female servants discussing sensation novels with their male employers or expressing concern that their beaus would run off with their female employers. The possibility of such transgressive cross-class and cross-gender behaviors was presumably the result of sensational fiction.[4] To combat an unprecedented phenomenon in which the largest reading public ever known seemed to be gaining control over the nation's culture and acquiring common ground with members of the middle classes, Rae entreated middle-class readers to exercise the taste appropriate to their class by rejecting the dangerous genre: "It is not enough that a work should interest, it must be capable of being perused without the reflecting reader being induced to lament the time he has lost over its pages. No discriminating reader ever laid down these volumes without regretting that he had taken them up, and that their authoress should have so misemployed her undoubted talents as to produce them" (187). Appealing to a middle-class sense of duty, Rae insists that if readers belonged to respectable society they would reject the genre that threatened the sanctity of the nation's culture.

However, the idea of preserving an elitist conception of middle-class values did not appeal to the upwardly mobile audience who flocked to Braddon's *Belgravia Magazine* as a way of signaling their recent movement into the middle classes. Rae was all too aware of the fact that Braddon's fiction would bring to any "magazine to which she contributes . . . a large circulation" that would "enrich its fortunate proprietors" (180). Braddon almost seems to have taken the idea to launch *Belgravia* from Rae since she used it to contradict critics like him. Considering Braddon's hold on the public and the general resistance to female power in the public sphere, the establishment of her very own literary magazine was sure to bring with it a heightened sense of anxiety among reviewers like Rae, who would begin to use increasingly hyperbolic language to condemn her work and her readers. Indeed, both sensation novels and *Belgravia* were boundary-breaking texts that revealed the difficulty of making clear distinctions—regardless of whether they were between classes, genders, or cultural modes—within a culture in which the increasing fluidity of boundaries made their strict containment even more crucial to the (ruling class) public's sense of stability.

Despite the financial and professional advantages of conducting her own magazine, Braddon was aware of the risks. She was (at least outwardly) apprehensive about taking on a public role as defender of women and sensationalism because she understood that this position would make her an even more obvious target for critics. Consequently, she apologetically announced her bold new literary position as a magazine editor to Bulwer-Lytton: "You will wonder after this–if indeed you honour so insignificant a person with yr wonder–to see my name blazoned anon on hoardings & railway stations in connection with a new Magazine–but I think that it is not me–but some bolder & busier spirit which worketh *for* me" (Wolff, "Devoted Disciple" 136). Indeed, Braddon had cause to distance herself from the endeavor, which was distinctly unfeminine in its prominent display of the name of its "conductor" on its cover, with the name of her married lover and publisher in a subordinate position, so that the magazine itself became closely allied to the sensationalism that she symbolized as mistress and novelist. Braddon's anxiety about her literary status and her overly sensational image prompted her at first to belittle her own agenda for the magazine. She explained to Bulwer-Lytton that she was "going in for a strong sensation story for 'Belgravia' not because I particularly believe in 'sensation,' but because I think the public shilling can only be extracted by strong measures" (ibid., 138–39). However, I argue that the popularity of *Belgravia* and the culmination of criticism directed at Braddon motivated her to articulate a philosophy of sensationalism that reflected more than a desire to make money. She very quickly began to use this new publication genre to champion herself, her readers, and her genre.

"Miss Braddon in Her Daring Flight": Beating the Critics at Their Own Game

Braddon paid a high price for her ambitious endeavor to turn her sensationalistic tendencies into a sustained critical philosophy. The kinds of critical assaults exemplified by Rae increased and intensified soon after, and, I maintain, as a result of, the successful founding of *Belgravia*. An *Athenaeum* review of Braddon's *Belgravia* serial *Birds of Prey* (October 1867) reveals concern for her tendency–encouraged by having her own magazine–to palm "off on society this mass of crude and incomplete penny-a-lining, and [call] it 'a novel in three volumes'" (461). Likewise, attacks by Margaret Oliphant in *Blackwood's* (September 1867), by Frederick Greenwood in the *Pall Mall Gazette* (September– October 1867), and by *The Saturday Review* (April 1868)

FIGURE 7. "Miss Braddon in Her Daring Flight." *The Mask* (June 1868): 139.

were particularly concerned with Braddon's increased power and visibility. Robert Wolff remarks that the critical onslaught against Braddon "reached a climax in 1867," but he does not connect this increased furor with her editorial position (*Sensational Victorian* 188). Braddon's role as editor seems to me to be a crucial and overlooked factor influencing her critical reception.

The most graphic depiction of the power of Braddon's new literary position can be found in a June 1868 cartoon from *The Mask* titled "Miss Braddon in Her Daring Flight" (Figure 7). While an accompanying article praises Braddon's work for its ability to hold the public's attention without corrupting its morals, the illustration portrays Braddon somewhat ridiculously as a circus performer led by ringmaster

John Maxwell. She simultaneously balances on a Pegasus with "Belgravia" printed on its collar and jumps through hoops labeled with the names of her novels, including her recent *Belgravia* serials, *Dead Sea Fruit, Birds of Prey,* and *Charlotte's Inheritance.* This cartoon undermines Braddon's authority by depicting her as a performer (rather than an artist) who will do anything to seize the attention of her audience.

By implying that Braddon's actions are dependent on Maxwell's direction, the cartoon also portrays her as a puppet rather than an autonomous individual. As Kate Mattacks argues, Braddon herself becomes a spectacle, a "body on display" (77). This body, packaged as it is in a leotard and tutu, also calls attention to Braddon's illicit sexual relationship with Maxwell; in fact, her hands seem to reach for him as she precariously balances in midair. Despite the combination of these belittling components of the cartoon, Braddon looms large, her position as editor preventing ridicule from diminishing her presence in the literary world. She wears a dignified expression on her face, and her head (from which her ideas and words presumably flow) dwarfs her tiny body (which makes her the personal subject of scandal). Braddon is supported and carried forward by a Pegasus, the mythological figure of poetic inspiration, bearing her magazine's name. Thus, the cartoon seems to suggest that Braddon's magazine might ultimately facilitate her success in spite of the critical circus that surrounded her. Regardless of whether *Belgravia* allowed Braddon to prove she was an artist instead of a circus performer, it certainly furnished her with a major and visible means of defense that many critics clearly saw as a threat.

Though Braddon told Bulwer-Lytton that she intended to disregard her critics, she devoted many pages to refuting them in *Belgravia.* Indeed, *Belgravia* was so caught up in debates with Braddon's critics that the magazine developed an interdependent relationship with them, premised upon the idea that sensation fiction had been unfairly maligned by biased and anonymous literary critics who were more sensational than the sensationalists. Despite her critique of the outrageous tactics her enemies used, Braddon was not afraid to invite the critics she hired to produce equally sensational criticism on her behalf. In fact, she skillfully followed other journalists of the period who, as Broomfield suggests, cranked up the rhetoric in order to increase circulation figures. However, *Belgravia* was so filled with sensation and Braddon was so invested in increasing her artistic credibility that it would be difficult to claim the magazine's agenda was manufactured solely for profit. Braddon of course wanted to sell her novels and sustain a hearty readership, but she seems to have sincerely desired to refute her enemies with the force of her own views as well. She also made an effort to refute some of their critical practices, particularly the use of anonymity. Most of the critics who wrote for *Belgravia* revealed their identities in the magazine, thus creating the appearance of a more honest and open forum for literary opinions that did not emanate solely from Braddon. That Braddon used this new periodical format effectively is, I think, indicated by the rising number of attacks launched immediately after the founding of *Belgravia* in November 1866.

For example, Oliphant's "Novels" combines anxieties about Braddon's personal life with anxieties about her public visibility and power over the reading public. Oliphant assails Braddon personally by declaring that she could not know "how young women of good blood and good training feel" (260). She is particularly concerned about what she characterizes as Braddon's "intense appreciation of flesh and blood," which is recklessly presented as "the natural sentiment of English girls" (259). Like Rae, Oliphant links Braddon's unconventional life with her fiction, implying that her inappropriate behavior prevents her from depicting proper women in her novels. Declaring that "It is a shame to women so to write," Oliphant reprimands Braddon on behalf of womankind (275). In fact, Oliphant suggests that Braddon's immorality could infect her otherwise presumably innocent readers. According to Oliphant, Braddon's readers were in danger of turning into Braddon or one of her heroines. Oliphant tries to prevent this by scolding readers with the same tone and language she uses to scold Braddon: "[I]t is a shame to the women who read and accept as a true representation of themselves and their ways the equivocal talk and fleshly inclinations herein attributed to them" (ibid.). Thus Oliphant makes the writers and readers of the genre as sensational as the fiction itself and cites Braddon as the root of the problem.

Oliphant's "sermon," as she appropriately calls it, may have characterized Braddon's personal life as sensational, but it was followed up by a smear campaign in the *Pall Mall Gazette* that effectively made Braddon's career sensational as well. In a series of articles printed between September 16 and October 9, 1867, Frederick Greenwood, the *Pall Mall* editor, relentlessly attacked Braddon and her magazine by accusing her of plagiarizing *Circe*, a *Belgravia* serial published under the pseudonym of Babington White.[5] Greenwood claims the "right to protect a proceeding so fraudulent" and implicates Braddon, despite her use of a pseudonym, by naming both *Circe* and Braddon's novel *The Doctor's Wife* as examples of unethical adaptations that "should be publicly

acknowledged and formally placed upon record" ("'Dalila' and 'Circe'"
9). Greenwood crossed the line of professionalism when he forged a
letter from Braddon claiming that the "discovery of the theft" had "fall-
en like a thunderbolt" on her senses and offering to refund the magazine's subscription costs to readers for the atrocity ("Mr. Babington
White's New Novel" 3). Though Braddon refuted this statement in her
own letter to the editor on September 20, the *Pall Mall* continued to
ridicule her, stating that "most people . . . will very much prefer the [let-
ter] that is said to be forged" as it expressed "a proper sense of mortifi-
cation and regret at the appearance in her magazine of an imposture"
("Mr. Babbington [*sic*] White's 'Circe'" 4). Greenwood's sensational
stunt came to a climax with the publication of evidence that Maxwell
had wrongly attributed a quotation used to promote *Circe* in his advertisements to the prestigious *Edinburgh Review* rather than the unknown
Daily Review, in which it was actually printed. The controversy surrounding these events was quite distressing to Braddon. In a letter to
Bulwer-Lytton she confessed that she was "most deeply stung" by the
"uncalled for and unjustifiable" charges. She believed she had been
selected "as the scape goat for the sins of this generation of second &
third rate novelists" by these critics who had "at last stung [her] into a
most savage state of mind" (Wolff, "Devoted Disciple" 142–45).

Braddon relieved her "savage state of mind" by responding to
these attacks in "A Remonstrance" (November 1867). Here Braddon
mocks Greenwood, the *Pall Mall Gazette,* and the shroud of anonymity
that enabled such cutthroat critical practices by taking on the guise of
Captain Shandon. Under the gentlemanly persona of Shandon–editor
of the fictional *Pall Mall* in Thackeray's *Pendennis,* after which the real
periodical had been named–Braddon sought to protect her own credibility while refusing to admit that she was in fact Babington White. In
this article Braddon draws a distinction between adaptation and pla-
giarism, defending both White's writing practices and "his" anonymity
in the face of similarly false and anonymous critics. "Captain" Braddon
accuses the *Gazette* of going beyond the limits of legitimate criticism to
"carry on a crusade, not against the writer of the work you dislike, but
against the lady who conducts the Magazine in which the work
appeared." Identifying her position as editor as the cause of the attacks,
Braddon declares Greenwood "guilty of a paltry and cowardly proceeding, eminently calculated to bring lasting discredit" to his own
magazine (81). She offers a reward for the discovery of the person who
forged a letter in her name, thereby placing her editorship in peril in a
very unchivalrous manner that is "more characteristic of the disap-

pointed author of two or three unappreciated novels than of the gentleman editor who writes for gentleman readers" (86). Braddon suggests that Greenwood, a minor novelist who had failed to achieve the wild success that she had won, was motivated more by professional jealousy than by strict moral and literary standards.

A few years earlier, Braddon had responded in a similar manner to Rae's attack. In a letter to Charles Kent, who had made himself known to her as a repeat defender of her work in *The Sun,* she attributes Rae's vehement dismissal of her work to his own failure as a writer:

> The Post has this moment brought me *The Sun* for this evening in which I discover your most kind, most disinterested, and able defense of me against the furious onslaught of "The North British Review." I had heard of the latter, but I have been and indeed am still too busy . . . to send for the Review or to trouble my head with an attack at once so virulent and malignant. I have been informed that the criticism in question is written by a novelist whose failure to excite public attention should at least have made him more charitable to a fellow labourer. (September 12, 1865[6])

Once she became editor of her own magazine, Braddon was no longer dependant on the chivalry of kind reviewers like Kent. Instead, she was able to use her editorial clout to accuse her attackers of professional jealousy, to defend popular writers as professional craftspeople,[7] and to hire other critics to defend her.

That Braddon grew accustomed to asking for critical support is apparent in a letter to George Sala, who was one of her most frequent and vehement defenders in *Belgravia:*

> I am becoming gradually more & more irritated by a stupid little paragraph wh. has gone the rounds of the papers to the effect that Miss Braddon has realised her ambition and made £ 100,000 by her pen . . . now I cannot imagine any statement more calculated to bring contempt & ridicule on a writer than this. . . . I have written for the love of my work quite as much as for money. . . . If you wd say a word to exculpate me . . . I should be greatly obliged. (no date[8])

Despite her initial statement to Bulwer-Lytton that a major goal of her magazine was to make a profit, she ultimately set forth an agenda intended to transform the critical landscape. Once she had attained popularity, Braddon hoped her magazine would help her achieve

CHAPTER 3

respect. As a result, the magazine's most forceful salvos were reserved for those who had established critical standards at her expense. She enlisted Sala and others to carry out a full assault on the values and skills of the critical elite, who she believed resented her success and impeded her attainment of respectability.

In "The Cant of Modern Criticism," Sala did in fact follow Braddon's directive by blaming the critical assault against sensation's reigning queen on "Hatred and jealousy and spite towards one of the most successful novelists of the age" (55). He casts aspersion on what he characterizes as the elitist profession of criticism as a whole for providing legitimacy to "dunderheaded libeler[s]" whose own lack of success leads them to attack others ("Cant" 55). J. Campbell Smith's "Literary Criticism" (April 1867) offers another typically Belgravian characterization of Braddon's opponents by sensationally criticizing the antisensationalists: "Critics are self-elected judges–men who consider themselves endowed with greater discernment, a purer taste, and a judgment superior to the rest of mankind. . . . If criticism were always fair and unbiased, it would exercise a genial and purifying influence upon literature; but when dictated by either favouritism or malice, or when the offspring of ignorance or conceit, it is productive only of evil" (226–27). The charge of bias could, of course, be made against *Belgravia*'s own critics; however, Braddon encouraged them to enter the critical fray armed to win the battle, and the only way to do that was to match the intensity of the charges lodged against her. In "Literary Bagmanship" (February 1871), T. H. S. Escott, a seasoned *Belgravia* veteran, portrays critics as mere quacks, as traveling salesmen of sorts who have unskillfully imitated "the cant jargon of the craft" of literary criticism and are full of "inflated ignorance and arrogant ability" (508–9). Escott wonders how the untrustworthy, uneducated, and inexperienced "literary bagman of to-day" can so jauntily presume "to pass judgment on men who have devoted their lifetime to authorship" (509). A supreme example of the bitter, vengeful, arrogant, and unskilled criticism described in *Belgravia* was displayed in the *Saturday Review*'s scathing analysis of Braddon's *Belgravia* serial *Charlotte's Inheritance,* which inspired its own counterattack within Braddon's magazine.

The *Saturday* reviewers focused on the character of Valentine Hawkehurst, who is cast as Braddon's literary alter ego in the novel. Though Hawkehurst begins as an associate of a con artist, he reforms himself and becomes one of the novel's heroes. Braddon characterizes him as a hard-working professional writer whose success has caused him to be metaphorically pelted with mud by "nameless assailants hidden behind the hedges." Hawkehurst's only consolation from his critics is an "indulgent public" that enables him "to accept the mud which bespattered" him "in a very placid spirit, and to make light of all obstacles in the great highway" (January 1869, 442). Braddon describes Hawkehurst's (and implicitly her own) critics as literary stalkers: "And, O, to be sure the critics lay in wait to catch the young scribbler tripping! An anachronism here, a secondhand idea there, and the *West End Wasp* shrieked its war-whoop. . . . The critics were not slow to remark that he worked at a white-hot haste, and must needs be a shallow pretender because he was laborious and indefatigable" (September 1868, 475–76). Clearly intended to defend Hawkehurst–and Braddon–as hard workers who had been unfairly accused of literary crimes, this comment was instead used by the *Saturday Review* as proof of Valentine's–and by implication Braddon's own–plagiaristic practices. The *Saturday* turned Braddon's commentary on Hawkehurst's critics against her by claiming that her struggling literary hero was

a professional blackleg, who . . . turns author, and exhibits his predatory propensities by a series of audacious plagiarisms. Miss Braddon shows a wonderful fellow-feeling with this literary freebooter, and is very noisily angry with the imaginary critics who set their faces against him. . . . In an ideal state of society, where ignorance reigned supreme, and sensation novels were the highest development of literature, the energy which he displayed in concocting and giving to the world his little hodge-podge of untrustworthy and slip-shod trash would no doubt have received its due recognition from the critics of the day. (459)

The reviewer ridicules what he sees as Braddon's effort to use *Belgravia* to create "an ideal state of society" in which "sensation novels were the highest development of literature." It seems that the *Saturday's* response was inspired not only by Braddon's latest novel, but also by the power and visibility accorded to it as a result of its place within the writer's own periodical, a periodical her critics saw as devoted to "educating her admirers, and preparing them by a gradual renunciation of all their critical faculties for the ultimate enthusiastic reception of a thoroughly bad novel" (ibid.).

On Braddon's behalf, Edward R. Russell dealt the ultimate Belgravian blow to the *Saturday* reviewers by announcing that they were the founders of a kind of criticism that had become "as sensational in motive as the most sensational novel" ("'Thorough' in Criticism," November 1868, 39). Russell dubs this a "thorough" criticism that is unsociable and uncritical and intentionally severe: "The thoroughness is thorough recklessness; the sensationalism is at the expense of truth. Whether sensation be a good or a bad element in creative literature, it must be dangerous in criticism" (41). The only positive side effect such criticism can have, he argues, is if it convinces readers to "regard as merely entertaining articles which have hitherto been for a great portion of the middle classes absolute canons of literary judgment" (43). *Belgravia's* critical arguments urged its readers to disregard the biased proclamations of reviewers and instead trust their own judgments. By emphasizing the wrongs of the critics of sensation, Braddon's magazine effectively shifted the blame for the corruption of literature from the supposedly scandalous women writers and uncritical women readers to the critics of respected journals. In this way Braddon did exactly what the *Saturday Review* accused her of doing: She encouraged women readers to create alternative literary canons that would include women sensation novelists like herself and magazines like *Belgravia*.

"I Should No More Think of Dictating . . . What Kinds of Books She Should Read": Dispelling the Myth of the Diseased Woman Reader

In addition to defending herself against personal critical attacks, Braddon set out to reshape the critical discourse surrounding sensationalism by creating a positive image of those who were perceived to be sensation's primary victims: women readers.[9] Indeed, these dual goals were inseparable due to their incessant link in contemporary reviews. Given the audience and subject matter of family literary magazines, one would expect a defense of women's reading skills in *Belgravia*. However, Braddon's defense of women readers was a necessary component of her defense of the sensation novel. *Belgravia's* discourse was therefore more spirited than *Harper's* or the *Cornhill's* and more focused on establishing women's independence from critics. Braddon's agenda to promote the acceptance of independent women readers while continuing to debunk the critics of sensationalism was explicitly set forth in T. H. S. Escott's article "Vagueness" in the May 1868 issue of *Belgravia*.

Escott spoke out against the charge that women were uncritical–

and therefore corruptible–consumers of print by claiming that those who were most in danger of "a habit of slovenliness . . . which is absolutely destructive of all mental improvement or discipline" were not women but *critics* "who believe they see everything at once and feel they can grasp complexity and think that nothing can be hidden from their view" (412–13). "Vagueness," a concept equivalent to the "disease of reading," is defined as an indistinct view of the world caused by an overwhelming abundance of literature, which turns readers into "skimmers" and "skippers" who lack a full comprehension of what they read. Escott laments that dizzying proliferation of print since "every morrow brings with it . . . fresh newspapers to be read, fresh magazines to be skimmed, new works of fiction or science or politics through which [readers] must gallop at express rate, without cessation or pause" (410). In mentioning newspapers and scientific and political treatises, Escott implicates a male, rather than a female, audience, particularly one that quickly consumes texts for professional purposes. He makes it clear that professional men are the most likely victims of "vagueness" because they read under harried circumstances for money. The inherent arrogance of professionals–especially critics–and the intense pressure to make a reputation for themselves and their magazines put them in a more vulnerable position than amateur (women) readers who could take a more leisurely approach to the consumption of print. According to Escott, leisure allows thorough digestion of information and results in the formation of more thoughtful opinions. With this argument Escott acquits women of the slanderous charges frequently lodged against them and legitimates them as more skilled consumers of print (and implicitly of sensation) than critics themselves.

Belgravia not only elevated the reading practices of women above those of critics, but also argued that women readers could independently make good reading choices. Unlike *Harper's* and the *Cornhill,* *Belgravia* insisted that women's reading should be conducted apart from and without the guidance of men. Affirming this idea, George Augustus Sala maintained the right of women to choose their own books without the masculine regulation of critics, fathers, or husbands. He claims that "Novels are written for grown people and not for babes and sucklings"; therefore, "grown women should be free to choose whatever reading material they desire." He speculates that if he had a daughter, "When she came to be one and twenty, or got married, I should no more think of dictating to her as to what kinds of books she should read, than as to what kinds of stays she should wear–if she wore any at all" ("The Cant of Modern Criticism" 54). Referring to women's undergarments as equivalent to her reading material is a very clever strategy because it excludes men from having any say in the matter at all. Furthermore, it maintains that what women read is their own business and even that a man's intervention is somewhat unseemly. Under Braddon's leadership, the magazine legitimized women as autonomous readers who could read what they wanted, by themselves, in any way they chose. Unlike *Harper's*, which insisted its readers accept its definition of proper reading material, or the *Cornhill*, which endorsed a certain amount of Arnoldian regulation to ensure that women could distinguish between high and low cultural texts that they chose for themselves, *Belgravia* maintained that the opinions of the critics about cultural divisions were inherently flawed and should in fact be disregarded.

Belgravia's support for the independence of women readers is most striking in its illustrations. Just as Sala argues that what women read is their own business, *Belgravia*'s illustrations consistently depict women who read alone or with other women. Not only are these women reading independently, they are doing it for their own personal benefit rather than for the good of others. Braddon's magazine provides images of women who experience self-gratification and the development of intense female bonds as a result of reading. In each case, the magazine's depiction of what critics would consider dangerous reading practices leads to an outcome that remains compatible with the behavior expected from a proper, middle-class woman. The magazine thus enhanced its textual arguments in support of women readers with the positive visual images it displayed, emphasizing that reading was not so threatening after all.

The ability to read independently allows the woman reader in "In the Firelight" to explore her fantasies in a healthy manner through reading as she falls asleep with a book on her lap, the visions of her imagination swirling around her head (Figure 8). This woman reader lounges in a chair, one arm dangling at her side, one arm still clutching the oversized book. Her dream visions of dramatically costumed figures, just barely visible in the background, hover around her as she rests. As Sally Mitchell notes, women's daydreams are often pleasurable mental stories that "provide expression, release, or simply indulgence for emotions or needs which are not otherwise satisfied either because of psychological inhibition or because of the social context" ("Sentiment and Suffering" 32). "In the Firelight" presents reading as just such an emotional outlet that is satisfying but also safe because the final result of this self-indulgence, as we are told in the accompanying

FIGURE 8. "In the Firelight." *Belgravia: A London Magazine* (March 1868): 66.

poem, is a socially acceptable dream about marriage.[10] In the poem the woman imagines two lovers being torn apart against the background of the French Huguenot War. After witnessing the bloody turmoil of war, the scene brightens, and the separated couple happily emerge at the wedding altar. The vision ends when the woman unexpectedly awakens to recognize herself and Frank, presumably her real-life beau, as the main characters of her fantasy (66).

Surprisingly, the poem itself does not mention reading as the impetus for the dream. Instead of reading, the woman sits alone at night gazing into the fire. However, the fireplace is only a bit player in this illustration—we can just see the edge of the mantle at the left-hand margin of the picture. The fire is replaced by what many nineteenth-century critics saw as an equally dangerous element: a book. While Charles Dickens's Louisa Gradgrind notoriously gets into trouble by gazing into the fire and "wondering," *Belgravia*'s independent woman reader shows that such fancy can be healthy and normal, even when the flames are replaced with printed words. Whether the book in the woman's lap is a gothic romance (a forerunner of the sensation novel) or a historical account of seventeenth-century France, she is able to read it on her own without dangerous results. In fact, her imagination transforms a chaotic scene of death and destruction into a conventional courtship narrative that reinforces society's expectations for her as a woman. This image suggests that even if women allow their minds to

FIGURE 9. "The Elopement-Door."
Belgravia: A London Magazine (July 1869): 114.

wander into dangerous territory, they are not likely to present a real threat to patriarchal society.

Another potentially scandalous reading experience occurs in "The Elopement-Door," an illustration and poem in which the main character reads her beau's letter at the bottom of the same staircase that another legendary woman walked down to elope with her lover (Figure 9).[11] The reader's downcast eyes, her hair (which appears red as it is "dyed" in the "sunset glow"), and her position at the foot of the stairs suggest that she too might be "fallen." However, the narrator—who is the woman's male admirer—maintains that while she is caught up in the "glamour" of the "ghostly" locale "In a languorous dream of loving bliss," a "Less fortunate omen might well befall / Than that love's letter

FIGURE 10. "One Summer Month."
Belgravia: A London Magazine (August 1871): 197.

should thus be read" (115). It soon becomes apparent that the woman is engaged in a harmless reading activity that does not imply that she will follow through with an elopement herself. This picture and the accompanying poem attest to women's abilities to read thoughtfully and to make moral judgments about what they've read without being guided by critics or other male overseers. The main point here is that women can learn from the scandalous situations of others without being compelled to copy them. In fact, "The Elopement-Door" implies that the woman is better off reading alone; if her lover were present she, too, might be more likely to be led astray. The real threat is not the words on the page or the memory of a legendary fallen woman, but rather the threat of male interference at the woman's scene of reading. Though the poem is narrated by the letter writer himself as he imagines the scene that Blanche has described to him by return post, his vision of the scene is based on what she chooses to tell him. He remains secondary, outside of the boundaries of the illustration, and, most likely, out of the consciousness of the *Belgravia* reader, whose focus is directed toward the image of an independent reader able to enjoy male admiration while still resisting male temptation.

"In the Firelight" and "The Elopement-Door" both illustrate women's self-control in the face of potentially corrupting influences. However, along with "One Summer Month" (Figure 10), they also represent the ways in which reading can figure as a satisfying but safe, imaginative rebellion against repressive social structures (as the first woman envisions death and destruction before converting to marriage and the second imagines the possibility of elopement without acting on it). In "One Summer Month," a story accompanied by an illustration of the same name, Miss Royes, a self-denying governess, dreams of the satisfaction of reading a book for her own pleasure but never actually does so. Instead, she remains devoted to her ungrateful pupil and her aloof employer. Even after falling in love with a man who proposes to her, she sacrifices the opportunity to escape her drudgery by refusing the proposal. Instead, Miss Royes selflessly reunites her potential fiancé with his first love, from whom he has been estranged. In the story Miss Royes's sole pleasure stems from the fantasy of acting on her own will instead of someone else's by escaping from her oppressive duties to read something other than a textbook as she relaxes on the beach. It is as if merely imagining the fulfillment of independent reading is enough to prevent her from shirking her duties. Even though she does not take the opportunity to escape her servitude in the story, this pleasurable reading scene at the beach becomes the only visual representation of Miss Royes included in the magazine. Thus, *Belgravia* figures the enjoyment of reading—even if it is only imaginary—as productive rather than destructive, permitting the possibility of the healthy self-indulgence that Miss Royes otherwise goes out of her way to avoid.

While Miss Royes fantasizes about solitary reading pleasures, "Summer Reminiscences" (Figure 11) accompanies a poem in which two women form a communal reading relationship. The women's friendship is solidified when they read and ridicule a letter written by a male suitor, a "rival" whom they will not allow to "intrude" on their "single-hearted" souls (258). The illustration depicts two young women intimately huddled together over a letter, one woman's hands lingering on the other woman's lap as they read. However, the poem—subtitled "From Dora's Letter to Blanche"—signals a betrayal of confidence, a sensational event that is counteracted by the wholly positive image of intense female friendship—or even lesbian love—provided by the picture. The poem and the picture actually represent a period in these women's lives that has ended. The first verse reads like a love poem: "O Darling, What is there between us? / What shadow has fall'n on our loves?" (ibid.). The use of the plural form for love diverts attention away

FIGURE 11. "Summer Reminiscences."
Belgravia: A London Magazine (December 1869): 258.

from the fact that the poem seems to be a love letter from one woman to another and is not really about their separate "loves." After reminiscing about the previous summer, when they "deserted each he-side / And wandr'd with interlocked hands," vowing not to entertain male rivals who might separate them, Dora speculates that Blanche has not contacted her because she has broken their vow and "taken a lover" (ibid.).

Despite the potential subversiveness of a relationship that involves both a communal resistance to women's traditional roles through reading and a love vow between women, any danger is subsumed by the fact that one of the women has been conquered by a male lover or, even worse (from Dora's perspective), has become engaged to be married: "For 'tis certain mere distance could never / Have parted us, darling, like this" (ibid.). It is clear that the intense and youthful connection between the women has been broken by a more appropriate romantic relationship. While the women bonded by reading in opposition to a man, the man triumphs in the end. Once again Braddon's magazine highlights the positive aspects of women's reading while also acknowledging and assuaging public fears about its dangers. Braddon hoped that those who feared the boldness of women's independent reading would be appeased by the pictures they saw, for it would seem that women, given a bit of room to make their own decisions, would willingly use them to improve, rather than overturn, their traditional roles.

Unlike the *Cornhill*'s repeated use of images of women who read within a family setting, *Belgravia*'s illustrations depict middle-class women whose reading occurs apart from the family as it displays either an individual or communal feminine identity that empowers them both to think independently and to enjoy themselves while reading. In the pages of *Belgravia,* women saw illustrations that showed them how pleasurable and empowering reading could be if they could make their own choices and develop their own active reading skills that were not reliant on the interpretations of the men around them. Kate Flint argues that in nineteenth-century paintings "Reading . . . provided the means not only, on occasion, for the Victorian woman to abnegate the self, to withdraw into the passivity induced by the opiate of fiction. Far more excitingly, it allowed her to assert her sense of selfhood, and to know that she was not alone in doing so" (330). This claim applies equally well to *Belgravia*'s illustrations. However, *Belgravia*'s message is that while the reading material offered in its pages may have an element of escapism and fantasy that absorbs women as well as an element of self-assertion that empowers them, reading is a harmless and necessary way for women to maintain their proper selves.

While Braddon more boldly overturns acceptable cultural norms and with them popular notions about the dangers of women's reading, the magazine's images of women are more benign than those presented in the *Cornhill.* Even though *Belgravia*'s women are alone and able to experience personal satisfaction through reading, they are less threatening than the intellectual women with whom the *Cornhill* concerns itself. But Braddon's defense of her novels relied on proving that reading would not result in making women more dangerous. In fact, it was crucial for her to show that her novels—and her magazine—could actually produce *better* (and therefore safer) readers.

Demonstrating that women readers were capable of reading potentially corrupting material in ways that were socially acceptable allowed Braddon to argue that sensation fiction was suitable for women. She went beyond claiming that sensation was harmless to argue that by studying sensational plots and characters women could become more, rather than less, skilled at reading critically. Braddon most likely would have agreed with Flint's claim about the function of sensation in nineteenth-century culture. Flint argues that authors of sensation fiction goaded critics by mocking "the belief that women read uncritically" and refuting "the idea that a woman reader is mentally passive and accepting of what she consumes." Instead, Flint notes that the general emphasis of sensation novels is on women's "capacity for self-awareness and social analysis and judgment" (15). Braddon attempted to both goad critics and highlight women's capacity for critical thinking in the most prominent serials the magazine featured: *Birds of Prey* and its sequel, *Charlotte's Inheritance*. In these two novels, which dominated *Belgravia*'s first five years with an almost continuous run from November 1866 to February 1869, Braddon forcefully argued that sensation fiction taught women readers to be active and therefore productive and healthy readers. Nevertheless, before examining how she did this, it is important to understand the context in which this strategy for her *Belgravia* serials emerged.

Detecting the Birds of Prey and Protecting Charlotte's Inheritance: Sensationalism and the Production of Independent Women Readers

Before taking her post at *Belgravia* and establishing herself as the primary defender of sensation, Braddon attempted to navigate an alternative route to critical success with her 1864 novel, *The Doctor's Wife*. She said of *The Doctor's Wife* that it was a "turning point" that would determine whether she would "sink or swim" (Wolff, "Devoted Disciple" 25). She told Bulwer-Lytton that she had done her best to create a work of art that would appease "that set of critics" who "pelted" her "with the word 'sensational'" (ibid., 22–25). In her effort to change critics' assessments of her, Braddon wrote what she hoped would be seen as a realistic novel. However, she may have distracted critics from her purpose by also using the novel to poke fun at the dangerous reading practices of the heroine, Isabel Gilbert, and the outrageous writing practices of Isabel's friend and sensation novelist, Sigismund Smith. In contrast to the savvy women readers later depicted in *Belgravia,* Isabel's uncritical reading habits and her preoccupation with leading the life of a novel heroine fulfill the worst nightmares of the high cultural critics as they nearly result in adultery and suicide. Though *The Doctor's Wife* was Braddon's rewrite of Gustave Flaubert's *Madame Bovary,* Braddon's desire to pen a novel that would be acceptable to English critics led her to alter the tragic ending of her French model. Upon the deaths of both Isabel's mundane husband (George Gilbert) and her Byronic suitor (Roland Lansdell), she becomes a benevolent widow who devotes her life—and the inheritance she receives from the wealthy Lansdell—to helping others. Isabel begins as an ominously bad reader but turns out to be a respectable and charitable member of society. Though two men must die first, she is transformed into a sophisticated and mature reader whose life is far from sensational. In the end, then, Braddon tones down the rhetoric of anxiety about women readers at the same time she increases the sensational elements of the story that relate to the male characters.

Despite her contention that *The Doctor's Wife* was to be a "turning point" in her career, Braddon admitted to Bulwer-Lytton that she could not avoid inserting the element of coincidence in the novel that leads to a sensational turn of events in which Isabel's father kills Lansdell, who turns out to be an old enemy. Apparently prompted by criticism from her mentor, Braddon tentatively defends her decision to turn to this sensational secondary storyline near the end of the novel by stating that the "question about the inadmissibility of accident in art is always perplexing to me. . . . I know of so many tragedies that seem to have arisen out of accident, and yet I feel that you are right, & that art must be something above the experience of life" (Wolff, "Devoted Disciple" 26). Bulwer-Lytton's response to the conclusion of the story probably prompted Braddon to realize that the "turning point" she had hoped for was more likely to cause her to "sink" than to "swim."

Though *The Doctor's Wife* may have resulted in what Tabitha Sparks calls "an ultimately confused compendium" of sensationalism, sentimentalism, and realism that make it "an extraordinary document of competing epistemologies at work in Victorian fiction" (198), I contend that Braddon hoped to show that she could write realistically even while playfully engaging with elements of sensation. However, Braddon's critics did not agree, and her plan to recast herself as a realist novelist ultimately failed. In his assessment of *The Doctor's Wife,* Rae claims that while there are "fewer artistic faults in it" than in any of her other novels, it proves "how very nearly Miss Braddon has missed being a novelist whom we might respect and praise without reserve. But it also proves how she is a slave, as it were, to the style she created. 'Sensation' is her Frankenstein" (197). It may in fact have been more truthful to say that the critics were enslaved by their conception of Braddon as the embodiment of sensationalism. Nonetheless, Braddon was disappointed to find that the stigma against her was not lifted as a result of her efforts and that her work was still characterized as a monstrosity. Furthermore, she was displeased with the sales of *The Doctor's Wife* compared to her more sensational works (Wolff, "Devoted Disciple" 28). For her next novel Braddon insisted that she would "make the story one of character–& incident also–but I must write for my own public which demands strong meat" (ibid.). Braddon here articulates a new goal: to combine character and accident, realism and sensationalism in her own way to please her public and herself. It seems that the unfulfilling outcome of *The Doctor's Wife* precipitated a shift in the maturing writer's thinking that led directly to her Belgravian strategy to redefine the relationship between women readers and sensationalism rather than try to live up to the standards of realism.

With the serialization of *Birds of Prey* and *Charlotte's Inheritance,* Braddon abandoned Isabel Gilbert to create an independent woman who could read more skillfully and critically than anyone around her. This time, instead of attempting to please her critics, Braddon pulled out all the stops, writing a story that relied on the typical sensational themes of deception, theft, hidden identity, poisoning, and murder to prove that a woman could read the most outrageous situations critically and realistically. Braddon cast sensationalism as both pedagogical and realistic because it revealed the potentially disastrous consequences of middle-class respectability and female passivity through a detailed description of events that were intensely real, if rare, occurrences. Braddon used sensationalism to alert readers, women in particular, to the restrictive nature and devious possibilities that underwrote accepted class behavior and gender roles. Thus, her strategy was to subtly teach critical-thinking skills to women and to deflate the notion that readers of sensation would be easily corrupted.

With *Birds of Prey* (November 1866–October 1867) and *Charlotte's Inheritance* (April 1868–February 1869), the serial anchors of *Belgravia,* Braddon also–apparently accidentally–ventured on a new experiment in form.[12] These two connected works were conceived as a solution to a problem. When the original novel began to overrun its allotted space, Braddon halted its serialization and announced that it would be continued in an upcoming sequel to be commenced after the completion of *Dead-Sea Fruit* (August 1867–September 1868), which had overlapped with *Birds of Prey* for two months and was intended to be the next major serial featured in the magazine. However, Braddon's editorial note to her readers indicates that the conclusion to the series was in such high demand that she was obliged to apologize for a six-month delay between the conclusion of *Birds of Prey* and the beginning of its eagerly awaited sequel. To appease impatient readers who wanted to know how the series would end, the magazine was increased by thirty-two pages per issue to accommodate *Charlotte's Inheritance* even while Braddon was still completing *Dead-Sea Fruit* and beginning another new serial, *Bound to John Company* (July 1868–October 1869).[13] Braddon characteristically seized the opportunity to turn a problem into a boon by assuring the public that despite the alteration of the magazine's familiar format, "all the characteristics which have won for *Belgravia* its recognition as 'the best shilling magazine that England possesses' are preserved in their fullest integrity." She skillfully promoted the fact that the alteration allowed the magazine to include "the greatest quantity of printed matter ever offered in any monthly magazine, however high its price; and it is hoped that the quality of its literature will sustain the critical opinion–'Briskest of all the magazines is *Belgravia'* " ("Editorial Note to *Charlotte's Inheritance*," April 1868, 244). Since these novels are out of print and rarely–if ever–read today, I provide a brief plot summary before explaining how the novels worked to achieve *Belgravia*'s goal of defending sensation as appropriate reading for women.

In *Birds of Prey,* Braddon contrasts the appearance with the reality of accepted class and gender roles when she tells the story of the "eminently respectable" Mr. Philip Sheldon, who murders Tom Halliday, the husband of his former girlfriend Georgina, so that he can marry her and gain control of her dead husband's money. After Sheldon slowly poisons his rival, he quickly marries the ultrapassive widow and receives guardianship of her equally submissive daughter, Charlotte. The other "birds of prey" of the novel's title, Captain Horatio Paget and George Sheldon, are only mildly corrupt compared to the murderous Philip Sheldon. "Captain" Paget is a swindler who gains access to the rich through lies and deceit, using his former position, from which he has fallen, to gain access to free dinners and lodging as well as a line of credit large enough to support his lifestyle. George Sheldon conceals his brother's criminality and occupies his time searching for the heir to an unclaimed fortune, hoping to strike it rich by either fraudulently collecting the money or profiting from his services to the unknown inheritor. George's race to discover the missing heir entices both his brother and Paget to begin their own investigations into the matter. When all clues lead to Charlotte as the lucky heiress, it quickly becomes apparent that she will be the next target of her stepfather's murderous greed.

In *Charlotte's Inheritance,* Philip Sheldon begins to slowly poison his stepdaughter after he has duped her into taking out a life insurance policy that names him as the beneficiary. Meanwhile, Horatio Paget discovers that the real heir to the mysterious fortune is actually Charlotte's secret French cousin, Gustave Lenoble. Paget introduces Lenoble to his daughter Diana with the hope that the Frenchman will be overwhelmed by her beauty (which he is) and will propose to her (which he does) so that Paget can live out the rest of his life in comfort on Lenoble's inheritance (he dies before he is able to capitalize on his daughter's advantageous marriage). Valentine Hawkehurst, who is engaged to Charlotte, eventually discovers Sheldon's murder plot, and, with the help of Diana and those who suspected Sheldon of the earlier murder, he rescues Charlotte from imminent death by eloping with her, thus eliminating her stepfather's control over her finances. Paget belatedly discloses his knowledge of the true heir, and Philip Sheldon escapes to America but later returns to die in a snowbank in front of his stepdaughter's home.

As this brief sketch of the complex plot suggests, one of the major messages of these novels is that extreme respectability and gentlemanliness should not be trusted because they could mask impending danger and deceit. Despite Philip Sheldon's reprehensible acts, he maintains his public respectability well into the second novel in the series. Based solely on his appearance, his home, and his position, everyone in the community assumes that he must be irreproachable: "Of course he was eminently respectable. On that question no [one] had ever hazarded a doubt. A householder with such a doorstep and such muslin curtains could not be other than the most correct of mankind" (November 1866, 6). As we see in this example, the omniscient narrator, who sometimes takes on the voice of the public, maintains a running commentary full of misjudgments that must be recognized as ironic to be understood. Thus, readers would have to read critically in order to learn the true lesson of the tale. The fact that the comprehension of Braddon's moral messages required careful reading made even critics like Henry James, who admired her style, doubt the moral effectiveness of her claim that sensation was in fact a subtle form of didacticism.

The murder Sheldon commits goes unnoticed primarily because those who suspect him are afraid to come forward against such a "respectable" man; readers are meant to learn to separate themselves from the passive community through the lessons of the novel, which teach them to speak up for justice regardless of potential social embarrassment. George Sheldon is aware of his brother's plan to kill Halliday, but, even though the victim is a longtime friend of his, he fails to act, in part because he fears that his word will not prevail over his brother's reputation. Likewise, the doctor and the maid who attend the ill-fated Halliday are silently forced into compliance with Sheldon's recommendation that they take no action on the dying man's behalf due to their comparably low status in the community. Furthermore, the passive acceptance of appearances allows Horatio Paget to swindle wealthy patrons who believe he must be honorable because he is a captain. The narrator conveys a biting criticism of ignorant passivity in the description of Paget as "a gentlemanly vulture, whose suave accents and perfect manners were fatal to the unwary" and as a man involved in "those petty shifts and miserable falsifications whereby the birds of prey thrive upon the flesh and blood of hapless pigeons" (December 1866, 160). Braddon's motley crew of deceivers and criminals exemplifies the dangers of judging individuals solely on their outward appearances and apparent social positions. Her novels instead encourage the careful discrimination of character based on behavior rather than class status.

Even more importantly, Braddon encourages the development of active and independent women readers by illustrating that feminine passivity keeps women ignorant and unable to combat wrongdoing. She turns the critical assumption that women need to be protected from sensation fiction on its head by urging that her magazine and, in particular, her brand of fiction can cure feminine passivity and its concomitant susceptibility to corruption. Instead of employing an actual woman reader like Isabel Gilbert, Braddon uses metaphorical women readers to implicitly argue that the knowledge women gain from sensational themes will teach them to be more active, critical readers. First, Braddon illustrates the result of coddling women readers through the example of the docile Georgina Halliday. Georgina is so inept at reading events for herself that she unknowingly assists gold-digger Philip Sheldon in the murder of her husband. As if that were not enough, she marries her deceased husband's murderer and passively sits by as he proceeds to poison her daughter. Once Georgina marries Sheldon, she allows him to control every aspect of her life: "[S]o completely did Mr. Sheldon rule his wife that when he informed her inferentially that she was a very happy woman, she accepted his view of the subject, and was content to believe herself blessed" (January 1867, 279). The disastrous effects of Georgina's weakness carry on to the next generation, when Charlotte's submissiveness predisposes her to accept blindly a life-insurance plan that transforms her into easy prey for her stepfather. Charlotte literally refuses to read what is in front of her and, as a result, becomes the victim of attempted murder. Similarly, Mrs. Paget, described as "one of those meek, loving creatures who are essentially cowardly," is so passive that she does not even have the will to live under the dominant rule of her swindling husband, Captain Paget. Instead of resisting him by acting on her accurate readings of his duplicitous behavior, she withers away and dies, leaving her daughter Diana to be brought up in "the nest of vultures" that "every day . . . brought its new lesson of trickery and falsehood" (January 1867, 260). Significantly, it is only Diana who is able to break free from the destructive forces of feminine self-effacement and call attention to the criminal activity that she understands is taking place around her. Diana's scandalous life of deception strips away her passive femininity and enables her to become the strongest, most active woman in the series, reading clues that enable her to save her friend Charlotte from a slow death. By juxtaposing the helpless Charlotte with the independent Diana, Braddon suggests that the "ideal" of the inactive and dependent women is actually a threat to society.

Diana is essentially Braddon's proper woman reader of sensation: While she has knowledge of undesirable things that erode her innocence, she is better off than the innocent women in the story because she is able to detect the evil around her and is equipped to deal with men such as her father and Philip Sheldon. Diana illustrates Braddon's contention that women who read sensation novels were made aware of the possible gap between appearance and reality and therefore had a greater chance of detecting and preventing unrespectable behavior. Braddon opposed the assumption that women would be more moral if they maintained their innocence by pointing out that innocence is merely ignorant vulnerability. Braddon in effect argues that the education and simulated worldly experience provided by sensation fiction would allow women to become active readers of life and fiction who could make informed moral choices. By depicting feminine passivity as a naive and destructive ideal, Braddon encouraged women to think for themselves and implied (with the successful marriage of Diana to the noble French heir) that they would be rewarded for it. By debunking the ideal of innate gentility and reinforcing the concept of earned respectability Braddon allowed women readers to prevail over the eminently respectable critics who disparaged them. She attempted to create the same sense of independence for herself by redefining sensationalism as a respectable literary form despite the contrary proclamations of critics.

"Henceforward I Refuse to Bow the Knee to Their Narrow Rule": Sensation Fiction as a Bold, New Form of High Art

As Tabitha Sparks argues about *The Doctor's Wife,* "Isabel's claim that she wants to be a heroine corresponds to Braddon's own claim that she wants to be a realist writer. Both character and author already are what they aspire to be" (208). Braddon set out in *Belgravia* to prove that she was what she wanted to be: a new kind of realist writer. In *Birds of Prey* and *Charlotte's Inheritance,* Braddon abandoned her attempt to write a novel that suited critics' typical definitions of realism and instead began to forge what she characterized as a new form of realistic fiction intended to remedy the "deification of the commonplace" exemplified by traditionally realist writers such as Trollope and Thackeray (Wolff, "Devoted Disciple" 134). Despite her antagonism toward these realist icons, upon reading a negative review of Trollope's *Miss Mackenzie* in the *Saturday Review,* Braddon decided she had had enough of the fickle allegiances of critics who unhesitatingly turned on even the most revered writers. She darted off a curt letter to Bulwer-Lytton in 1866 stating that

> The realistic school has been written up so perseveringly of late—always to the disparagement of every thing romantic & imaginative—that I was beginning to lose all courage, & to bow my head to the idea that the subject of a respectable novel is bound to be all that is trite & commonplace. But I find that when these reviewers have made their Gods they turn upon them & rend them—and henceforward I refuse to bow the knee to their narrow rule. (ibid., 132)

In this letter Braddon reiterates her intense distrust of critics and rejects what she sees as their capricious standards. At the same time she

indicates that, as she was undertaking the editorship of a new magazine, she was formulating an alternative definition of realism that incorporated sensational themes and techniques to expose what she thought
was a less idealized reality. Her bold presentation of the harsh realities
of life was closely allied with the French novelists whose work Braddon
admired, translated, and sometimes copied. In the tradition of French
realists like Gustave Flaubert and Honoré de Balzac, Braddon hoped
to expose society's evils through what she defined as a new and previously misunderstood form of art.

Braddon drew a natural parallel between her work and French literature–both of which were considered by English critics to be morally suspect. Just as Braddon defended women readers to justify sensation fiction as proper reading material in *Belgravia,* she also defended
French literature to support her redefinition of sensationalism as high
art. In French romances like the interpolated tale of Gustave Lenoble
(apparently named after Flaubert) in *Charlotte's Inheritance* and in articles
such as "French Novels" (July 1867), "Glimpses at Foreign Literature"
(April 1868), and "Baudelaire" (October 1871), *Belgravia* denies "that the
moral condition of the world which French novelists portray is so vastly
different from" English society ("French Novels" 78).[14] The magazine
refuses the idea that the English have a monopoly on morality and
instead insists that there are immoral people in England as well as
moral people in France. In case readers persisted in their distaste for all
things French, *Belgravia* returns to the topic of women readers, claiming that the responsible reading practices of French women diminish
the dangers of reading their own nation's novels. *Belgravia* explains that
in France the lack of circulating libraries and the expense of novels
ensured that these books were read by educated adult women who
could make informed judgments rather than by girls who might be
more strongly influenced by what they read. Once again, the magazine
acknowledges a difference between child and adult readers in order to
defend middle-class women's rights to read whatever they desire. By
expanding the minds of the public beyond the narrow confines of
British moralism and its limited definition of realism, Braddon hoped
to create an atmosphere more amenable to sensation.

Despite her attempts to change attitudes toward the French,
Braddon was somewhat conflicted about the appropriateness of advertising the fact that she used French novels as literary models. In her correspondence with Bulwer-Lytton, Braddon expressed her doubts in discussions of Flaubert and Balzac. Although Braddon is fascinated by the
"unvarnished realism" of these writers, she fears that their work is "the

very reverse of poetry" because it dangerously peers "into the most hideous sores in the social body" (Wolff, "Devoted Disciple" 20, 27). Braddon's desire to please Bulwer-Lytton may have influenced her reluctance to endorse the reviled French novelists in her letters, but she also hesitated to overtly ally herself with them in *Birds of Prey*.

In the novel, the murderer, Philip Sheldon, classifies realist novels as "senseless trash" because "he had found that the heroes of them were impracticable beings, who were always talking of honor and chivalry, and always sacrificing their own interests in an utterly preposterous manner" (January 1867, 277). However, once he reads Balzac he is "riveted by the hideous cynicism, the supreme power of penetration into the vilest of wicked hearts; and he had flung the book from him at last with an expression of unmitigated admiration" (January 1867, 277). Sheldon's rejection of the extreme idealism and moralism of supposedly realist fiction articulates Braddon's own conception of it, though it is safely distanced from her by the fact that it is spoken by the villain of her tale. To further complicate matters, Sheldon's "flinging away" of the novel seems to contradict his feeling of "unmitigated admiration." Braddon's cautious handling of this scene indicates the hazards she faced by allying her work with the French realists. She was clearly concerned that this line of reasoning might fail to win the hearts and minds of both the public and the critics.

Braddon's mixed feelings about an "unvarnished realism" devoid of morality are also evident in the character of Valentine Hawkehurst, who expresses his wariness about French fiction. Despite Hawkehurst's birdlike name, he is not one of the novel's "birds of prey." Like Braddon, his name may insinuate something negative, but he (and she) are shown to be rather heroic within the pages of the magazine. Indeed, Hawkehurst closely echoes Braddon, as he proclaims that "There is an odor of the dissecting-room pervading all my friend Balzac's novels, and I don't think he was capable of painting a fresh, healthy nature" (March 1867, 9–10). The image of the dissecting room is reminiscent of the typical critical equation of both French and sensational fiction with the horrifying sights and pungent smells of a place in which living things are reduced to specimens (and monsters like Frankenstein's are created). However, Braddon's use of this metaphor is not wholly negative. Dissection rooms do not necessarily produce monsters; they can ultimately lead to scientific discoveries that are useful for humanity. According to Braddon's fictional philosophy, unpleasant dissections were required to build knowledge, and she was committed to violating the borders of respectability in order to do just that.

So, despite her qualms about embracing French realism, Braddon persisted in redefining her own style upon the French model.

Braddon's endorsement of French fiction was ultimately used to market her novel. In an October 5, 1867 *Athenaeum* advertisement for the three-volume edition of *Birds of Prey,* the *London Leader* is quoted as stating that the novel is written "with the true tact of an artist" in a moral style that is "pure and healthy. . . . Miss Braddon, at her best, unites all that is subtlest and most thrilling in the French school with all that is purest in the English" (446).[15] Though the *Athenaeum* ad touted the novel as Braddon's best work, the *Athenaeum's* own reviewers remained unconvinced of her "purity" and "tact." Both *Birds of Prey* and *Charlotte's Inheritance* elicited fervent responses in the journal.[16] The first novel was characterized as empty and audacious, a work that "contains next to nothing worth the toil of reading." The reviewer reminds us that "Audacity is [Braddon's] *forte*" and asks whether "it [is] wise to draw the boundary-line of unscrupulousness nowhere?" (461). As for the sequel, the reviewer admits that the tale "is told with force and reality" but concludes that "the general impression left by the book is painful and repellant" because "the reader feels only disgust, and no interest or sympathy" (418). As these reviews indicate, Braddon's attempt to ally herself with the French novelists was not well received. However, she had already told Bulwer-Lytton in 1866 that she would no longer be influenced by critical rejection: "I believe that if I listened to the howling of the critics and abandoned what they call sensation I should sink into the dullest namby-pambyism" (Wolff, "Devoted Disciple" 130). In her magazine Braddon held fast to her goal of legitimizing sensation as an acceptable form of realism that did not require the slavish adherence to morality and acceptable class and gender roles that she conceived of as dull "namby-pambyism."[17]

Belgravia took multiple approaches to establish respect for the genre of sensation fiction that were tangential to the genre's own merits: It questioned the validity of critical opinions, argued that women could enjoy sensation fiction without harming the social order, and allied sensation fiction with French realism as a way of broadening the nation's narrow definition of the real. However, the magazine also attempted to debunk the basic assumptions that relegated sensation fiction to a marginalized position within British culture. George Sala played a major role in the campaign to establish the genre as part of the English literary tradition. In "The Cant of Modern Criticism," Sala challenges Oliphant's claim that the English novel since Scott had been characterized by a tradition of "sanity, wholesomeness, and cleanness" that was suitable for all members of the family ("Novels" 257). Sala instead connected Scott to a countertradition of English literature that included the wild, ghastly, and immoral elements of writers such as Anne Radcliffe and Monk Lewis. By doing this, he implied that sensationalism was the true heir to the throne of British literature and that the boundaries Oliphant drew between the high and the low were not as stable as she imagined. Indeed, Sala argues that some of the best novels of the day, including Charlotte Brontë's *Jane Eyre,* George Eliot's *Adam Bede,* and Braddon's *Lady Audley's Secret,* are superior to Oliphant's supposedly wholesome canon because they are novels of "life and character and adventure" that are "outspoken, realistic, moving, breathing fiction, which mirrors the passions of the age for which it is written" (52). Thus, for Sala as for Braddon, sensationalism provided a real connection to contemporary life that conventional realist novels ignored.

In "On the Sensational in Literature and Art" (February 1868), Sala goes on to establish a high cultural heritage for sensation novels. He proclaims that the genre has a royal lineage of works by critically accepted writers such as Shakespeare, Ruskin, and especially Dickens, whom he characterizes as "the most persistently 'sensational' writer of the age" (454). Braddon herself continued the strategy of establishing the relationship of sensation to its respectable ancestors in "The Mudie Classics" (March and April 1868). This two-part series, published under the pseudonym of Babington White, playfully employs the wholesome reputation of Mudie's Circulating Library and the reverence for classical literature to defend sensation novels. The series satirically promises to be a mini-Mudie library that will deliver stories modeled on "the highest exemplars of art," the tales of classical Greece. These works are said to be offered in deference to those "wise" authorities whose "critical contempt for all stories of a sensational character has of late become a fact so notorious that the conductor of this magazine would be wanting in deference to those great Teachers who preside over the Literary Journals of this country, if she failed to recognize the necessity of an immediate reform in the class of fiction provided for the indulgent readers of BELGRAVIA" (March 1868, 41). In a mock attempt to reform the contents of the magazine, the series promises to include classic Greek dramas, which—it is ironically noted—are filled with bribery, adultery, assassination, matricide, bigamy, and murder. By humorously pointing out the predominance of such sensational events in classical literature, Braddon drew attention to inconsistencies of literary valuation and connected her fiction with well-respected literary traditions. As Robert Wolff notes, Braddon "proved her point: Indeed, she may have overproved it, since" the series "stopped short after two installments" (*Sensational Victorian* 217).

In addition to asserting sensationalism's connection to a high cultural tradition, *Belgravia* set out to prove that the genre outdid the current critical darling, the realist novel, in its honest depiction of reality. To accomplish this task, the magazine had to show that the reliance of realism on idealized morality weakened its social power. In contrast, sensationalism proclaimed that its supreme goal was to copy the details of life without the taint of idealism. Belgravian critics noted that the seemingly outrageous occurrences in sensation novels were based on real events that the newspapers often reported. Indeed, Sala defines sensationalism as a heightened form of realism that is no more harmful to readers than the daily news: "[I]n all these novels the people walk and talk and act . . . like dwellers in the actual, breathing world in which we live. If we read the newspapers, if we read the police reports . . . we shall take no great harm by reading realistic novels of human passion, weakness, and error" ("Cant" 53). He boldly declares that the public deserves such thrilling and real presentations and that adult readers–even women–can handle such fiction: "[We] want novels about that which Is, and not about that which never Was and never Will be. We don't want pap, or spoon meat, or milk-and-water, or curds-and-whey, or Robb's biscuits, or boiled whiting, or cold boiled veal without salt. We want meat; and this is a strong age, and we can digest it" (54). In this passage Sala tacitly declares that realist fiction is no more than a bland and lifeless idealization of human behavior (cold boiled veal without salt). Sensation fiction, on the other hand, is a heartier, stronger version of life that is nevertheless closer to "reality." For Sala and Braddon, realist novels were not "real" but "ideal" representations of life that did not deserve to be valued over sensation novels. Far from destroying the minds (or the digestive tracts) of readers, sensationalism, Sala argues, provides readers with a better understanding of the world as it is, rather than as it should be.

Preventing "Universal Darkness": Sensational Nonfiction and the Progress of Society

Despite *Belgravia*'s disdain for idealism in fiction, the magazine argued that sensationalism could ultimately move society toward a more ideal state. *Belgravia* claimed that sensationalism–whether in fiction or nonfiction—was a remedy for the entrenchment and stagnation of the cultural values of the past. Sala saw sensation as vital to the modern experience of living in a rapidly changing, industrial nation. Thus, the elimination of sensation would mean the elimination of experience as well as the end of interest in contemporary literature and life: "Don't let us move, don't let us travel, don't let us hear or see anything . . . and then let Dullness reign triumphant, and universal Darkness cover all." As he sensationally puts it, "In the opinion of dolts and dullards and envious backbiters, everything is 'sensational' that is vivid, and nervous, and forcible, and graphic, and true" ("On the Sensational in Literature and Art" 457–58). Understanding the progressive message of nonfiction discourse within the magazine helps to explain how Sala was able to make the proclamation that "*Belgravia* is a sensational magazine, and Miss Braddon is a dreadfully sensational novelist" ring with victory rather than with defeat (ibid., 457). This victorious tone pervades *Belgravia*'s sensational nonfiction, which calls attention to positive societal changes facilitated by sensational discourse.

Mortimer Collins strikes a tone of triumph in "Mrs. Harris" (December 1870), an article about an eighteenth-century writer in whose letters Collins locates the origins of sensationalism, which he sees as part of an inevitable evolution of feminine forms of writing. He contends that with the decline of women's letter writing and the advent of the penny post and the telegraph, "you are supposed to see everything in the paper. But then you don't see everything in the paper; journalists are not behind the scenes. They tell you, rather tardily, that one man has discarded his wife, and that another has disappointed his creditors; but they fail to furnish the true causes of such occurrences" (159). The woman letter writer, on the other hand, is the only one who can truly describe behind-the-scenes events in detail and offer explanations for the causes of things, but "publishers have found her out," and she now "devotes herself to three-volume novels" (ibid.). Collins claims that women's superior skills of observation and analysis that had been displayed for decades in the private and respectable form of the letter have recently been transformed into the public form of the sensation novel.

Even though Collins is nostalgic for the old letter-writing style, he endorses sensation novels as more detailed and comprehensive than the male-dominated news media because they delve beneath the surface to provide an in-depth analysis of contemporary life. Whereas most critics of the day bemoaned the abundance of women writers and readers of sensation, Collins celebrates the genre's "feminine" attention to detail and its superior ability over masculine forms to penetrate the truth about human relations. Naomi Schor argues in *Reading in Detail* that, since at least the eighteenth century, the detail has been seen as feminine, while the sublime has been characterized "as a masculinist aesthetic designed to check the rise of detailism which threatens to hasten the slide of art into femininity" (22). However, Collins here uses the detail to empower rather than diminish women's artistic abilities. Indeed, Collins promotes this "feminine" skill as a sign of progress that is essential to creating believable novels as well as truthful analyses of modern society.

Just as Collins links sensationalism to the intimacy and accuracy of letter writing, the author of "A Day in the Telegraph Office" (September 1869) links it to more modern forms of communication. The author argues that being a telegraph operator made him aware of the sensational elements of real life: "I do not suppose that if I were to chronicle the messages of grief, despair, entreaty, telling of crime, remorse, poverty, and death . . . that passed before me [at the telegraph office], I should be credited. But there it was, attested to by their signatures and in their own handwriting. Believe me, there is no romance like reality" (318). Like the genre of sensation fiction, telegraph messages, which were high-tech versions of the letters written in the previous century, described extreme events that were nonetheless real. More advanced technologies in the printing and publishing industry were at the root of mass culture, symbolized by sensation fiction, and were thus prime targets for the high culture critics, who feared the effects of rapid change on the literary and cultural traditions of the country. Technological progress, then, was equated with the threat of popular culture and with sensation. *Belgravia*'s articles, however, usually characterized such progress as not only inevitable but also as salutary.

Despite the magazine's generally positive outlook on technological progress, its articles acknowledge that scientific developments could threaten society if not thoroughly understood. Articles such as "Before the Mirror" (July 1867), "Cosmetics" (December 1867), "Beautiful Forever" (April 1868), and "Cosmetics for the Hair" (May 1868) uncover the health hazards that commonly worn fashions and beauty products presented, while "The Pitman's Perils" (February 1867) publicizes the hidden causes of coal-mining deaths and "The Gorilla as I Found Him" (August 1867) explores potentially false scientific claims about gorillas and the implications of Darwinian theory. Such articles turn a more critical eye on new developments, urging the public—as *Belgravia* urged women readers—to become actively involved in learning how to avoid potential threats to their health, their lives, and their beliefs.

Most notable for exposing and critiquing scientific theories is Robert Patterson's series "Sensationalism in Science," which not only points out that respected scientists used sensational techniques, but also indicates the role sensation plays in initiating critical thinking about important epistemological issues.[18] This series opens ominously with the claim that

> It is often said as a reproach that literature, as a whole, and especially fiction, has become "sensational"—that it loves to produce excitement by descriptions of imaginary crimes and unnatural incidents. But what are all the startling scenes portrayed in novels—though we question if there is any of them which has not had its counterpart in real life—to the dreadful catastrophes predicted for us and for all creation in the pages of science? (June 1868, 555)

Patterson supports Braddon's agenda by claiming that sensation fiction has its roots in the real world, whereas a supposedly more objective and professional discourse like science might not reflect reality at all. The "Sensationalism in Science" series freely explored disastrous scientific predictions such as the depletion of the nation's coal supply ("Our Coal Fields" June 1868), the death of the sun ("Is the Sun Dying?" July 1868), and the existence of life on other planets ("More Worlds Than One" October 1868). These articles were intended to both titillate readers with the possibility of terrifying phenomena and convince them to think through the theories and reach their own conclusions about whether to place their faith in modern science to divert such catastrophic events or to dismiss the wild speculations on the grounds of faulty reasoning.[19] For example, "Is the Sun Dying?" begs readers to "gather [their] startled senses" in light of the claims of some "modern high-priests of science" that the sun will eventually burn itself up and "ray out darkness" because the fact is that "even if their theory of combustion was right, the basis of their calculations is entirely wrong" and the sun "will last as long as Matter itself endures" (71–81). Such "reasonable" conclusions to outrageous claims reinforced the magazine's contention that sensationalism stimulated thought and discouraged the blind acceptance of "the authorities," whether they happened to be scientists or literary critics.

Investigative journalism was another sensational discourse that

Belgravia claimed both questioned authority and encouraged advances in the scientific community that would benefit society. For example, "An Adventurous Investigation" (November 1866) uncovered the need to research new treatments for the insane. Written in a sensational style that included adventure and suspense, the article's investigation was even inspired by a sensation novel, Wilkie Collins's *Cornhill* serial, *Armadale*. The article's narrator and his companion, Smith, examine the exact location where "Wilkie Collins introduced Allan Armadale and Midwinter to the wreck of *La Grace de Dieu*. . . . And near to which . . . you may see the veritable cottage where the lunatic was confined whose shriek so horrified the Armadales on that terrible night." The investigator tells Smith that he has set out to find the lunatic featured in *Armadale* and to spend time with him, studying the causes of mental disease. Smith is at first skeptical about his friend's claims: "But that's all nonsense, you know . . . Pooh! The empty creation of a sensation novelist" (57). However, the narrator insists that he has already successfully identified the lunatic and written a newspaper article about him. Upon discovering this fact, Smith responds with fear: "Look here; if you, alone and single-handed, attempt such a mad thing as exploring the ins and outs of this island, and hunting up lunatics by day and night, why, you'll get stuck in a bog, or stabbed, or something else as bad or worse" (ibid.). Despite Smith's anxieties and his inference that the narrator may himself be "mad," the narrator persists in pursuing his "adventurous investigation" in order to "stir up the public interest to provide remedies for [lunacy]; to alleviate the misery and neglect of such poor unfortunates, to, if possible, ultimately create for them a proper and commodious system" of treatment (57–58).

"An Adventurous Investigation" indicates that some seemingly fictional events that take place in sensation novels are actually based on real-life occurrences and can, as Mortimer Collins claims, give readers a deeper understanding of society as well as bring about positive social change. Likewise, another *Belgravia* article on "Insanity and Its Treatment" articulates a rationale for exposing the horrors of insane asylums that coincides with the magazine's rationale for exposing women to sensational subjects in everyday life:

> We have taken the readers of *Belgravia* for a while out of their own geographical district to . . . places and subjects which are hardly congenial, however important they may be. But it is good for us sometimes to see the "night-side" of things—to have laid bare our social

scourges both of the moral and material kind, in order that we may
with one heart and mind unite in striving to rectify those evils which
madden peoples and hurry nations to premature decay. (478)

Belgravia's articles stress that although sensationalism dwells on the
"night-side" of life, taking readers away from the safety of their homes
into the brutal world, the genre prevents rather than causes cultural
decay. In both *Belgravia*'s fiction and nonfiction, then, sensationalism
was defined as a legitimate force for education and reform that could
make the public aware of societal problems that might otherwise be
hidden or ignored. As a genre associated with modernity and social
progress, sensation was touted as a sign of the nation's cultural health
and of women's centrality to the progress of the nation.

Under Braddon's leadership, *Belgravia* articulated a critical assessment of sensationalism that appreciated its ability to be simultaneously entertaining, educational, and artistic: to, in Braddon's words, serve
both God and Mammon well. While *Harper's* and the *Cornhill* each
appealed to women readers to demonstrate their ability to master the
differences between the high and the low in order to prove their critical abilities, *Belgravia* asked women readers to overtly reject those critical divisions because they were established by untrustworthy critics.
Harper's and the *Cornhill* were interested in using the critical divisions
to their advantage and in teaching women to follow suit. *Belgravia,* on
the other hand, championed women readers and sensation fiction as a
way of moving Braddon's own professional agenda forward. As a
result, Braddon created a popular family literary magazine that refused
to safely parrot the more elite journals while attempting to replace
them for middle-class readers. Braddon had nothing to lose and was
therefore able to dispense with the literary knowledge and authority of
the elite critics altogether and establish an alternative ideology of literary valuation. The discussion carried out in *Belgravia* was explicitly
meant to transform attitudes toward women readers and popular literature by imagining the woman reader as independent, free, and
informed and by redefining the genre of the sensation novel as realistic, artistic, and instructive. Both of these rhetorical moves aimed to
bring women readers and writers into the public and professional
realms while preserving their sense of propriety.

⟶⟶ 4 ⟵⟵

VICTORIA'S SECRET:

The Woman's Movement from Reader to Writer/Critic, 1863–1868

A FOUNDING MEMBER of the Langham Place Circle, Bessie Rayner Parkes, summarized the organization's goals in the following lines reprinted in *Victoria Magazine:*

> Let women be thoroughly developed.
> Let women be thoroughly rational.
> Let women be pious and charitable.
> Let women be properly protected by law.
> Let women have fair chances of a livelihood.
> And lastly, let women have ample access to all stores of learning.
> ("Miss Parkes' Essays on Woman's Work" 173)

Parkes and her Langham Place colleagues encouraged activities that would improve women's lives intellectually, economically, and politically, while using rhetoric that would preserve the "pious and charitable" qualities that dominated the Victorian public's conception of the fair sex. Emerging alongside family literary magazines like the *Cornhill* and *Belgravia,* the comparably marginal and considerably less profitable feminist magazines produced by the members of the Langham Place Group–the *English Woman's Journal,* the *Englishwoman's Review,* and *Victoria Magazine*–called for a reformed society in which women could support themselves financially and live independently without threatening the social order.[1] Though each of these publishing ventures attempted to effect changes that would benefit women, their approaches were distinct. While the *English Woman's Journal* and the

Englishwoman's Review focused on changing the daily lives of women, *Victoria* aimed to provide good literature alongside its feminist social agenda. Conducted, printed, and published by Langham Place members Emily Faithfull and Emily Davies along with the progressive group of working women at the Victoria Press, *Victoria* clearly descended from the more politically focused Langham Place publications; however, it had greater literary aspirations and modeled itself after the family literary magazines, especially the successful and respectable *Cornhill.*

Many recent critics have contended that *Victoria's* "chief value" lies in its chronicling of the women's movement (Westwater 443) and in its "special purpose" of providing women with a successful public forum for two decades (Herstein, "The Langham Place Circle" 27; see also Nestor). Despite supporting this assessment, Martha Westwater acknowledges that the magazine had "definite literary pretensions" in addition to its feminist goals (443). Alvar Ellegård sees the magazine's "literary pretensions" as its focus rather than as a footnote to its activist tendencies. Accordingly, he describes *Victoria* first as "a fiction magazine," adding that it also contains "some useful information on feminine subjects" (35). I concur with Ellegård, and I want to focus here on *Victoria's* attempts to conform to the successful genre of the family literary magazine (while also transforming it) by examining how *Victoria's* "literary pretensions" reinforced its "special purpose" of furthering women's rights. Indeed, I argue that *Victoria's* focus on becoming a successful family literary magazine allowed it to emerge as the first mainstream feminist magazine in England. *Victoria's* seventeen-year run from 1863 to 1880 and its competitive circulation of 20,000 in 1865 indicate that it achieved some measure of success in meeting its goals, though it remained financially troubled (Ellegård 32). As Maria Frawley accurately points out, the magazine's cultural capital far exceeded its commercial success ("Feminism, Format" 40). In this chapter I analyze how the magazine achieved a cultural status that Braddon never quite obtained with *Belgravia* and examine its impact on the Victorian literary scene despite its failure to match the *Cornhill* in profits.

Due to the prohibitive cost of serializing "first-rate" novelists, *Victoria* was unable to obtain authors with the same status as those who contributed to the *Cornhill.* As a result of *Victoria's* inability to rely solely on fiction for its reputation, the magazine emphasized its literary criticism as a way to compete with its wealthier and more popular rival, whose serial novels it regularly reviewed. *Victoria's* criticism thus emerged as the crowning glory of the magazine. *Victoria* insisted on a broad range of reading for women and used its reviews to guide that reading toward the most productive texts. Moreover, the magazine combined its women's rights and literary agendas by mapping out a distinctly feminist conception of realism in its reviews. Within the magazine's feminist critical formulation, works were lauded as realistic examples of "good" literature based on their depiction of moral, intelligent, and independent female characters who could serve as role models for the "new woman," while works were defined as sensational or "bad" because of their portrayal of women characters who were immoral criminals or passive victims of crime. Unlike the other family literary magazines in this study that troubled the boundaries between high and low culture in order to support the interests and needs of women readers, *Victoria* reinforced the high/low cultural split that the elite critics espoused while vociferously opposing those critics' dismissive views of women readers and writers. I argue that *Victoria's* endorsement of cultural divisions allowed the magazine to gain authority for its feminist critical voice as it made a sustained effort to move women from the margins to the center of the profession of literary criticism. In this way, the magazine contributed to the production and definition of the emerging literary canon and increased the status of women readers, writers, and critics. *Harper's* asked American women to read properly in order to live up to and even surpass the standards of British culture; the *Cornhill* urged women readers to educate themselves in the service of upwardly mobile gentlemen; *Belgravia* encouraged women's independence as readers; and *Victoria Magazine* redefined the woman reader as a writer and critic, thus casting women in roles that allowed them to contribute to the definition and production, as well as the consumption, of literary culture.

"A Happy Augury of Victory": The Establishment of the Victoria Press

In order to explain how *Victoria* both built upon and diverged from the feminist magazines published by the Langham Place Circle, I will briefly trace the history of the organization and the publications it produced. The Langham Place Group and its publications—of which the *English Woman's Journal* (1858–1864) and its descendant, the *Englishwoman's Review* (1866–1910), were the most successful—initially developed as a result of the first Married Woman's Property Campaign.

In 1855 Parkes and Barbara Leigh Smith (later Bodichon) organized what Sheila Herstein calls the first "group of women [who] met together in England to discuss and organize political action to change the status of the sex" ("The Langham Place Circle" 25). When the campaign for property rights failed in 1857, these middle-class women channeled their frustration in a positive direction by forming the Langham Place Group, named after the location of their headquarters.

The organization began the *English Woman's Journal* and developed ties with groups such as the National Association for the Promotion of the Social Sciences (NAPSS), the Society for Promoting the Employment of Women (unfortunately called SPEW), the Ladies' Sanitation Association, and the Female Middle-Class Emigration Society. As a result of SPEW's efforts to find work for women, Parkes purchased a printing press with the intention of training women as compositors. In March 1860 Emily Faithfull stepped forward to take charge of the project that she called the Victoria Press. From the beginning, then, the group united its philosophical mission to advance women's rights with very practical endeavors that engaged women in the newly conceived field of social work as well as in writing, printing, and publishing. These activities ingeniously kept women employed while also ensuring that they were doing tasks that could be linked to a more acceptable tradition of middle-class women's charitable organizations on the one hand (the work of NAPSS and SPEW, for example) and that could serve as a publicity and recruitment tool on the other hand (the work of the press). But, while the Victoria press gave the group the power to control its own image, it also became a lightning rod that outside forces inevitably focused on in their critiques of the Langhamites.

As Faithfull writes in the *English Woman's Journal,* Victoria Press marked "a happy augury of victory" for the organization. The press, she explains, was established in

> Great Coram Street, Russell Square, which, by judicious expenditure, was rendered fit for printing purposes; I name the locality because we were anxious it should be in a light and airy situation, and in a quiet and respectable neighborhood. We ventured to call it the Victoria Press, after the Sovereign to whose influence English women owe so large a debt of gratitude, and in the hope also that the name would prove a happy augury of victory. I have recently had the gratification of receiving an assurance of Her Majesty's

FIGURE 12. "Victoria Press." *Illustrated London News* (June 15, 1861): 555.

interest in the office, and the kind expression of her approbation of all such really useful and practical steps for the opening of new branches of industry for women. ("Victoria Press" 122–23)

The Queen's stamp of approval was a vital legitimization of a project that immediately sparked controversy. The hostility of male printers toward the Victoria Press was so great that they attempted to intimidate the women workers and sabotage their equipment (Stone 57). Faithfull countered arguments by printers' unions that hiring women workers would trigger a decrease in their wages by maintaining that such false claims were "also urged against the introduction of machinery, a far more powerful invader of man's labour than women's hands, but this has fallen before the test of experience" ("Women Compositors" 38). Furthermore, Faithfull asserted what came to be the Langhamite mantra, that it is "sound common sense" in accordance with "the spirit of Christianity" to train young, middle-class women for professions to prevent "some unforeseen calamity" from plunging them into "utter destitution, at an age when it is difficult, I had almost said impossible, to acquire new habits of life" (ibid., 40). The Victoria Press proved to be one successful–if limited–solution to what Faithfull, the Langham

Place women, and even the *Cornhill Magazine* identified as a rampant social problem: women's inability to provide for themselves.

However, Faithfull also had to combat complaints about the nature of the work women did at the press. She justified hiring sixteen female compositors by emphasizing the genteel work atmosphere. This included working a regular eight-hour day, going home for an hour-long lunch break or eating meals in the specially designed kitchen, and getting paid adequately for occasional overtime work, during which the women would break for tea. To refute the assertion that printing was an unhealthy industry for women, Faithfull contended that the negative effects of the job arose "in great measure from removable evils" including bad ventilation, the heavy consumption of alcohol, and the habit of standing all day. Faithfull's press remedied these problems by maintaining a bright and open work space, forbidding alcoholic beverages, and designing special stools for her workers ("Victoria Press" 124–25). As if to prove Faithfull's claims, a woodcut drawing of Victoria Press printed in the June 15, 1861 *Illustrated London News* featured nineteen well-dressed women and one apron-wearing girl carrying and setting type in a clean and wholesome atmosphere (Figure 12). These neatly kempt women work intently on their stools or leaning over tables. They appear well organized, professional, and able to work productively alongside the men who assist and (possibly) watch over them. The illustration of the printing office confirms Faithfull's intimations that women could maintain private dignity in a public workplace. Maria Frawley points out that Faithfull's claims about Victoria Press "reveal well the ways that [she] was able to capitalize on certain features of domestic discourse in her endeavor to control portions of the print industry. . . . Likening the press to a middle-class household, Faithfull's rhetoric enabled her to destabilize, even erase, the implied opposition between public and private–to ensure that her workplace had domestic appeal" ("The Editor as Advocate" 91–92). In this way Faithfull's press embodied the ideal later established in her magazine: that of the genteel working woman whose domesticity remained intact.

In the face of great opposition, the Victoria Press proved that women could contribute to the successful production of literary culture, not only through writing but also through the mastery of the physical process of printing. In fact, as Frawley contends, Faithfull's press enacted a relationship to print culture that was consummate with women's natural reproductive functions by emphasizing the work of women printers as "literally a reproductive task" because it "required resetting in type words already written in ink" (ibid., 90). Faithfull hoped symbolically to suggest that the women of Victoria Press were able to fulfill their reproductive functions as they gave birth to words by printing the *English Woman's Journal*, the yearly reports of NAPSS, and a variety of pamphlets by Frances Power Cobbe, Mary Taylor, Isa Craig, and other members of the Langham Place Circle. In addition, the 1861 publication of *Victoria Regia*, a literary anthology edited by Adelaide Proctor and dedicated to the Queen, indicated that women could produce high-quality printed material. The beautifully bound book with a decorative gilt and morocco cover was meant to showcase the skills of the women at the press as well as the contemporary authors it featured, including Harriet Martineau, Caroline Norton, Alfred Tennyson, William Thackeray, and Anthony Trollope. In fact, this remarkable gift book won the prize for excellent printing at the International Exhibition and consequently led to Faithfull's appointment as Queen Victoria's official printer and publisher (Fredeman 153–57). Notwithstanding the success of *Victoria Regia*, the *English Woman's Journal* remained the press's best-known publication before the founding of the *Victoria Magazine*. The *Journal* maintained an average monthly circulation of 1,000 copies in 1860, matching the figures for the well-established journal of the educated elite, the *Westminster Review* (P. Levine 296).

The *English Woman's Journal*, like its "parent" Victoria Press, focused on advancing women's professional status while maintaining feminine gentility. The hallmark of the magazine was its effort to include work written only by women. On the basis of the magazine's practical efforts, George Eliot declared the *Journal* to be a publication that "must be doing good substantially—stimulating women to useful work and rousing people generally to some consideration of women's needs" (Letter to Barbara Bodichon. December 5, 1859. Haight, 225–26). However, Eliot refused to contribute to the magazine, disparaged its literary merit, and urged its editors to attend to the quality of the contributions rather than the sex of the contributors if they wanted to glorify women's work (Herstein, "*The English Woman's Journal*" 66–69). Despite Eliot's reservations about purely feminist journals, the magazine had no trouble establishing an audience within the feminist community. But maintaining and expanding a steady readership proved to be more problematic. As a result, the *Journal's* main problem was paying contributors. Despite selling 1,000 copies per month, the magazine could pay writers only half of what they would make writing for mainstream periodicals backed by major publishing houses (Rendall 133). Furthermore, as Parkes noted, "the conditions of the

periodical market" in the 1860s were changing dramatically as competition increased and "each journal [was] pitted against the other." This
"very uncertain" economic situation was even more problematic for
feminist magazines like the *Journal* (ibid.). Philippa Levine succinctly
explains the financial difficulties these magazines faced: "[P]ayment for
work was a means of valuing women's labours . . . but at the same time
it represented a heavy drain on their funds which their returns did not
begin to replace. The question of professionalism was a difficult one.
The proprietors themselves . . . were unpaid and indeed often funded
their ventures from their own private means, and yet sought to reward
their writers pecuniarily" (297). When, in 1864, the *Journal* could not
sustain in practice the feminist principle of proper remuneration for
women's work, the magazine's six-year run was reluctantly brought to
a conclusion.

The *Journal* briefly merged with the *Alexandra Magazine,* but this
enterprise ended in less than a year. Despite the establishment of
Victoria Magazine in May of 1863, the *Englishwoman's Review,* founded
by Jessie Boucherett in 1866, was seen as the only legitimate child of
the *Journal.* As Boucherett wrote in "The Work We Have to Do," an
article featured in the inaugural issue of the *Review:*

> It is, indeed, our intention to follow the plan traced out by those who
> established the *EWJ,* and if this review shall prove equally effective
> in calling the attention of the public to the wants and condition of
> women, we shall be well content; for we believe the favorable
> change of opinion, and the more respectful tone with regard to
> women, which may be observed in the literature of the day, to be in
> no small degree due to the influence of the *EWJ.* (4–5)

The *Review,* then, carried on the tradition of the feminist magazine
while *Victoria* attempted to accomplish something slightly different.

In addition to recording the incremental accomplishments made in
advancing women's education and employment with frequent progress
reports on women's admission into institutions of higher education,
their success in university examinations, and their attempts to enter
professions, the great achievement of *Victoria Magazine* was the transformation of feminist educational and economic principles into a feminist literary criticism.[2] *Victoria* paired its feminist criticism with the cultural power and general middle-class appeal of the family literary magazine, becoming a hybrid born of the influences of both the feminist
magazine and the family literary magazine. However, before turning to

Victoria's unique feminist literary discourse—which included redefinitions of both women readers and realism—I examine the ways in which the magazine maintained the goals of the feminist journals while courting mainstream audiences by invoking the figure of the queen, inviting male professionals to support the feminist cause, and revising societal assumptions about women's roles.

"As Much of It as They Will Swallow": Victoria's Feminist Agenda

In its namesake, the Queen, *Victoria* found an apt symbol of its intent to provide "an outlet for the expression of moderate & well-considered opinions on those questions, which while bearing more directly on the condition of women, are in their wider aspects, of the highest importance to society generally" (Emily Davies, letter to Barbara Bodichon. March 12, 1863). That the Queen became the driving force behind the magazine is not surprising considering Faithfull's well-advertised appointment as "Printer and Publisher in Ordinary to Her Majesty." This appointment lent credibility to the Victoria Press, and the creation of a magazine of the same name highlighted the prestigious connection, which appeared emblazoned on the title page of every issue.

Faithfull promoted *Victoria* as an organ of reform that "forwarded the industrial and educational claims for women . . . gradually moulded public opinion and at last led to reforms therein advocated as necessary for the free and harmonious development of women's physical, mental, and moral nature" (quoted in Stone 76). From Faithfull's perspective, the use of Her Majesty as icon enabled *Victoria* to advance women's entry into the public sphere without seeming to violate societal expectations about the importance of women's domesticity and morality.[3] As Frawley succinctly puts it, the image of the queen allowed Faithfull to "negotiate the uneven boundaries between the private and the public that the Queen herself seemed to embody" ("The Editor as Advocate" 93). The Queen thus became an icon for the magazine's hybrid woman: the domestic professional.

The poem "Victoria Regina," which pays tribute to the Queen's influence on the magazine's conception of womanhood, opens the first volume of *Victoria.* Despite the poem's description of the Queen as "True woman, but the more a Queen," overall it depicts Victoria as a regular woman who mourns the death of her husband. The poem recognizes that the Queen has both a public and a private life (just like the magazine's own working women) and that each of these is integral to developing a complete identity. While recognizing the significance of one's private life to one's public duties, the poem calls for the nation's figurative leader to reemerge from her private sanctuary of mourning and resume her public role:

> Once happy wife of noble mate, Victoria!
> Sacred in wedlock's holy state;
> Most sacred now, when desolate,
> Death does thy life's love consecrate, Victoria! . . .
> Bid the last cloud of mourning flee, Victoria!
> The world expectant turns to thee:
> Thy name itself is Victory;
> And thou wilt conquer worthily, Victoria! (May 1863, 1–2)

While Victoria's devotion to her husband is characterized as admirable, she is proclaimed to be incomplete in her private role as widow. She will live up to her name only if she returns to a life that balances her public and private roles. The poem suits the inauguration of the magazine because it asks for a more balanced conception of womanhood that is implicitly applied to middle-class Englishwomen like those who produced and read *Victoria Magazine.*

The June 1864 opening article, "Elizabeth and Victoria from a Woman's Point of View," further emphasizes the magazine's insistence that the nation's queens represent common, middle-class women. The article urges the public to forgive Queen Victoria for sending relatives to fulfill her public duties because "the life of a nation is not its ceremonial but its moral life," to which she "contributes more than the holding of a hundred drawing rooms" (102). In its conclusion that "womanhood is higher than queendom" (ibid.) and that the true life of the nation is its moral life, *Victoria* seems to support the private over the public functions of women. However, the conception of the Queen's real power as essentially feminine allows the magazine to use her as an example of how womanly virtues actually make typical, middle-class women suitable participants in public life. Likewise, "The Queen as Ruler" emphasizes that a woman's ability to unify and strengthen the family can be carried into both the workplace and the nation. Despite the turmoil of war and rapid changes in the British Empire, the Queen has been able to "knit together all ranks and classes in the bonds of common feeling" (January 1864, 194). Victoria's ability to create national harmony is rooted in her domestic skills. Thus, her feminine traits are what have allowed her to walk "a quarter of a century with steady, unfaltering, and almost or altogether unerring steps" (201). By rhetorically constructing Queen Victoria as the ultimate example of the public and private spheres, *Victoria Magazine* rationalized and legitimized its feminist project.[4]

Victoria's feminist articles written by male "experts" similarly worked in the interest of making its agenda acceptable to a broader audience. Following a suggestion by the Langham Place Circle's Anna Jameson that such a journal required "the masculine power–the masculine hand" to attract male readers (quoted in P. Levine 300), *Victoria* featured writers such as Matthew Arnold, Thomas Hood, Nassau Senior, and Thomas Adolphus Trollope to lend respectability to its feminist endeavor. As managing editor Emily Davies declared, "We mean to employ chiefly men [as contributors] at first & not to press our special subject till we have got a character. *Then,* when we have once gained a hearing, we shall give the public as much of it as they will swallow" (Letter to Barbara Bodichon. March 12, 1863). Reversing the goals of the *Journal* along the lines George Eliot suggested, Davies wanted the new magazine to "represent good *men* as well as women" (Letter to Barbara Bodichon. January 14, 1863). Indeed, the first volume avoided stating outright that the magazine was conducted by women: Davies's name was absent, Faithfull was listed only in her capacity as publisher, and, as Solveig Robinson notes, the contents did not include the typical direct address from woman editor to woman reader ("Amazed at Our Success" 168).[5]

Many of the magazine's male contributors focused on women's education in ways that might appeal to a masculine audience. The arguments they presented frequently adhered to the *Cornhill*'s claim that women should be educated for the benefit of their class and nation. Like pieces written by Thackeray and Stephen in the *Cornhill,* "The Influence of University Degrees on the Education of Women" (July 1863) argues that education would not make women masculine, but would instead expose them to higher culture and thus improve the cultural status of the middle class and the nation. This unsigned article, written from a male perspective, downplays fears about the changes women's formal education would bring about by maintaining that, in fact, "A very small proportion of girls would attempt to take [a college degree]; fewer still would succeed; fewer still would take honours; But every school-girl in the land would very soon become aware of the fact, that women might hope and strive for a thorough culture, which has never yet been generally offered to them" (268). W. B. Hodgson takes a similar approach in "The Education of Girls, Considered in Connexion [*sic*] with the University Local Examinations" (July 1864). Hodgson, too, calls for women's access to education on the basis of preserving a healthy culture rather than solving women's financial woes: "[I]t is, in truth, the power not to rival, but to understand, and sympathetically to appreciate, that makes all *men* akin to those great thinkers; and so it is . . . that places woman side by side with man. . . . It is on the inward community of human nature, not on the outward similarity of employment, that the right to an equal culture is really founded" (251–52). Hodgson emphasizes the similarities between men and women by pointing out that neither educated women nor educated men would likely become Shakespeares, Dantes, or Michelangelos; however, both would be more apt to contribute to the maintenance of the nation's culture. Echoes of the controversy caused by the women compositors at Victoria Press can be heard in these articles as they downplay the threat that educated women would compete with men for jobs. To justify women's education, these writers rely on a sense of cultural nationalism rather than on the inherent right of women to have equal educational or professional opportunities.

Other male "experts" commissioned by *Victoria* resort to the more traditional argument, used most frequently in *Harper's* but also prominent in the *Cornhill,* that educated women make better wives and should therefore be cultivated and desired by educated men. In "The Education of Women" (March 1864), J. G. Fitch, for example, appeals to husbands who want to improve their marriages. The school inspector explains that in women's education as it currently stands "nothing is required . . . but a blind mechanical obedience" to dates, tables, events, and needlework stitches, which allow women to become skilled copyists but not thinkers (436). Fitch suggests that women be encouraged to move beyond this mechanical function into higher thought processes in order to allow both wives and husbands greater fulfillment in life. Fitch fears that "so long as the worthiest thoughts which a man has in his mind are those which his wife cannot share . . . his marriage is imperfect, and whatever may be its outward fitness and propriety, must often be unsatisfactory to himself as well as to her" (442). Fitch shows how education for women can benefit both sexes, but his argument stops short when it comes to women's infringement on public institutions: "If women asked for a system of mixed education, for admission to academic lectures, to the bar, the church, or the legislature, the reply to such demands would be very simple. We cannot imperil the social order" (447). Early on, then, *Victoria* follows Emily Davies's plan to employ "chiefly men" as writers and to avoid pressing too firmly on the "special subject" of the magazine until it had "gained a hearing." These articles were intended to show the general public that there were men willing to support increased education for women and to set forth reasonable arguments on their behalf. However, *Victoria's* message became increasingly forceful as it did, indeed, "give the public as much of it as they [would] swallow" with a series of hard-hitting essays by Mary Taylor, published by Victoria Press in 1870 as *The First Duty of Women.*[6]

Taylor's articles explicitly attempt to reshape societal assumptions about women's roles. Like the articles about Queen Victoria, Taylor's essays were prominently featured in the magazine, usually as the opening item. Signed by the gender-neutral "T," these articles take on a masculine viewpoint by referring to women as "they" rather than "we." This, however, is the only effort to soften the arguments intended "avowedly to inculcate the duty of earning money" and that "contained much that was startling at the time" (Herstein, "The Langham Place Circle" 26).[7] Taylor forcefully reiterates the primary feminist concern of Faithfull and the Victoria Press as she repeats, under various headings, that women should be educated and trained to work. Her arguments fulfilled *Victoria's* agenda in a way that conformed to its queenly namesake by turning the domestic space inside out and placing the proper Victorian woman intact outside the home.

Each essay begins with the statement of an assumption that is then skillfully refuted. Each refuted claim leads to a common conclusion that women must be allowed to educate and financially support themselves. "Feminine Honesty," for example, begins by questioning the popular presumption that women must be honest to properly fulfill their domestic duties. Taylor interrogates the practicality of this supposition by arguing that women must have more knowledge of and control over their sources of livelihood in order to be truly honest:

> It is dishonest to incur debts which you cannot pay; is it honest, then to know nothing of your means of paying? . . . It borders on dishonesty to know so little of your future means as to have no assured provision for your future wants; . . . It is needful therefore to know whence your income arises, to have the power of judging its permanence, and, if it is liable to fail, to be taught some means of replacing it. (7)

By redefining the common understanding of honesty, Taylor points out that the ignorance of women promoted by the social order not only encouraged, but, in fact, also required them to act dishonestly.

Likewise, in "Feminine Work" (September 1867), Taylor attacks the expectation that women should keep themselves occupied within the home by illustrating that in the present condition of women's lives, meaningful occupation is impossible:

> It is the pride of well-doing women, and a duty they always urge on those whom they have to educate, never to be idle. It is a wise rule, and experience taught them it. . . . But the want of this clear insight into the consequences of their own rules has made them, generally, satisfied with employment that is little better than digging holes and filling them up again. (403)

The article begins by agreeing with the common belief that idleness breeds danger; however, it concludes that the repetition of inconsequential activities often taken as fit occupations for women can be as harmful as idleness itself. Instead of accepting clichés about women, Taylor uncovers the contradictions that are inherent in traditional views of women's roles by attacking the angelic stereotype of middle-class women, which she claims are built on false ideas about women's nature. Over and over Taylor argues that idleness and lack of knowledge make women pitiful beings who leave "most of their wants and wishes" unsatisfied and therefore "have little motive for activity." The result is that "doing nothing, they escape doing wrong" but come to embody all that is futile, unproductive, and destructive to the individual and the family ("Feminine Idleness," November 1867, 1).

In "Feminine Knowledge" (June 1867), Taylor goes even further, asserting that women are physically as well as emotionally endangered by threats such as disease, violence, and bad advice because they are ignorant and uneducated. To emphasize her point, she characteristically begins with a question:

> Would any of us choose, if we could have our choice, to belong to that large class of the human race who pass through the world knowing nothing of the causes of their good or evil fortune, and powerless consequently to help or avert it? Who see, for instance, their numbers thinned by small-pox or ague, without knowledge of the help or rescue that may yet be within their reach. (99)

The answer to these questions is obvious: Women must be better educated and have a wider scope in which to do good for society. Increasing women's access to books becomes one way to address the problems that face them. Taylor, in fact, sees reading as women's only comfort because as readers they can absorb knowledge in an unmediated form, without facing censorship or the prejudices of others. For Taylor and for *Victoria*, access to books and the development of critical reading practices were vital to sustaining a culture of women's knowledge that could eventually prepare them to enter the public realm.

"Escaping the Natural Danger of Her Quiet Home Life": Victoria's *Critical Readers and Actual Critics*

One unifying characteristic of the family literary magazine is its devotion to women readers. I have shown how each of the magazines in this book invokes the woman reader as vital to the health of the nation's literary culture. As *Victoria* contributed to creating an image of the critical woman reader that the other family literary magazines in this study also imagined, it went one step further. *Victoria* invited its readers to become critics by speaking out within the pages of the magazine. Together, the magazine's reprint of Reverend Brooke Herford's "Importance of Newspapers to Women," its two-part "Mr. Ruskin on Books and Women," and its "Correspondence" section indicate the ways in which *Victoria* revised the conception of reading as a "disease" by defining periodicals not as dangerous threats to women's reading practices, but as vital resources that allowed them to enter the public realm both virtually and literally as they became critical readers and actual critics.

Herford's December 1866 article was copied from the *Manchester Guardian* into *Victoria's* "Miscellanea" section, which often featured reprints relevant to *Victoria's* agenda. Herford stresses the importance of reading, especially periodical reading, for women. He argues that newspaper and magazine reading are "more important to women than to men" because "women in their quiet household life, may go on for weeks hardly hearing a word of what is passing in the great world outside." Not only does Herford define periodical reading as healthy for women as individuals, but he also blames incompatible marriages on the restriction of women's reading practices. His primary solution for a rocky marriage is for the husband to end his wife's dependency on him for knowledge, to stop explaining and interpreting things for her, and instead to let his wife "read the newspaper for herself, not merely for half an hour's amusement, but with the definite object of escaping the natural danger of her quiet home life, and keeping an open eye, and an understanding mind, for the passing history of nations, and the great interests which are stirring the heart of the world" (176–77). Herford reconsiders the idea that reading is dangerous, suggesting that a graver danger lies in ignorance of rather than exposure to the thoughts that prevail in the public sphere. Reading is cast as a moral and political good because it allows women to gain greater intellectual equality with men, which, in turn, preserves (while admittedly transforming) the institution of marriage. Herford combines the appeasing approach to women's learning exemplified by many of *Victoria*'s male contributors with Taylor's bold crusade against women's ignorance as he focuses on reading itself as the primary way to improve marriage, culture, and women's lives. Thus, *Victoria* conceives of a healthy society that not only encourages but also requires active women readers.

"Mr. Ruskin on Books and Women," featured in the November and December 1865 issues of *Victoria,* challenges Ruskin's "Of Queen's Gardens" as it more sharply delineates the magazine's conception of the active woman reader who is able to transform herself from a consumer to a producer of literary culture. Sharon Aronofsky Weltman declares that this article constitutes "one of the most favorable contemporary reviews of 'Of Queen's Gardens,'" confirming her own position that "While a queen's garden may sound fenced in, the point of Ruskin's essay is to open it up . . . to redefine those gardens to include all of England" (121–23). Indeed, the article generously credits Ruskin with acknowledging that women deserve to be educated–to be "'turned loose' into the library and let alone"–and praises him for arguing that a "girl's education should be more earnest, and in the spirit of it more serious, than the boy's" (November 1865, 75–76). However, I contend that *Victoria*'s review takes Ruskin to task for defining women readers and the purposes of women's reading too narrowly. *Victoria*'s reviewer emphatically disagrees with Ruskin's belief that "Girls ought to be highly educated, and their minds fully cultivated . . . and yet . . . their minds are to stop short at certain points, and to present a perfect vacancy on some subjects, in spite of the fact that when a mind is once thoroughly awakened and active, everything which comes before it must be thought about and judged" (December 1865, 131).

Victoria's countermanifesto provides ample evidence that women's minds should not and could not be "stopped short." The reviewer criticizes Ruskin for equivocating on the status of women as intellectual readers, urging a wider and more substantial program of reading for them while maintaining that they could not enter the intellectual ranks of men:

> Mr. Ruskin is teaching us what to read and how to read, so that we may lift ourselves up into higher mental and moral regions; yet, at the same time he tells us that we can never reach them; for if we are to discard all thoughts of our own, it will avail us little to acquire (if indeed it were possible on such condition) all the thoughts of the highest thinkers in the world. The human spirit is not a mere vessel to be filled with good things, but a living organism, the law of whose nature it is to grow, and expand and clothe itself in beauty of its own. (November 1865, 69)

In addition to objecting to Ruskin's characterization of women's reading as passive, *Victoria* asserts that his contradictory ideal is at the root of a charming but inhuman conception of womanhood that makes women into one-dimensional creatures. *Victoria* opposes Ruskin's implication that all women should conform to this single dimension by preparing for marriage. To the contrary, the reviewer contends, there is a surplus of at least half a million women who must not merely be trained to sympathize with a husband's pleasures: "If [a woman] is to be educated with any theory respecting marriage at all, it would be wiser in these days to adopt the very possible contingency of her never marrying" (December 1865, 132). Despite *Victoria*'s frequent use of the argument that better education for women would guarantee better wives and stronger marriages, in this case the reviewer rejects that formulation as the only legitimate one. Instead, the reviewer maintains that the woman reader is capable of sustaining both a happy marriage and an active, intellectually fulfilling single life.

Not surprisingly, then, *Victoria*'s biggest protest arises in response to Ruskin's failure to recognize women's need to educate themselves toward professional purposes. While Ruskin inspires "spirit-stirring" gratitude for "nobly" conceiving of woman's mission, he ignores "the one great urgent question of the day . . . which still keeps sounding in our ear": "that woman has to work, not only in queen's gardens, but in the busy mart, and for the coarse bread of life; that she is not only the helpmate of man—the dispenser of all that is loveliest in home—but that she has often, alone and unsupported, to live without a home to sweeten, and wander forth in the rough and stony places of the world's highway" (November 1865, 76). *Victoria* points out the limitations of Ruskin's "Queen" in the "Garden" and brings forth a new species that exists but has not yet been reckoned with. This middle-class, working woman is the critical reader who must think independently and be self-educated in order to be self-supporting if it becomes necessary. She is the reader who can become the critic, the angel who transforms herself into the professional woman through books, conversation, and, eventually, public reform.

Victoria takes as its mission to push women's powers further than Ruskin imagined by creating a public forum for the expression of women's critical reading skills in its "Correspondence" section. *Victoria's* "Correspondence" was set up "to admit free discussion on the social questions of the day" by "freely" printing "letters containing various opinions . . . to give expression to the thoughts of various minds" (December 1865, 183). Here, women readers were invited to show off the same kind of intellectual prowess that was modeled for them in the magazine by contributing to the conversation themselves. Since the editor refused to endorse the opinions submitted, readers were even encouraged to disagree with the magazine—which they in fact did from time to time. *Victoria's* correspondence section is especially interesting because it is an atypical feature of the family literary magazine as a genre. *Harper's,* the *Cornhill,* and *Belgravia* each invite women to read in particular ways that they proscribe but do not invite them to demonstrate that they have followed the magazine's proscriptions by raising their critical voices. In fact, as I already noted, when Thackeray invited the *Cornhill's* women readers to contribute, he quickly proceeded to withdraw his invitation and reject the flood of submissions he received. *Victoria's* "Correspondence" provides a striking example of reader interaction that went far beyond that allowed by other magazines of this class.[8] Regardless of who these correspondents were—whether they were ordinary subscribers or members of the Langham Place Group—the placement of their letters in the correspondence section sent an important message about the magazine's faith in its women readers to write opinions worth publishing. Indeed, *Victoria's* willingness to print a section of readers' responses—not just in the form of questions addressed to the editor, as such sections were formulated in most women's magazines, but as genuine contributions to contemporary debates—indicates the respect *Victoria* had for its readers and the fluidity of its conception of the woman reader/critic. While most women's magazines offered advice to women correspondents, *Victoria's* letter writers offered their ideas and advice to the magazine's editors and readers.

The "Correspondence" section made *Victoria's* goals concrete by transforming women readers into women critics who were empowered to express their views in a public forum. One of the most effective letters, from a reader named "Henrietta," was published in August 1867. In its length alone—which took up seven valuable pages—this letter exemplifies the importance given to readers' responses, but it is the writer's ability to fit seamlessly within the narrative of the magazine that is most striking. Henrietta is the embodiment of *Victoria's* proper woman reader: She reads widely, thinks deeply, and responds critically in writing. Her letter opens with a slyly sarcastic tone, declaring that she "has the misfortune to be . . . one of those frivolous beings . . . pursued by the *Saturday Review*"—a young lady:

> I confess to being tolerably sentimental; I own to having read novels occasionally before twelve o'clock A.M. [*sic*], and to taking a wicked interest in Tennyson's poetry. But I read something else the other day which was neither exactly a novel or a poem. I took upon me—ambitious task!—to unfold the ample pages of the Times, and to dive into the awful depths of Parliamentary debate. (336)

The sense of self-deprecating but confident defiance this passage conveys reflects the magazine's attempt to empower its women readers not only to engage in political debates, but also to write back, and to write themselves into the larger discussions (dominated by men) taking place in current literary journals such as the *Saturday Review*. Andrea Broomfield argues that, despite its high-brow reputation, the *Saturday Review* "was less intellectual in its tone and content than many critics have assumed" as its "success lay in its ability to generate a constant stream of scandalous or audacious opinions" and to construct a "symbolic readership composed of well-educated, intellectual gentlemen that appeared to be much larger and powerful than it actually was" ("Anti-feminist 275)." *Victoria* frequently responded to the scandalous tone and male intellectual tenor of the *Saturday* with an annoyance that indicated its desire to reduce the journal's perceived power. For example, *Victoria's* "Miscellanea" section sometimes reprinted sections of the journal's particularly audacious articles in order to refute them. The sole purpose of including reprints from the *Saturday*, it seems, was to increase *Victoria's* critical authority over what it conceived of as a misogynist journal. In writing against the *Saturday's* prestigious critical voice, Henrietta makes her own brave and biting statement against its critical dominance and becomes the reader/critic that the magazine imagines.

Furthermore, Henrietta successfully combines literary analysis with feminist concerns in a way particularly well suited to *Victoria*. As if she had divined the significance that Coventry Patmore's "Angel of the House" would have for defining perceptions of the Victorian woman for years to come, Henrietta zeroes in on Patmore's "angel" Honoria as an icon of proper womanhood. While praising Honoria's embodiment of femininity, Henrietta points out that such angelic qualities are too often "less her own fair possessions than wrung and wrested from her by force either for the gratification or caprice of men." Thus, "If woman were to be all that angels are, without the wings, and her virtues the outgrowths of necessity and chance rather than the productions of will and responsible act and thought, they are . . . of a morally useless character" (338). Like Taylor, Henrietta argues that women must be able to make a conscious choice to be moral rather than merely appearing to be so because they conform to society's expectations. She sees in Honoria a more assertive self that she implies lurks in all women:

> While every debt which is due to poetry and idealised womanhood is paid, Honoria herself, the heroine of the simple tale, remains an average woman, neither transcendently gifted in heart or brain. . . . I can imagine Felix and Honoria talking—yes, oh reader—on politics together . . . [and Honoria] registering with her own delicate fingers the vote which gives at once substance to thought, and value to judgment. (340)

Henrietta concludes, in opposition to the *Saturday,* that "it is impossible for woman to be 'too intellectual.' I think she cannot be too highly educated. Though she were charged with the knowledge of all the world, she would be woman still" (342). Just as the magazine adapts the image of the Queen for its own purposes, this woman reader adapts the prototypical "angel of the house" to her advocacy for woman's intellectual and political rights.

Articulating the magazine's dual feminist and literary purposes, Henrietta shows how easily women readers could become critics who were able not only to act rationally and monitor their own reading, but also to suggest productive ways of reading for others. Jon Klancher notes that in such interactions "Reading and writing are not fixed functions but performing roles to be exchanged" (22). In this case the letter writer performs her role as reader/critic for *Victoria* successfully, matching wits with professional writers from one of the most revered literary reviews. Thus, *Victoria*'s goals prevail as regular readers enact its tenets by becoming active critics who advocate the educated, professional, and political woman who is, according to Henrietta, an angel without wings.

"I Could Not Edit a Light Magazine": Emily Davies and Victoria's *Literary Aspirations*

Victoria's wingless angels—the women readers/critics it imagined and ultimately produced—linked the magazine to its feminist predecessors, but it was its focus on literature that secured its status as a family literary magazine. Whereas the Victoria Press feminist magazines had no intention of competing with the popular literary monthlies, *Victoria* intended to do precisely that. *Victoria* was conceived as a very different feminist project, one that would emphasize "Literature, Art & Science" without excluding "Theology and Politics" (Emily Davies, letter to Barbara Bodichon. March 12, 1863). Before beginning her partnership with Faithfull as acting editor of *Victoria* in May 1863, Emily Davies had collaborated with Bessie Rayner Parkes on the *Journal*. Davies left her post as editor of the *Journal* (which she occupied from September 1862 until March 1863) primarily because Parkes rejected her idea to compete with major commercial magazines as "hopeless and absurd, and indeed self-destructive" (quoted in P. Levine 299).[9] Together Davies and Faithfull hoped to achieve exactly the combination of the feminist and the mainstream that Parkes feared would compromise a woman's rights agenda. Davies in particular insisted on creating a more literary focus by featuring fiction, poetry, and criticism in the magazine.

Victoria Magazine was therefore founded with the idea of transcending the bounds of the traditional feminist magazine audience in order to reach the general public. While most family literary magazines made an effort to include "the ladies," *Victoria* made an effort to include the men of the house. *Victoria* was to be a family literary magazine that happened to have a feminist agenda. Davies hoped to create a magazine that would:

> take the line of a good general magazine assuming throughout that men & women are interested in the same things, tho [*sic*] taking care to give information as to anything new or special which is being done by or for women, & advocating the removal of grievances as

injurious to society generally, tho [*sic*] in their *direct* action, bearing upon women only. (Letter to Barbara Bodichon. January 14, 1863)

Davies overtly states her intention to "go in for a rivalry with Fraser, Macmillan, and Blackwood" (Letter to Barbara Bodichon. March 12, 1863). I would add to this list of rivals the *Cornhill*, which Davies mentions as a good forum for the publication of feminist opinions "suited to commonplace people" (Letter to Barbara Bodichon. No date). The magazine's attempt to follow the new and highly successful genre would have inevitably led to the emulation of the leader of the pack, the *Cornhill*. Indeed, Davies did her best to recruit *Cornhill* contributors to work for *Victoria*. Among the famous contributors *Victoria* had in common with the *Cornhill* were Matthew Arnold ("Marcus Aurelius," November 1863), Margaret Oliphant ("A Story of a Voice," August and September 1863), and a Trollope, though not the one associated with the *Cornhill*'s hot-selling premiere issue. After receiving polite refusals from G. H. Lewes and Anthony Trollope, Davies and Faithfull commissioned the second-string Trollope, Thomas Adolphus, to serialize his novel *Landisfarn Chase* in *Victoria* (May 1863–August 1864). Despite Davies's efforts, it soon became clear that *Victoria* could not financially sustain writers of the *Cornhill* caliber. In place of the reputable writers Davies desired to hire to lend credence to the periodical, Faithfull commissioned her friends to contribute for little or no pay (Stone 74).

Victoria substituted the hiring of *Cornhill* contributors with merely making references to the magazine it endeavored to make its peer. Accordingly, *Victoria* included articles that responded to works or authors featured in that well-respected magazine. For example, *Victoria* included an essay that refuted Arnold's *Cornhill* contribution on the positive influence of literary academies (March 1867), a response to a *Cornhill* article on the spirit world (May 1863), a poem on William Thackeray's death (February 1864), and correspondence about a *Cornhill* article on female education in Germany (April 1867). Most importantly, *Victoria*'s early literary reviews were dominated by favorable responses to *Cornhill* serials including Anne Thackeray's *The Story of Elizabeth* (May 1863), George Eliot's *Romola* (August 1863), Anthony Trollope's *The Small House at Allington* (May 1864), Frederick Greenwood's *Margaret Denzil's History* (January 1865), and Matthew Arnold's *Essays in Criticism* (March 1865), as well as reviews of works by other *Cornhill* contributors such as Elizabeth Gaskell and Margaret Oliphant.

Victoria became a full-scale "literary review" in a way the *Cornhill* was not in order to make up for the fact that it could not afford the high-quality fiction it would take to make it an equal to its competitor. This feature of the magazine also linked it to older, review-oriented journals such as *Blackwood's* and the newer academic reviews like *Fraser's*. However, *Victoria's* self-conscious use of the *Cornhill* as an intertext indicates that Davies and Faithfull wanted readers to associate their magazine with the new phenomenon of the family literary magazine that was attracting much wider audiences than the reviews. While establishing *Victoria* as connected to but separate from its feminist predecessors and as a descendant of the new genre of the family literary magazine, Davies was able to carve out a unique niche for the magazine.

From the beginning Davies knew that she could easily produce and guide the production of feminist criticism to fulfill the goals of the magazine. As Robinson points out, all of the Langham Place journals relied on a form of feminist literary criticism; but Victoria's stake in that criticism was altered by Davies's efforts to shape the magazine into a literary, rather than a solely activist, publication.[10] Davies was aware that, as she put it, "the story is our great difficulty. First-rate writers have not got long serials lying on their hands, & cannot strike them off at a month's notice" (Letter to Barbara Bodichon. March 12, 1863). She believed that the magazine's inability to recruit high-quality fiction writers jeopardized her vision of Victoria as a legitimate rival to the Cornhill. As she bluntly put it, "Thomas Adolphus . . . murdered us" (Letter 337a. January 12, 1864). Davies felt so strongly about the detrimental effect of Landisfarn Chase on the success of the magazine that she wanted to bring it to a premature conclusion. Faithfull's refusal to cut the novel short led Davies to publicly deny responsibility for the serial, and this created an immense amount of tension between the two women.[11] Ultimately, Davies concluded that "I could not edit a light magazine, nor can I edit one at all, unless I may go to the best writers, and pay them properly" (Letter to A. D. [Anna] Richardson. March 15, 1864). In February 1864, after struggling along for almost a year with what she saw as Faithfull's mismanagement of the magazine, Davies resigned her editorship, and Faithfull took over.

Davies agreed to stay on as book-review editor for an unspecified period, although she had never been properly paid for her editorial duties, let alone her written contributions to the magazine. After Davies's resignation, the magazine drifted slightly away from the literary agenda she advocated. However, her emphasis on sustaining a feminist literary philosophy in the magazine's fiction and reviews had a significant impact. The development of *Victoria's* literary content to complement its social feminist agenda was Davies's primary contribution and lasting legacy to the magazine. Her literary philosophy permeated the ideas about reading conveyed in the magazine and had visible effects on the magazine's women readers, who, as I have shown, began to use their own critical voices in the magazine. Those women readers/writers followed the critical model Davies set up during her relatively brief involvement with the magazine.

"An Excellent Picture of Life": Realism and the Creation of a Feminist Literary Criticism

In an April 1863 letter to her friend and *Victoria* book reviewer Anna Richardson, Davies presented guidelines for her "Literature of the Month" section:

> My "idea" of the notices is this. People see a book advertised, and wonder whether it would be worth while to order it. They ask one what is it about? Is it worth reading? Is it trustworthy as far as it goes? Is it beyond the comprehension of ordinary readers? In writing a notice, I should try to answer these questions. Of course this is not a thorough review, but I think it is useful information. If you have read the notices in the Westminster Review . . . you can understand the sort of things I mean, only that our notices must be shorter as we have not much space to spare. (*Family Chronicle* 3, 289–90)

Davies set up the *Westminster Review* as a model for her own work, paying homage to her friend George Eliot's impressive reviewing practices in that journal several years earlier. Just as Eliot saw writing criticism for the *Westminster Review* as a move toward becoming a true professional (Robinson, *Good Literature* 59), Davies saw writing and editing *Victoria*'s criticism as a way to assert professional authority not only for herself but also for women generally. Robinson claims that Eliot explored what professional authorship meant for women while developing nongendered literary standards (ibid., 60–63). Davies deeply respected Eliot's views and used them as a starting point; however, she developed a decidedly gendered definition of realism that required not only verisimilitude, complex characters, and a moral purpose (all commonly recognized components of the form), but also female characters who could serve as role models for strong, intelligent women.

Many critics, including Nicola Diane Thompson, have argued that nineteenth-century literary criticism in general produced "a distinctly gendered aesthetics of reception" that reflected a polarized and patriarchal culture by designating male writers as creators of original, intellectual art and female writers as producers of superficial, domestic, low cultural works (10, 20). While it was typical, then, for gender to impact Victorian literary criticism, *Victoria* transformed the way gender functioned in literary reviews. Whereas works by women tended to be labeled and criticized for their sentimentality or sensationalism, *Victoria* made an effort to praise works by women for their artistry and their social value. Still, *Victoria's* critical framework was predicated on a high/low cultural split that elevated realism at the expense of sensationalism and thereby validated what was seen as a predominantly masculine form over a feminine one. Thompson contends that this kind of critical argument reflects an internalization of the patriarchal voice aimed at both consolidating women's "precarious hold on literary authority and respectability" and being "taken seriously and accepted as part of the patriarchal establishment" (12). *Victoria's* case, however, is more complex. Davies's review section was partly modeled on Eliot's work—which Thompson describes as the quintessential example of internalizing the patriarchal voice—and incorporated the critical conceptions of the weightier journals as a means of legitimating *Victoria* in the field of literary criticism. *Victoria,* however, struck out on its own by basing its gendered evaluation of realist texts on feminist rather than patriarchal values. By insisting on the importance of progressive representations of women in high art, Davies succeeded in simultaneously gaining critical authority and maintaining her feminist goals.

Davies articulated her own definition of realist-feminist fiction in her personal letters as well as in the magazine.[12] For example, in her correspondence Davies proclaims that after reading Charles Reade's *Hard Cash,* her opinion of the writer rose "immensely" due to his presentation of a "very beautiful & clever girl in it, such as a common man could not have imagined" (Letter 337b. January 2, 1864). She also writes of Eliot's *Felix Holt* that she is "delighted" with its presentation of "a view of women that we want to have looked at" (Letter to Barbara Bodichon. No date). Such passing comments to her friends were transformed into a formal aesthetics in *Victoria's* "Literature of the Month" section, in which Davies formulated a literary criticism that co-opted some of the authority wielded by the elite reviews by tying the magazine's feminist perspective to the high cultural value of realism. The magazine made this seemingly precarious bond by altering the standard definition of realism that relied on the valuation of character over plot to also require that "real" characters be morally respectable women who were intelligent, independent, and worthy of serving as role models for progressive women like those in the Langham Place Group.

That Davies wanted to defy the idea that women were inherently worse writers than men (also a goal of Eliot's "Silly Novels by Lady Novelists," published in the *Westminster Review* in October 1856) is apparent in the support *Victoria*'s reviews show for the artistry of women writers. The reviews repeatedly highlight the originality, time-liness, and moral strength of realist women writers in order to prove that they are worthy of high cultural status. For example, *Victoria* enthusiastically cites Anne Thackeray's former *Cornhill* serial, *The Story of Elizabeth* (May 1863), as such an exciting literary production that it requires "no external passport to recommend it" (95). However, *Victoria* goes on to construct its own "passport" anyway. The reviewer praises Thackeray's ability to provide a moral example of a woman working tri-umphantly within the confines of her role and "strikingly" illustrating "the tone of women's minds at the present moment" (ibid.). While Thackeray's status as heir to her father's literary reputation and her solid place within the *Cornhill* recommend her as an ally to *Victoria*'s mission, it is even more crucial that her novel is presumed to accurately reflect contemporary women's lives: "If we do not actually know of a similar story in real life, we feel that such an [sic] one might very easily come within the range of our experience" (ibid.).[13] Thus, Thackeray repre-sents the kind of realist woman writer the magazine endorses because she is well known, well respected, and well suited to the magazine's goal of creating a countercanon of realist women writers.

Elizabeth Gaskell, another prominent *Cornhill* contributor, also became a part of *Victoria*'s alternative canon of realist women writers. A review of *A Dark Night's Work* (June 1863) highlights the important literary contribution made by this eminent woman author, to whose "masterly hand" the world "already owe[s] so much" (190). This work is recommended for the "clearness of its moral teaching" and praised because "Not being overcrowded with incident, there is room for the characters to work, and to display a strongly-marked individuality" (ibid.). Gaskell combines originality, morality, and verisimilitude in precisely the way *Victoria* values. The review notes that "Even a care-less reader can scarcely fail to be struck with the reality of Mrs. Gaskell's characters. The style of the book is simple though forcible; the persons are too natural to be other than many-sided" (191). Gaskell's reliance on complex characters to drive her fiction is cited as proof of her artistic superiority. The fact that she also uses her artistry to produce serious work that reflects women's lives makes her a model author for *Victoria*'s readers.[14]

Despite the contemporary issues Thackeray addresses and the realistic characters Gaskell offers, in the pages of *Victoria* no writer surpasses the literary genius of George Eliot. *Romola* (August 1863) is given the highest praise possible when it is described as a work written "in what Mr. Matthew Arnold might call the 'grand style' of fiction" (383). While this compliment indicates that Eliot's work in some ways transcends gender-based critiques of writing, the magazine also draws attention to Eliot's "ambitious" depiction of a woman's life that reflects "The highest and most tragic human interests, both in the family and in public life." Eliot's movement beyond the private concerns of a fifteenth-century woman into the complex realm of Italian politics is the trait that is most compelling to *Victoria*'s reviewer. While the novel's subject might "repel a careless reader," the "singular wealth of learning" that Eliot "lays out . . . upon the details of the narrative," the magazine urges, is well worth the effort it takes to read (383). Not only does Eliot create an intellectual heroine, but she also displays the "intellectual power" and "richness" of her own art (ibid.). In Davies's review section, well-known women novelists such as Thackeray, Gaskell, and Eliot become synonymous with *Victoria*'s mission to privilege high cultural realist works that cast women writers as artists and models for other women. *Victoria*'s compendium of worthy women writers emerges as an imaginary Langham Place Circle of fiction writers to rival the Langham Place activists.

Novels that were not written by members of *Victoria*'s elite list of women writers were still evaluated based on gendered criteria. Reviews of these novels often focused on whether the female characters accurately portrayed the lives and attitudes of the progressive women of the day, thus providing "real" women as feminist role models. Perhaps surprisingly, Anthony Trollope's female characters were the most frequent targets of *Victoria*'s gendered critical evaluations, regardless of the approval he received for his realistic reflection of society as a whole. The key to *Victoria*'s single laudatory review of Trollope, written about the *Cornhill* serial *The Small House at Allington* (May 1864), is the novel's superior ability to teach readers by holding "up to English society a mirror in which its superficial aspect is faithfully reflected" (93). Trollope's realism as well as his "moral lesson" about "the worthlessness of [superficial] success" keep him in line with the magazine's valued women writers. Furthermore, it is in his favor that "the interest does not depend either on the plot or the leading incidents, but on the gradual working out of the story, the development of the characters, and their mode of thinking and acting under varying circumstances" (ibid.). Thus, Trollope exhibited most of the qualities that *Victoria* valued in literature, including verisimilitude, morality, and complex characters. *Victoria*'s amenability to Trollope would seem even more likely given his association with the success of family literary magazines (particularly the *Cornhill* and his own *Saint Paul's*) and the fact that he was friends with Emily Faithfull (Margaret King 311). In addition, Trollope's increasing feminization throughout the 1860s as a result of his popularity as a circulating library author, his concentration on the details of domestic life in his fiction, and his intense interest in women characters would seem to put him in good stead with the magazine (Thompson 81).

However, instead of honoring Trollope for his appeal to women readers and his unconventional female characters, *Victoria* complained that his daring women did not go far enough. A case in point is *Victoria*'s critique of *The Small House at Allington*'s "old maid" Lily Dale. Lily is criticized because "the exalted courage with which she meets [rejection by her true love] appears unreal" and "no sufficient sustaining motive is disclosed" for her decision to remain unmarried (May 1864, 93). *Victoria*'s objection to Lily, an otherwise progressive female character, focuses on the fact that while she is an independent woman, she is not given an independent and fulfilling occupation:

> We never hear of her doing anything whatever but looking after her clothes, drawing, riding, and playing croquet. These innocent sports may or may not be very well as filling up a few vacant years before marriage, but they can scarcely be regarded as adequate sustenance for a whole life. Still less does it seem possible that these occupations could suffice to fill the terrible void which such a disappointment as Lily's must have caused. She tries to think it enough to live for her mother, and it is very good of her to try, but in the course of nature this can only be a temporary relief, not a permanent satisfaction of her needs. (ibid.)

The reviewer is unsatisfied because it seems that Lily should be unsatisfied. In fact, Lily's focus on clothing and sports belies a void in intellectual interests essential to the *Victoria* staff. Trollope failed to seize the opportunity to illustrate the soundness of the Langham Place platform on the necessity of women's education and employment; therefore, his daring woman was determined to be merely disappointing.

Victoria printed similar reviews of Trollope's leading ladies in *Miss Mackenzie* and *Can You Forgive Her?* Again, these novels explore the lives of single women who consider bucking expectations by willfully remaining unmarried—lives that would seem to be of interest to the women of Langham Place. However, Trollope's Miss Mackenzie is maligned on the grounds that she remains an inconsequential character despite her potential to be a Langhamite role model: "Miss Mackenzie makes our acquaintance as a gentle lady between thirty and forty, who finds herself, after a youth of self-devotion to a sick brother, alone in the world, with 800 £ a year. Throughout the first volume it is chiefly in relation to the said 800 £ a year, that we are induced to think of Miss Mackenzie at all, so very undecided and shadowy is the lady" (April 1865, 566). The reviewer admits that "On the whole" the novel provides "an excellent picture of life." However, the novel's weak heroine leads to the reviewer's conclusion that "We have no right to quarrel with Mr. Trollope for selecting dull or mean and stupid people for his characters" (ibid.). Miss Mackenzie was pronounced a dismal model for *Victoria*'s single women readers and was therefore dismissed.

Victoria's standards required an exciting as well as a strong-minded female lead. However, the boundary between excitement and immorality was easily crossed, as an October 1865 review of Trollope's *Can You Forgive Her?* indicates. The reviewer answers the question asked in the book's title with a definitive no: "We cannot forgive her." This response is attributed to the heroine Alice Vavasor's inexcusable infidelity:

> Mr. Trollope will forgive us, we trust, for a verdict as unhesitating as it is unconditional. He has pleaded his cause well, but has lost it. . . . Lucy Robartes [*sic*] had, at least, a show of reason in refusing the young Lord Lufton; but Alice Vavasor alternately jilts John Grey, the worthy man, and George Vavasor, the wild man, without rhyme or reason. . . . Alice Vavasor is represented as a woman of sense, and do women of sense change lovers as easily as gloves . . . ? (574–75)

Despite the objection to Alice's fickleness, it seems that her realization that living an independent life was an idea based on pure folly may, in fact, have been just as disturbing to Davies and her staff. The following passage from the novel makes *Victoria*'s reaction understandable: "[Alice] had taken her fling at having her own will, and she and all her friends had seen what had come of it. She had assumed command of the ship, and had thrown it upon the rocks, and she felt that she never ought to take the captain's place again" (11). Trollope's conception of women's inability to take a leadership role would be enough to raise the hackles of any *Victoria* reviewer. Margaret King goes even further, arguing that Trollope's novel was based on his knowledge of and interactions with the women of Langham Place. King claims that *Can You Forgive Her?* is ultimately his unabashed rejection of the group's values. Though King does not make reference to *Victoria*'s review of the novel, she agrees with its conclusion. King states that Trollope's portrayal of Alice lacks realism because it is mired in "hyperbole." This hyperbole, King concludes, is "part of a strategy for silencing the threat posed" by Langham Place feminism (308). Whether Davies and her staff recognized caricatures of themselves in these portrayals, according to their standards, Trollope's women seemed idle, silly, and even immoral. They were thus unworthy of the designation of feminist realism, which required the pairing of unconventional strength and conventional morality in realistic female characters.

Trollope was not the only writer the magazine criticized for failing to meet Davies's standards of feminist realism. Considering *Victoria*'s view of Trollope, it is not surprising that the magazine denounced Charlotte Yonge's *The Clever Woman of the Family* for its unpleasant depiction of a strong-minded woman, a depiction that directly satirized SPEW, the Victoria Press, and *Victoria Magazine* by attributing folly and pomposity to women like the Langhamites (April 1865). Here again the review neglects to mention the direct connection between the heroine Rachel Curtis and the Langham Place Group, but the magazine's complaints must have been informed by Yonge's biting satire of the group whose SPEW is transformed into FULE (the Scottish word for "fool").[15] Despite the unveiled attack on Langham Place—which includes Rachel's disastrous founding of an orphanage where girls are supposed to be taught printing and engraving but are actually abused, and her failed attempts to publish her pompous and uninformed polemical writing—the review concedes that the novel displays many of Yonge's "well known excellences." However, these are noted to be sadly "accompanied by exaggerated defects" (573) that build to "a feeble protest against what the author oddly conceives to be intellectual and social ambition in women" (576). The review attributes Yonge's negative portrayal of the "strong-minded woman" to a misunderstanding of the primary reason behind the movements for women's education and work, which is not ambition, but necessity. The review states that

Yonge "has missed a good aim in her delineation of a strong-minded character. . . . [S]he has worked it out clumsily, and has fallen far short of an adequate representation of the follies and mistakes incidental to energy and action as displayed by women, and the real difficulties through which they are likely to pass" (574). While the reviewer acknowledges that there could be comical elements to the situations in which "strong-minded women" find themselves, Yonge is taken to task for exaggerating the trivial aspects of her character's activities and ignoring the real challenges and potential results of such work. The novel is ultimately deemed to be unrealistic because it gives the impression that "the necessary effect of a cultivated mind was to be overbearing, abrupt, and unpleasant to the last degree" (ibid.). In the end, the reviewer concludes, Rachel "attains a satisfactory ideal of weakmindedness," giving up her ambition in order to marry a soldier (575). In this review *Victoria* defended its feminist critical standards in response to a novel that presented the ideal feminist heroine as an impossibility.

While *Victoria* seemed to demand idealized female role models in fiction, the reviewers took umbrage at idealizations that did not coincide with the magazine's feminist goals. A September 1863 review of *Margaret Stourton* exemplifies this by calling the novel's romantic depiction of the life of a governess irresponsible:

> It would seem scarcely necessary to point out the glaring unlikeness of this picture to the life it professes to represent. . . . The fable is too fabulous to bear the moral appended to it. Half-educated girls engaged in or preparing for governess life, on whom alone the book can be supposed to have any influence, may find in it materials for castle-building. They certainly will not learn from it to respect their work, or to accommodate themselves cheerfully to the real exigencies of their position. (477–78)

A more realistic depiction of governessing would alert both the public and young girls to the difficulties they should be prepared to encounter in earning their own living. *Victoria*'s conception of a feminist realism also asks, then, that the challenges women faced in Victorian society be honestly depicted in order to prepare women for the harsh realities of life. With this review and the critique of Yonge's failure to deal with the real problems independent women faced, *Victoria* demanded that literature serve an activist purpose by encouraging readers to support changes in the status quo that would improve the lives of women and indeed improve society as a whole. However, fiction that effectively exposed the ills of society was not always embraced in the magazine. When those ills were dramatized in sensation novels, the magazine concluded that the potential benefit of such literature was exceeded by the potential harm. Despite the fact that the genre was dominated by women writers and championed convincingly by Mary Elizabeth Braddon in *Belgravia, Victoria* rejected sensationalism as an embodiment of a dangerous, low cultural phenomenon that threatened the respectability of womankind.

"Noxious and Offensive Specimen[s] of Womankind": Victoria's *Critical Diatribes and the Domestication of Sensation Fiction*

Victoria's discussion of Margaret Oliphant's *Miss Marjoribanks* offers a striking example of the magazine's valuation of realism over sensationalism. The June 1866 review provides a "cordial welcome" to the new novel, declaring that

> It is quite an unusual luxury in these days to meet with a story which does not contain a single murder, or one case of bigamy, by an author who is able to make the career of a girl ambitious of becoming a leader of society in a small country town, interesting from the first page to the last of a three volume novel. Not being overcrowded with incident, the characters have room to work, and to display a strongly marked individuality in which the true merit of the story lies. The men and women in it are real people, living and acting in the society of a provincial town, which is pictured vividly, but without exaggeration. (187)[16]

All the traits the magazine deplores—criminal story lines that are overcrowded with incidents and plagued by exaggerated characters—are embodied by sensation fiction. *Victoria*'s increasing opposition to sensationalism was therefore a logical extension of the literary values already promoted by the magazine's elevation of feminist realism. Since a successful realist novel had to provide a positive and plausible feminist role model, *Victoria*'s rejection of sensation fiction—a form that relies heavily on plot and on female characters who are often either criminals or victims of crime—was in line with Davies's critical values despite the fact that the genre was dominated by women writers.

From *Victoria's* inception, sensational writers were criticized for their outrageous plots and characters in consistently brief—usually one- or two-sentence—reviews that were somewhat dismissive. However, the critiques of women sensationalists like Mary Elizabeth Braddon and Mrs. Henry (Ellen Price) Wood were initially quite mild. Braddon's *Henry Dunbar* was identified in July 1864 as a member of "the sensational school, which is said to be so mischievously exciting, and has the necessary elements of murder and mystery." But the dangerous effects of the novel are downplayed: "A reader must, however, be very sensitive indeed to be in any danger of suffering from the gentle strikes administered in *Henry Dunbar*" (283). In part, the defense of the novel relies on the magazine's construction of the woman reader as rational and critical and therefore unlikely to be one of those "very sensitive" readers who could "suffer" from reading such novels. In this way *Victoria* echoed the *Cornhill*'s view of sensation: that it was fine as long as readers understood it was purely for entertainment. Similarly, Wood's *Oswald Cray* was excused in January 1865 as "a spirited story, which will help sustain Mrs. Wood's reputation as being one of the most rapid producers in the present day of novels with improbable plots" (287). In trusting its readers to recognize these improbabilities, the reviewer finds the novel otherwise harmless. *Victoria*, it seems, was giving these women writers a break by declaring their novels to be exciting but innocuous and silly rather than dangerous. Their lack of importance is indicated by the brevity of the commentary devoted to them.[17]

The magazine's negative attitude toward sensationalism was more pronounced in February 1864, when Charles Reade's *Hard Cash* was panned in spite of its strong female lead (and Davies's positive response to the novel in a letter to Bodichon quoted earlier in the chapter). The review declares that "The select few may be lured from the beginning to the end by an untiring interest in the heroine—as beautiful and lovable as she is clever and original." However, those who are enticed will have to "shut their eyes to a host of impossibilities (improbabilities is too mild a word), and will pass lightly over many other transgressions of the laws of high art." This would be fine if not for the fact that "to the multitude the transgressions are the attraction" (380). Reade is cast as a more insidious writer, one who will not merely amuse his readers but might actually thrill them with unsavory subjects. Reade, then, is not treated as flippantly as Braddon and Wood. Regardless of his admirable heroine, his work was thought to so egregiously violate the standards of high culture that both the novel and its audience are denounced for their mutual interest in "transgressions," presumably both moral and artistic.

By April 1868 the absence of both Davies and Faithfull allowed the development of *Victoria*'s hard line against sensationalism. Despite the profound and lasting impact Davies's editorship had on *Victoria*'s literary character, her resignation was followed by a significant shift in the magazine's critical approach. In February 1865, a year after Davies had deserted her editorial chair, several changes instituted in the review section seem to indicate that her proprietorship over the reviews had also come to a conclusion. These revisions include the shortening of the title from "Literature of the Month" to "Literature," an increase in the length of the section, and a decrease in the number of fiction reviews. Faithfull's response to Davies's departure contributed to the changes that were underway. In August 1867 Faithfull sold half of the magazine to William Wilfred Head, who seems to have managed *Victoria*'s affairs until 1873.[18] Head was a Langhamite sympathizer who had already developed a successful partnership with Faithfull in managing the Victoria Press.[19] When Faithfull took a leave of absence from the magazine in November 1867, Head implemented an even more pronounced change in what was now called the "Reviews of Books" section, a title that indicated the steadily decreasing focus on "literary" works. The "Reviews of Books" included more reviews, but they were shorter, more cursory, and much more frequently focused on autobiographical, historical, and political works. Faithfull's and Head's plans to decrease costs and increase circulation figures moved *Victoria* even further away from Davies's vision of the magazine. While *Victoria*'s stint as a full-scale literary review tapered off when Davies resigned, the important role the magazine played in establishing a feminist critical voice in the mainstream periodical marketplace remained significant, nonetheless. Regardless of the changes in format, *Victoria* continued to initiate what Robinson calls "a feminist project of establishing a pantheon of notable women writers, proudly drawing attention to contemporary women's literary achievements . . . [and shaping] nearly 40 years of criticism in Victorian women's periodicals ("Amazed at Our Success" 162).

The changes made in *Victoria*'s review section under Head's tenure were coupled with an increasing number of scathing critiques of sensation novels in the magazine. For example, the novel *Little Miss Fairfax* was sharply criticized in April 1868 for its plot about a sensational villain who denounces marriage yet seduces every woman who crosses his path, plans a thwarted murder by poison, and, worst of all, escapes punishment. In a lengthy tirade *Victoria* maps out its objections to such fiction:

> In this work the author aims at producing effective scenes and strik-
> ing conversations, by dint of bold colours and hardy words. The
> lights are rather too strong and the shadows too dark to suit our taste.
> . . . The public may, however, think differently, as nothing seems too
> hot or spiced to swallow, while the rush-along style now in fashion
> precludes the possibility of taking time to note whether harmony
> exists either in the conversations of the speakers or their actions. If
> this book, and others of like description, give indeed true pictures of
> our times, then we are far advanced on the road downwards, and not
> upwards, as is by some fondly believed. (571)

Victoria acknowledges that the novel clearly intended "to show the evil therein depicted, and to prove that virtue is a reality," but the novel is dismissed as a failure of art because of its dependence upon a fast-paced plot and bold contrasts rather than on well-developed characters (ibid.). This review marks an intensification of the magazine's view of sensation fiction, which began to take on a more menacing character as a harbinger of cultural decline. Though such reviews seem to be a direct result of Head's increasing control and what Robinson refers to as his "frequently . . . incoherent, reactionary discourses on the decline of contemporary culture" ("Amazed at Our Success" 169), the values articulated remain consistent with Davies's elevation of realist charac-terization and disparagement of "overcrowded incident." Under Head's control, the arguments became more vehement, but Davies's definition of good literature prevailed.

In the March 1868 article "Sensational Novels," however, *Victoria's* assertion of its literary critical authority began to impinge on its femi-nist values. The magazine blames critics who have "fallen into a servile worship of what is too willingly welcomed and read, and abjectly bowed to the great idol of success" for the general public's inability to distinguish between high and low culture (455). By declaring other crit-ics to be lax in their duties, *Victoria* raised its own status as a critical authority. Nevertheless, *Victoria* risked contradicting its mission by attacking the motives of the sensation novelists themselves. Since so many of these novelists were women trying to make a living, a cause that the magazine otherwise wholeheartedly promoted, *Victoria* was in danger of alienating its core audience. The article scandalously declares that:

Instructing and profiting, purifying and ennobling their readers, do not enter into the thoughts, are not the ambition of [sensation] writers. . . . Their highest aim is to write what will be read, and thus secure the golden booty. Ephemeral notoriety and a publisher's solid thanks seem effectually to stifle any disagreeable twinge of conscience, [sic] literary prostitution may at times be supposed to give rise to. (456–57)

Equating prostitution with writing sensation fiction is shocking because it contradicts the magazine's campaign to make women's work acceptable—to in fact distance women's work from immorality. Braddon, who embodies this class of literary prostitutes, comes directly under fire for her role as the "founder and flagrant example" of the noxious school of literature (464). *Victoria* belligerently proclaims that "If ladies will seek notoriety in an unenviable and vicious province of literature, they have only themselves to thank for well-merited and (it is to be hoped) salutary castigation" (ibid.). In abandoning its championship of women writers and in this case attacking a prominent woman editor whose magazine was in direct competition with *Victoria,* Head even more closely allied *Victoria* with journals like the *Saturday Review,* which generated controversy to draw attention to itself and to perpetuate its conservative literary values.

Despite the increasing venom of *Victoria's* attacks on sensation, the values remained rooted in Davies's demand for realistic female characters who would serve as role models for readers. In fact, female sensation characters—"noxious and offensive specimen[s] of womankind, in reality the victim[s] of ignorance, vanity, selfishness"—emerge as the primary reason for the magazine's hostility toward sensation novels (459). Sensational characters are blamed for damaging the public's respect for women and delaying progress for womankind by

traduc[ing], calumniat[ing], and blacken[ing] the character of Englishwomen. . . . What, we may ask, will ultimately be the estimate of the other sex, if men put faith in such portraitures? It must rapidly sink to the lowest depth a Sensational author can crawl to, and principle, fidelity, and honour in a woman, will come to be regarded as unattainable. (460–61)

Authors of sensation novels, whatever their intention or their sex, are condemned for tainting the reputations of Englishwomen and thereby crippling the goals of the Langhamites.

188

However, *Victoria*'s dismissal of sensationalism and championing of realism is complicated by the acknowledgement in "Sensational Novels" that such fiction exposes "Evils in our social system" that should be addressed (457). While it is conceded that sensationalism is "real" because its themes are ripped from the daily newspaper headlines, the failure of the genre lies in its refusal to show readers explicitly what moral lesson they should take from their reading:

> [R]epresentatives of the sensational or realistic school assert that their intention is to portray life as it is, without a tinge of idealism, without seeking to point a moral. . . . Here, they say, we lay before you a picture. Do not turn your eyes away from the horrors, ghastly vices, and social depravity we have dissected and unfolded, but answer us–is it accurate or not? If it is, our purpose is fulfilled. You, reader, must draw your own conclusions–and moral, if possible– from it. (ibid.)

Victoria contended that regardless of sensation fiction's hyperreality, its lack of moral guidance coupled with its dangerous portrayal of women barred it from entering the ranks of acceptable art.[20] Once again, under Head's guidance, *Victoria* came dangerously close to contradicting one of its most important goals, in this case promoting the critical-thinking skills of its women readers who would presumably be able to draw their own conclusions and morals from sensational works.

In its impassioned reviews of sensational works as well as its more laudatory analyses of realist novels, comments about the multitude of vulnerable and careless readers betray the tensions *Victoria* faced in attempting to put forth a feminist agenda while also establishing a respectable critical voice. It is largely in its comments about uncritical readers–who are notably *not* identified primarily as women–that *Victoria*'s desire to assert its critical authority by mimicking the concerns of other elite reviewers becomes evident. Still, the magazine's empowerment of women readers outweighs its condescending remarks about uncritical readers in general, and the confidential tone of the magazine's comments seems to indicate that its own readers are certainly not among those who are in danger of being corrupted. One reader's objection to *Victoria*'s tirade against sensationalism in the April 1868 "Correspondence" section illustrates that its readers still felt empowered to express their own critical voices. "H. P.," one of *Victoria*'s active reader-critics, contends that sensation serves a necessary function in modern society, in which science has nearly eliminated the experience of the mysterious and the unknown. Sensation novels, H. P. argues, provide a balance to scientific attempts to eradicate supernatural beliefs, filling the imaginative void of the unknown: "Though witches and fairies with all their kith and kin are no more, not even a poor ghost lingering behind, the craving for excitement, the degenerate offspring of wonder, still lives, and, too listless to rise to healthier regions, grovels in the infected marshes of sensationalism" (537). While acknowledging the inferior artistry of sensation fiction (and thereby demonstrating her ability to distinguish between high and low culture), *Victoria*'s rebellious reader contends that the genre serves a deeper purpose, connecting modern citizens with the wonders of a pre-scientific age. Head's agenda may have slightly derailed some of the magazine's goals, but its readers clearly remembered the example Davies had set and continued to emulate it by proving their own worthiness as critics. Despite Davies's dismissive attitude toward sensation novels and Head's amplification of the genre's dangers, the thrills of sensationalism were embraced not only by *Victoria*'s readers, but also by the magazine's own fiction.

Perhaps surprisingly, given the clear divisions *Victoria* upholds in its criticism, the magazine's short fiction tended toward the sensational from the magazine's inception. Two closely related factors account for this seeming contradiction. First, a shortage of funds prevented the hiring of the most revered realists, leaving the magazine with limited options and a reliance on short fiction rather than major serials to attract readers. Second, the need to sustain a wider audience to boost the magazine's profits may also have resulted in a bid to find fiction that would excite and attract as many new readers as possible. Since sensation fiction outsold realist fiction, the magazine would naturally gravitate toward the genre for sales purposes. But *Victoria* did not completely abandon its critical assessments, nor did it hypocritically pander to popular tastes, as *Harper's* rivals accused it of doing. The *Cornhill* insisted that its readers could determine the differences between enriching fiction and entertaining fiction and therefore had no problem including both. *Victoria*, on the other hand, had to reconcile its harsh condemnation of sensation with the incorporation of sensational elements in its own fiction.

Victoria did this and stayed true to its original critical values by making sure that its sensational story lines featured redeemable female characters who delivered moral lessons that adhered to the magazine's definition of feminist realism. *Victoria* included works like "Why I Never Married" (August 1864), the story of a spinster whose former fiancé jilted her in order to save her from his secret mental illness; "A

Long Lane and a Turning" (August 1864), about a respected young clergyman's relationship with a woman whose father's forgery conviction is overturned just in time to save the couple from marrying in disgrace; and "The Story of a Scandal" (August 1865), an account of a country doctor who is the subject of a misunderstanding that turns into a sensationalized rumor perpetuated by a community of "old maids." All of these stories—as well as the two I examine in greater detail, Margaret Oliphant's "A Story of a Voice" (August and September 1863) and the unsigned story "Written for My Daughter" (August and September 1865)—could be considered realist texts in *Victoria*'s terms because they offer effective moral lessons, attempt to depict events that could really happen to fairly well-developed characters, and provide positive images of strong, unconventional women. In fact, four of these five stories contain characters who are independent, single women variously referred to as spinsters or old maids.[21] The plots of "A Story of a Voice" and "Written for My Daughter" involve even more potentially sensational events that go beyond gossipy scandals caused by false accusations, petty crimes, insanity, and jilted lovers to include assault, kidnapping, murder, and detective work. These plots are uniformly resolved in such a way that the villains are punished, the women maintain their moral standards, and a lesson is subtly but didactically communicated to the reader. Thus, *Victoria*'s stories tend to adapt the sensational to the real, thereby fulfilling the magazine's critical and feminist agendas by domesticating the genre of sensationalism.

Oliphant's highly entertaining and humorously written "A Story of a Voice" traces the events that follow a murder witnessed by the stout and lovable old bachelor Mr. Oldham. The only way that Oldham can identify the murderer is by the haunting sound of his "strange, spasmodic voice—a voice which seemed to catch upon special words, and clench the teeth on them" (August 1863, 303). All he knows is that the murderer was a gentleman who struck a deadly blow to a humble man after repeatedly asking where he had put "the child." After Oldham hears this scuffle beneath his window, his obsession with finding the murderer transforms him into a bumbling investigator, a sort of anti-detective, who knows "nothing of the arts of detectiveism" and, even worse, does not "understand how to hold his tongue" (September 1863, 407). He somehow manages to stumble upon clues accidentally and to hide evidence from the police though he cannot restrain himself from talking incessantly about what he knows. He is ridiculed by his friends, who think his interest in the case is silly and self-important because he believes that "justice in the world can no longer go on without him"

(August 1863, 311). When Oldham sets out to locate the address written on a slip of paper he confiscated from the dead man's pocketbook, he meets an old maid named Miss Mead, hears the voice of the murderer, and finds the kidnapped child safe and sound living with Miss Mead's maid.

However, the closer Oldham comes to unraveling the mystery, the less interest he has in it. His obsession with the crime is transferred to Miss Mead, an "experienced" and "quick-witted" woman of forty with "pretty grey ringlets" that "stirred softly on the sweet bloom of her cheeks" (September 1863, 403). Miss Mead saves Oldham from his bumbling detective work with her practical advice. She is "the centre of her little society," the manager of the community who makes him understand "the inferiority of the male portion of the creation altogether" (ibid., 412–13). In the end, Oldham and Miss Mead are married, the kidnapped child is returned to his mother, and the murderer is caught as a result of their teamwork. Good and evil are clearly delineated, those who commit crimes are punished, and the old maid saves the day and gets the man. Clearly, this upholds *Victoria*'s feminist purpose by depicting a strong female lead, while also flirting with sensational themes that would attract readers. Moreover, with Oliphant's added reputation for moral strength (and her public abhorrence of all things sensational), the magazine's needs were well met by the story. In her discussion of Oliphant's *Salem Chapel,* Marlene Tromp argues that the supposedly conservative author who was a favorite of the Queen "defies her own admonitions" against sensationalism in that novel (156), as I claim she does in this story. Both Oliphant and *Victoria* incorporated sensational themes within a more acceptable (realist) notion of domesticity, to, as Tromp says, "provide an alternative to sensation" and to demonstrate how sensation "could evolve out of a picture of life" (198).

In "Written for My Daughter," realism again flirts with sensationalism as the seemingly villainous narrator, Margaret Oglevie, writes the secret story of her life for her daughter to read after her death. The narrative voice cleverly places the reader in the position of the daughter and asks the audience to read the tale critically in order to derive a moral lesson from its sensational events. Margaret Oglevie is a self-described "woman of a cool head, but fiery heart" who is "proud, selfish, and self-willed" (August 1865, 363, 367). Because of the strictures of society, Margaret's desire to leave home and strike out on her own can, ironically, be fulfilled only by marriage. Therefore, she submits to the first proposal she receives, which is from John Baldwin, a mild-mannered family friend who showers her with admiration. Margaret states that she "had no notion of prematurely resigning my liberty, nor of sinking into my proper place, with regard to him; for, so far, I led and influenced him completely" (367). During her extended engagement with John, Margaret falls in love with Roland Oglevie, a dark, passionate figure who is a better match for her intellect and will. The couple decides to elope despite the fact that she is engaged and Roland has been promised to his cousin–Margaret's frail and angelic, boarding-school roommate. Therefore, they begin their lives together "stained with unfaithfulness and dishonour," leaving two victims in their wake (370). So far, this seems to be the beginning of a typical sensational tale in which the evil villains triumph over their weak fiancés. However, the story had to be more complex than that to suit *Victoria's* brand of domesticated sensationalism.

Indeed, the tale takes an unexpected twist toward that domestication when Roland and Margaret come to represent an ideal marriage. They have a baby and seem to be on their way to living happily ever after–if not for the wrath of the formerly docile John Baldwin. Despite the couple's remorse and the hardship of being exiled from their families and friends, they lead a quiet, respectable, and happy life together. Baldwin, however, will not accept that Margaret left him of her own free will; he is convinced that she has been brainwashed and corrupted by Roland. In fact, to justify stalking Margaret, he creates his own delusional sensation plot. Finally, John's obsession leads to a psychotic rage, during which he beats Roland in the face with a whip, blinding him and eventually causing his death. Thus the strong-willed woman is punished for her transgressions by the tragic death of her husband; however, her decision not to marry John is justified since he turns out to be the real villain of the tale. Surprisingly, Margaret turns out to be both a model wife and an independent woman whose mistakes serve to educate single girls. Her story warns girls not to marry too soon and encourages them to trust their own opinions and desires.

Victoria's fiction illustrates the difficulties the magazine faced as it attempted to balance its sometimes conflicting goals. *Victoria* hoped to simultaneously establish its own critical authority in ways that promoted women's involvement in the production of high art, to provide a sound feminist analysis of society, and to compete on a literary level with other family literary magazines. However, *Victoria's* decision to attack sensationalism in an effort to gain critical authority separated it from the family literary magazines it otherwise emulated. Finding direct competition impossible, *Victoria* adopted a more elitist critical stance than other magazines of the genre, which, like the *Cornhill,* featured and defended some sensation novels or, like *Belgravia,* built its market niche by elevating the sensation genre to the level of high art. As a result of its conflicting financial constraints and philosophical commitments, the magazine was forced to walk the line between sensationalism and feminist realism. The magazine participated in creating a form of domesticated sensationalism that maintained an overt moral message that was more covert in the typical sensation novel. Thus *Victoria* tried to expand the functions of the family literary magazine while maintaining the genre's essential format and goals.

Victoria's conflicted character did not lessen its importance as a vehicle for establishing a feminist critical voice that enabled the woman reader to become a critic; it only guaranteed that the magazine would have strict moral guidelines for women who wrote, guidelines that would ensure that professional women maintained their social acceptability within the existing ideals of Victorian womanhood. *Victoria*'s domestic and moralistic feminism follows the model set forth by Faithfull's defense of her female compositors at the Victoria Press, who would carry out their womanly reproductive and domestic functions within a nontraditional profession as they transferred words onto the printed page to be circulated around the nation, thus spreading culture throughout the British empire and beyond. Maria Frawley argues that Emily Faithfull's "experimentation with a variety of textual forms" produced by the Victoria Press "reveals her keen awareness of the vexed relationship between commercial success, cultural authority, and the activist agenda she promoted" ("Feminism, Format" 40). This propensity for experimentation with form plays out within the single textual example of *Victoria Magazine* as its conflicting purposes create what is often a chaotic array of messages without diminishing its influence as the first mainstream feminist family literary magazine.

AFTERWORD

THE IMAGES OF influential women readers (in *Harper's*), intellectual women readers (in the *Cornhill*), independent women readers (in
Belgravia), and feminist women readers/critics (in *Victoria*) successfully
gave women an opportunity to participate in defining literary culture
and paved the way for changes in women's education and roles in society that family literary magazines characterized as part of an inevitable,
evolutionary development. These magazines provided women with a
mainstream forum that invited them to develop their own ideas about
literature and to engage in the kinds of critical discussions from which
they were typically excluded. As a result of the phenomenon of the
family literary magazine, women like *Victoria*'s correspondent
Henrietta were confidently able to raise their voices in favor of the
intellectual development of women. In her letter to the editor,
Henrietta overtly expresses the message that underlies this magazine
genre:

> The epithets of "bluestocking" and "strong-minded" have been too
> often thrust in the faces of many of the most refined and modest of
> women, whose higher natures instinctively followed a law to which
> more frivolous or ill-trained minds were strangers, but which pre-
> serving the outward semblance of womanly goodness, passed
> muster when those others were censured and discouraged. The most
> capable, the most intellectual among women have ranked among
> the gentlest, kindest, and most devoted of wives and mothers. The
> largest view allowed to her, the more clearly she discerns her true
> sphere, her noblest mission. I know of no argument more cogent

than that of the right to grow. It ranks above all others, it is mighty for all time. I think I do not overstate a conviction founded on observation and a calm though deep-rooted interest in the subject, when I say, I think it is impossible for a woman to be "too intellectual." I think she cannot be too highly educated. Though she were charged with the knowledge of all the world, she would be "woman" still. (341–42)

As a genre, these magazines empowered women to read in new ways that were fervently justified as beneficial to the status of the entire middle class and the cultural health of the nation. Thus, the women who read and wrote for family literary magazines were able to influence the valuation of literary culture in important ways that were characterized as acceptable within the middle classes. Uncovering these alternative representations of women readers is crucial to our understanding of Victorian culture because it was partly as a result of such female-friendly but not female-exclusive forums that women would increasingly gain access to education and to previously male-dominated professions. These magazines reached a broad audience and effectively worked to change public opinion about women's roles in the literary world as well as in society at large.

However, the advances in thinking represented by these magazines had evidently become invisible to early-twentieth-century writers like Virginia Woolf, perhaps due to arguments like Henrietta's, which continued to focus on women's education as a force that would improve family life rather than transform it. Woolf, whose father edited the *Cornhill* from 1871 to 1882, famously lamented the lack of a woman's literary and critical tradition, apparently disregarding all of the "Henriettas" (including her Aunt Anne Thackeray Ritchie) who read and contributed to family literary magazines like the one that occupied so many years of her father's life. In *The Forgotten Female Aesthetes,* Talia Schaffer argues that "Woolf was well read in the literature produced by women at the turn of the century and was indeed intimately acquainted with many of the women themselves." However, "the woman who insisted 'we think back through our literary mothers'" actually established modern feminism and the modernist movement by excluding her mid-to-late-nineteenth-century literary foremothers (194). In addition to the ascendance of a new generation that disregarded the activities of its immediate Victorian predecessors, several major changes in the publishing industry and the system of higher education at the turn of the century apparently muffled the voices to which

I have drawn attention in this book. The demise of the serialized novel and the circulating library, which effectively ended the dominance of the family literary magazine; the increasing specialization of magazines into distinct target audiences, which further separated male and female readers; and the development of English literature as an acceptable field for academic study, which entrenched the profession of criticism as a predominantly male pursuit, worked to exclude women from mainstream literary and cultural discourse despite the gains they had made at mid-century. These changes led to the exclusion of women from the development of the literary canon as readers, authors, and critics until the late twentieth century. However, we cannot forget that, if only for a brief time during the middle of the nineteenth century, women had a mainstream forum that invited them to create and influence culture rather than to consume it passively.

Though the modernists may have forgotten or dismissed the family literary magazines, studying such cultural texts is important not only for what they teach us about the past, but also for what they teach us about the present. In her postscript to *Victorian Afterlife: Postmodern Culture Rewrites the Nineteenth Century,* Nancy Armstrong argues that postmodernism is the culmination of the Victorian cultural modernization process that shifted "political action from government onto culture" (313). The importance of culture to women's power in mid-Victorian society and, particularly, to the nation's imagined identity prefigures our contemporary "culture wars" in which the identity of the nation is represented as much by its culture as by its land and institutions (ibid., 312). Thus, through the study of nineteenth-century commodities like family literary magazines, which figure cultural knowledge as status, we can trace the origins of the democratization of the public sphere that fueled the anxieties of nineteenth-century critics, elicited the rejection and suppression of all things Victorian by the modernists, and has inspired the cultural play as well as the culture wars of the postmodernists.

NOTES

Notes to Introduction

1. Despite vast national differences, I treat British and American literature as a single discursive field in which similar and parallel critical trends were emerging–particularly in relation to the function of critics, periodicals, and women readers. Likewise, I use the term "Victorian," which is technically applicable only to Great Britain during the reign of Queen Victoria, to refer to the corresponding time period in the United States. While this is a convenience in a book that focuses on more British than American periodicals, it is also a practice that some American historians have followed.

2. For more on the conception of reading as a disease, see Kate Flint, Pamela K. Gilbert, and Kelly J. Mays.

3. Though *Temple Bar* belongs to the genre of the family literary magazine, which I define more thoroughly below, it seems that–at least during the 1870s–it was more conservative than its contemporaries.

4. *Putnam's,* a rival to *Harper's,* also belongs to the category of the family literary magazine. The fact that it focuses on the power of women readers and shifts the fears of reading to girls indicates that it took a more progressive stance in tune with the magazine genre even while it justified the role of the critic.

5. In addition to Mary Elizabeth Braddon's editorship of *Belgravia* and Emily Faithfull and Emily Davies's editorial posts at *Victoria,* Ellen Price Wood edited the *Argosy,* and Anna Maria Hall edited *St. James's.*

6. See my qualification of these numbers as they apply to William Thackeray's editorial reign over the *Cornhill* in chapter 3.

7. While this index includes the family literary magazines the *Cornhill, Macmillan's,* and *Temple Bar,* it is dominated by more elite journals.

8. For an account of the ways serial novels coincided with the Victorian worldview, see Linda Hughes and Michael Lund's *The Victorian Serial* (Charlottesville: University of Virginia Press, 1991).

9. See the special issue on "Critical Theory and Periodical Research" (*Victorian Periodicals Review* 22 [Fall 1989]) for an important series of articles about studying the genre and form of periodicals.

10. The most ambitious bibliographic attempts made thus far have been the cataloguing of a wide range of British periodicals in the *Wellesley Index to Victorian Periodicals* and *Waterloo Directory of Victorian Periodicals* (ed. Michael Wolff, John S. North, and Dorothy Deering. Waterloo, Ontario: Wilfrid Laurier University Press, 1977)—both of which are now available in fully searchable CD-ROM formats—as well as the *Union List of Victorian Serials* (ed. Richard D. Fulton and C. M. Colee. New York: Garland, 1985). The *Nineteenth Century Masterfile*, a new web-based subscription search engine for nineteenth-century magazines, and *The Athenaeum Project*, an online database of reviews published between 1830 and 1870, are recent useful electronic resources.

For publication information and thorough descriptions of thousands of magazines, Edward Chielens's *American Literary Magazines* and Alvin Sullivan's *British Literary Magazines* are also invaluable. For historical surveys, Frank Luther Mott's *History of American Magazines* and John Tebble and Mary Ellen Zuckerman's *Magazine in America* (New York: Oxford University Press, 1991) prove to be the most comprehensive studies on the American front.

11. See Margaret Beetham's *A Magazine of Her Own* for a detailed examination of the function of British women's magazines. For information on American women's magazines, consult Jennifer Scanlon's *Inarticulate Longings: The Ladies' Home Journal, Gender, and the Promises of Consumer Culture* (New York: Routledge, 1995) and Ellen Gruber Garvey's *The Adman in the Parlor: Magazines and the Gendering of Consumer Culture, 1880s to 1910s* (New York: Oxford University Press, 1996).

12. For a comprehensive study of Mudie's, see Guinevere Griest's *Mudie's Circulating Library and the Victorian Novel* (Bloomington: Indiana University Press, 1970).

13. For other recent accounts of the complex and contradictory nature of realism, see Nancy Armstrong's *Fiction in the Age of Photography: The Legacy of British Realism* (Cambridge: Harvard University Press, 1999) and Katherine Kearns's *Nineteenth-Century Realism: Through the Looking-Glass* (Cambridge: Cambridge University Press, 1996).

14. For more about the generic characteristics and cultural implications of sensation fiction, see Thomas Boyle's *Black Swine in the Sewers of Hampstead: Beneath the Surface of Victorian Sensationalism* (New York: Viking Penguin, 1989); Anne Cvetkovitch's *Mixed Feelings: Feminism, Mass Culture, and Victorian Sensationalism;* Pamela K. Gilbert's *Disease, Desire, and the Body in Victorian Women's Popular Novels;* Winifred Hughes's *Maniac in the Cellar;* and Marlene Tromp's *Private Rod.* On sentimentality, see Anne Douglas's classic study *The Feminization of American Culture* (New York: Alfred A. Knopf, 1977), Lori Merish's *Sentimental Materialism,* Marianne Noble's *The Masochistic Pleasures of Sentimental Literature* (Princeton, NJ: Princeton University Press, 2000), and Jane Tompkins's *Sensational Designs: The Cultural Work of American Fiction 1790–1860* (New York: Oxford University Press, 1985).

Notes to Chapter 1

1. The magazine was called *Harper's New Monthly Magazine* from 1850 to 1900. From 1900 to 1925 the name was shortened to *Harper's Monthly Magazine,*

and in 1925 it was changed to its current title, *Harper's Magazine.* For the sake of convenience, I refer to the magazine by its shortest and most commonly used name, *Harper's.*

2. Technically speaking, the works copied from British magazines into *Harper's* pages were reprinted legally and were therefore not pirated. However, *Harper's* developed a reputation for piracy despite the absence of laws preventing its reprinting practices.

3. McGill only briefly discusses *Harper's* in her "Coda" (271–72).

4. In *Transatlantic Insurrections* Paul Giles identifies a need for more scholars to acknowledge and trace "reciprocal transatlantic influences" as they relate to "versions of national identity" in the literatures of Britain and America (15). For another account of literary history that reverses the traditional transatlantic flow, see Nancy Armstrong and Leonard Tennenhouse's *The Imaginary Puritan: Literature, Intellectual Labor, and the Origins of Personal Life* (Berkeley: University of California Press, 1992).

5. See John Gray Laird Dowgray's *A History of Harper's Literary Magazines, 1850–1900* (25–27) and Laurel Brake's chapter, "*Harper's New Monthly Magazine:* American Censorship, European Decadence, and the Periodicals Market in the 1890s," in *Subjugated Knowledges* for more details about the English version of the magazine.

6. As Mark W. Turner points out in his book *Trollope and the Magazines,* periodicals embody Bakhtin's notion of intertextuality as multivocal texts with plural meanings (233). Cynthia L. Bandish affirms this notion by suggesting that Bakhtinian analysis serve as a model for periodical studies.

7. The featured serial novels for the first issue were Charles Lever's *Maurice Tiernay, Soldier of Fortune* from *Dublin University Magazine* and Anne Marsh's *Lettice Arnold* from *The Ladies' Companion.* Other works included the short story "Lizzie Leigh," attributed to Charles Dickens (but actually written by Elizabeth Gaskell for Dickens's *Household Words*); a biography of Samuel Johnson and an article on George Sand from *Bentley's;* and an article on William Wordsworth from the *Athenaeum.*

8. The June 1850 features taken from *Household Words* are "Lizzie Leigh," "A Tale of the Good Old Times," "Francis Jeffrey," "A Child's Dream of a Star," "Illustrations of Cheapness," "Short Cuts across the Globe," "Ghost Stories–An Incident in the Life of Mademoiselle Clairon," and "Work! An Anecdote." In July 1850 the following articles are attributed to Dickens's magazine: "The Miner's Daughter," "The Railway Station," "Globes and How They Are Made," "A Paris Newspaper," "Two-Handed Dick the Stockman," "The Uses of Sorrow," "Alchemy and Gunpowder," "Ignorance of the English," "The Planet–Watchers of Greenwich," "Father and Son," "The Appetite for News," "Greenwich Weather-Wisdom," "Young Russia," and "The Orphan's Voyage Home." Of these pieces taken from *Household Words* between its inception on March 30, 1850, and June 8, 1850, "Ghost Stories–An Incident in the Life of Mademoiselle Clairon" is listed in Anne Lohrli's table of contents for the magazine without the phrase "Ghost Stories," and "Globes and How They Are Made" and "Ignorance of the English" are not listed at all. It is likely that the titles of these selections were changed before they were reprinted.

9. Dickens received $1,728 for the advance sheets of his novel (Exman, *Brothers Harper* 310).

10. While authors such as Dickens and Edgar Allan Poe fought for an international copyright agreement, publishers were generally not supportive of the idea and claimed that book prices would rise dangerously, jeopardizing most Americans' access to books and threatening the American book trade abroad (Barnes 234–38). As early as 1844 Wesley Harper joined the American Copyright Club, which pushed for more extensive international copyright laws, but this did not seem to interfere with the company's piratical practices (Exman, *Brothers Harper* 157). Apparently, Harper and Brothers' relationship to the push for an international copyright law was precarious: On the one hand, the company wanted to be recognized for its efforts on behalf of authors; on the other hand, it did not want to endanger its own profits. The copyright controversy raged on and awareness of the problem grew, but the rights of readers and manufacturers held sway over those of authors until 1891, when an international copyright agreement was finally reached.

11. John Abbott's *Napoleon Bonaparte* was highly profitable for both author and publisher. It was published in two volumes with engravings from the magazine on June 15, 1855 (Exman, *House of Harper* 329). Contracts for "Abbott's Napoleon" of February and March 1852 show that the company agreed to pay $100 an article and an advance of $1,000 for travel to Europe to sell the plates and the copyright of *Napoleon* if Abbott split the profits of those sales with Harper and Brothers (*Archives* A1, 177–79). Jacob Abbott was paid five dollars a page plus expenses not to exceed one additional dollar per page, and he was promised a ten-percent royalty should it be "deemed expedient at any future time to publish any portion of said articles" (ibid., 171).

12. Travel writer and essayist Donald G. Mitchell, also known as Ik Marvel, occupied the "easy chair" from its inception in 1851 until October 1853, when he began to share the responsibility with George W. Curtis, a young journalist associated with the Brook Farm intellectuals. According to Gordon Milne, Curtis took over the "chair" in April 1854 (75). Curtis was considered the more "literary" as well as the more "political" of the two editors, though both had a strong stake in strengthening the reputation of American writers. Curtis in particular supported Herman Melville and was instrumental in getting his work (including "Bartleby") published in *Putnam's*, where he simultaneously worked until 1857 (ibid., 68, 75). However, both Mitchell and Curtis conformed their editorial commentaries to *Harper's* agenda.

13. As Zboray illustrates, literacy instruction in nineteenth-century America often fell to women, who were expected to reinforce their children's reading practices at home. This feminization of reading and other literate practices gained strength as women increasingly participated in public institutions such as churches and schools that promoted reading (88).

14. The vexed nature of Esther's narrative has been a favorite topic of critics. Some articles that have examined her role as narrator over the years include William Axton's "The Trouble with Esther" (*Modern Language Quarterly* 26 [1965]: 545–57); Valerie Kennedy's "*Bleak House:* More Trouble with Esther" (*Journal of Women's Studies in Literature* 1 [1979]: 330–47); Michael Kearns's "'But I Cried

Very Much': Esther Summerson as Narrator" (*Dickens Quarterly* 1 [4] [1984]: 121–29); John Frazee's "Character of Esther and the Narrative Structure of *Bleak House*" (*Studies in the Novel* 17 [3] [1985]: 227–40); Jasmine Yong Hall's "What's Troubling about Esther? Narrating, Policing and Resisting Arrest in *Bleak House*" (*Dickens Studies Annual* 22 [1993]: 171–94); and Eleanor Salotto's "Detecting Esther Summerson's Secrets: Dickens's Bleak House of Representation" (*Victorian Literature and Culture* [1997]: 333–49).

15. Nina Baym notes of this particular review that "the work seen by the *London Leader* as particularly American would not have been accepted as worthy of the up-and-coming nation, and indeed in allotting work reminiscent of the European Dark Ages to the American mind, the British journal was patronizing" (245). This view of Melville's fiction as "uncivilized" could further account for *Harper's* rejection of the novel for serialization.

16. See *Herman Melville: The Contemporary Reviews,* edited by Brian Higgins and Hershel Parker (Cambridge University Press, 1995), for a complete collection of reviews of *Moby-Dick.*

17. For an account of Melville's relationship with Harper and Brothers throughout his career see Exman, *House of Harper,* 282–302.

18. See Brian Foley, Sheila Post-Lauria, Pearl Chesler Solomon, and Robert Weisbuch. Foley suggests that Melville's purpose in writing "Bartleby" was "to show not just that an American writer can write a Dickensian story as well as Dickens can, but that he can write one better" (247).

19. Sheila Post-Lauria and Michael T. Gilmore both offer analyses that follow this line of reasoning.

20. For more on *Israel Potter, Harper's,* and *Putnam's,* see Post-Lauria (191–201).

21. In fact, Dickens was responding to critics, G. H. Lewes in particular, who attacked his work for being unrealistic.

Notes to Chapter 2

1. The *Cornhill's* own advertisements suggested that initial sales were as high as 120,000, but according to John Sutherland, the exact figure was 109,274. The sales figures for the remaining issues during the first year are as follows: February–March, 100,000; April, 92,000; May–June, 90,000; and July– December, 87,500 (106). These numbers are astounding when one considers the 1860 circulation figures for precursors to the *Cornhill* such as *Blackwood's* (10,000) and *Bentley's* (5,000) and for reviews such as *Fraser's* (8,000) and the *Saturday Review* (10,000) (Ellegård 22, 32). The *Cornhill's* sales figures remained around 80,000 for the first two years and are recorded as follows by George Smith for December of each subsequent year under consideration here: 1862, 72,500; 1863, 50,000; and 1864, 41,259 (Glynn 143).

2. The *Saturday Review* was particularly opposed to the *Cornhill Magazine* because of bitterness over William Thackeray's successful bid to obtain several of *Saturday's* frequent contributors. Fitzjames Stephen, Henry Sumner Maine, and John Ruskin were among the defectors to the *Cornhill* (Bevington 28). In his "Roundabout Papers" (August 1860, October 1860, and July 1861), Thackeray

protested what he saw as the *Review*'s unfair critiques of himself and his publisher, George Smith. The *Saturday* reciprocated with unfavorable reviews of Thackeray's works (ibid., 173–74) as well as with an attack on Stephen's *Cornhill* campaign for women's economic independence.

3. During Thackeray's tenure as editor, articles on many serious and controversial subjects made their way into the magazine. The *Cornhill* included articles that covered topics such as liberal political and social philosophy ("Liberalism," January 1862), industrial reform ("Life and Labour in the Coal Fields," March 1862), continental wars and politics ("Invasion Panics," February 1860; "How I Quitted Naples," August 1860; and "The Dark Church in Vienna," March 1863), and the Civil War ("The Dissolution of the Union," August 1861, and "Negroes Bond and Free," September 1861), as well as numerous articles on British courts, parliament, and laws, particularly those regarding women, criminals, and the insane. Furthermore, the magazine's inclusion of a novel like Wilkie Collins's *Armadale,* which the author felt compelled to defend against the "claptrap morality of the present day" as a book "daring enough to speak the truth" ("Foreword" 5), illustrates the *Cornhill*'s proclivity to take risks, especially after Thackeray's editorial reign had ended.

However, Thackeray did in fact reject Trollope's story *Mrs. General Tallboys* and George Meredith's poem "The Meeting" because of his fears of offending lady readers. When he reluctantly and with profuse apology turned down Elizabeth Barrett Browning's poem "Lord Walter's Wife" on the grounds that "there is an account of unlawful passion felt by a man for a woman" against which "I am sure our readers would make an outcry" (Ray, *Letters* 227), she replied with a convincing defense of women readers: "I am deeply convinced that the corruption of our society requires not shut doors and windows, but light and air–and that it is exactly because pure and prosperous women choose to *ignore* vice, that miserable women suffer wrong by it everywhere" (ibid., 228). It seems that Browning's defense was supported by George Smith, who played a role in tempering Thackeray's moralistic intent. Smith considered the rejection of Barrett Browning's poem an unnecessary fuss and insisted on printing controversial articles on public school reform that Thackeray also opposed. These widely debated articles led to the *Cornhill*'s emergence as a champion of public school reforms.

4. In addition, Thackeray was generously paid for his serials. According to Sutherland, Thackeray received the bulk of the magazine's payments to contributors; in September 1860, for example, he received about 358 of 538 pounds in payments (106). Thackeray conducted the magazine from January 1860 until May 1862. From May 1862 until August 1864 the magazine was run by an editorial board consisting of George Smith, Frederick Greenwood, and G. H. Lewes. When Lewes resigned in 1864, Greenwood became the sole editor until 1868, when Lewes, Dutton Cook, and Smith took over. Finally, in 1871 Leslie Stephen was hired, giving the magazine a unified editorial identity once again, but with a continued decline in sales (Huxley, *Smith Elder* 118).

Thackeray and Smith agreed that they would have equal veto power over contributions, an arrangement that–coupled with increasing financial worries–may have eventually led to Thackeray's resignation, although the partnership was successful overall. The facts surrounding Thackeray's resignation remain fuzzy.

However, the existing letter recording the incident, written March 4, 1862, states: "I have been thinking over our conversation of yesterday, and it has not improved the gaiety of the work on wh[ich] I am presently busy. Today I have taken my friend Sir Charles Taylor into my confidence, and his opinion coincides with mine that I should withdraw from the magazine. To go into bygones now is needless. . . . And whether connected with the Cornhill Magazine or not, I hope I shall always be sincerely your friend" (Ray, *Letters* 256). In fact, Thackeray continued to write for the magazine until his death in December 1863.

5. Spencer Eddy's comparison of the *Cornhill* cover with the stodgy *Macmillan's* cover indicates the positive impact it probably had on the public. As further evidence of this impact in a transatlantic context, Eddy notes that the ailing American magazine *The Knickerbocker* looked to the *Cornhill's* cover design as a model for transforming its own image (16–17).

6. Typical of most issues, the premiere number included two fiction serials, one of which opened the magazine—Anthony Trollope's *Framley Parsonage*—and one that was inserted amidst the "factual" material—Thackeray's *Lovel the Widower*. Most issues contained seven serious articles and two or three poems. The January 1860 issue featured the first part of G. H. Lewes's scientific series "Studies in Animal Life," which encouraged the hands-on study of biology among amateurs; John Bowring's account of his experience as a British diplomat in the Orient, including a description of Chinese women and daily life in "The Chinese and the Outer Barbarians"; John Burgoyne's "Our Volunteers," which warned of the dangers of French militarism and the need to bolster the nation's military forces; Thornton Hunt's biography of his father, Leigh Hunt; excerpts from Allen Young's journal (complete with an elaborate fold-out map) about his search for Sir John Franklin's lost Arctic expedition; the first of Thackeray's *Roundabout Papers;* and the poems "Father Prout's Inaugurative Ode to the Author of *Vanity Fair*," a piece by Reverend F. Mahoney glorifying Thackeray as editor, and "The First Morning of 1860," a wartime poem urging peace by Mrs. Archer Clive. This issue included six, rather than the standard seven, articles due to the length of Young's excerpt. Despite this, Peter Smith maintains that the first number has certain qualities that became typical of the magazine: "[T]here is a topicality, not in the sense that it deals with the news, but that it treats of ideas and facts which are of concern; secondly, there is the variety of subjects considered, and finally, there is the fact that the contributors are all men of authority in their subjects" (31).

7. For some less enthusiastic reviews of the *Cornhill*, see Andrew Maunder's "Discourses of Distinction: The Reception of the *Cornhill Magazine*, 1859–60" in *Victorian Periodicals Review* 32 (3) (Fall 1999): 239–58.

8. Schmidt points out that Smith's habit of signing authors to write serials after they had completed their most popular works tended to leave the magazine with authors of great reputation and works of less astounding popularity ("Novelists" 148). For example, John Sutherland claims that by December 1862, in the middle of *Romola's* serial run, sales of the magazine had dropped from 70,000 to 50,000 copies while expenditures doubled (107). G. H. Lewes lamented that *Romola* had "unfortunately not been so generally popular as I hoped and believed its intrinsic beauty would have made it" (quoted in Glynn 140). Though *Romola* did not recruit more readers, Smith stuck to his promise. The novel maintained

its honorary position at the beginning of every issue and included two illustrations by Frederic Leighton per installment–double the usual number–for ten of its twelve parts.

9. Accepting the editorial post of the *Cornhill* seemed to be the best way to ensure the future comfort of his daughters. As an editor, Thackeray would gain a position of great prestige and earn a generous and steady income. This would have been a less arduous means of supporting his family than embarking on lecture tours as he did in America in 1852 and 1856.

10. The 12.5 percent written by women during Thackeray's editorship includes twenty-one works of fiction, thirteen poems, and three nonfiction articles. The total of 297 contributions excludes nine poems whose authors remain unidentified. My figures are based on the list of prose contributors provided by *The Wellesley Index*, as well as on a survey of the tables of contents of the *Cornhill* to determine which poets contributed to the magazine. Many of these poets are also discussed in articles by Robert A. Colby and Rosemary Scott.

11. During the ten-month period between these two essays, only Thackeray's daughter Anne (who had one story and one article included in the magazine), the famous poets Elizabeth Barrett Browning and Adelaide Proctor (who contributed two poems each), and Charlotte Brontë (who had one poem posthumously published) appeared in the magazine.

12. For accounts of some of the "thorn letters" not mentioned in Thackeray's essay, see Robert Colby's "Goose Quill and Blue Pencil" in *Innovators and Preachers: The Role of the Editor in Victorian England* (ed. Joel H. Wiener, London: Greenwood, 1985: 203–30).

13. See "Why Are Women Redundant?" in *The National Review* 14 (28) (April 1862): 434–60.

14. The *Cornhill's* argument seems to have disturbed someone at the feminist Victoria Press whose November 1863 article "The *Cornhill* on Men and Women" in the *English Woman's Journal* complains about what it interprets as the *Cornhill's* crass call for women to be *like* men. While the *English Woman's Journal* feared that women would lose their moral authority if they became too masculine, the *Journal* was probably also reacting to the fact that the *Cornhill's* liberatory project for women was presented primarily as a protection for men rather than as an improvement for women; as a result it offered little practical advice for women seeking professional opportunities.

The *Journal* is specifically offended by the September 1863 *Cornhill* article "Anti-Respectability," written by Fitzjames Stephen. This article argues that women are not inherently more virtuous than men but are only more moral because of the restrictions society places on them. Stephen calls for the expansion of women's rights but suggests that once societal restrictions on women's behavior are lifted, women will lose their moral superiority. The *Journal* argues instead for a time when "men and women . . . shall reverence and uphold everywhere that virtue which is of no sex–which is the offspring of God's love, not of man's prudence" (181).

15. On the Victorian idea of the gentleman, see also James Eli Adams's *Dandies and Desert Saints: Styles of Victorian Masculinity* (Ithaca, N.Y.: Cornell University Press, 1995) and Shirley Robin Letwin's *The Gentleman in Trollope: Individuality and*

Moral Conduct (Cambridge: Harvard University Press, 1982).

16. For a more extensive analysis of Leighton's illustrations for *Romola* see Shawn Malley, "'The Listening Look': Visual and Verbal Metaphor in Frederic Leighton's Illustrations to George Eliot's *Romola*" in *Nineteenth-Century Contexts* 19 (3) (1996): 259–84. See also Mark W. Turner, "George Eliot v. Frederic Leighton: Whose Text Is It Anyway?" in which Turner notes that "Almost no work has been done on the ways periodical illustrations in the nineteenth century were consumed. While there is an ever-increasing body of work on Victorian images, there is little work that theorizes ways for twentieth-century viewers to encounter nineteenth-century visual culture" (19). Turner suggests some important questions that should be asked about Victorian illustrations, which I address in my discussion of magazine images of women readers: "[H]ow do these drawings relate to the literary text? How do they relate to other visual images within the magazine? How does each individual image stand apart from the series?" (19).

17. That Eliot believed her heroine symbolized the potential of educated women is evidenced by the fact that with her fifty-pound donation to Girton College she identified herself only as the author of *Romola*. It was also rumored that Barbara Bodichon–cofounder of Girton College with Emily Davies–was the model for the character of Romola.

18. The object Phillis holds–which appears to be a rolling pin–is unmistakably phallic and is thus an additional sign of the threat she presents to her cousin.

19. Although Reader inadvertently states that this census occurred in 1865 (a year in which there was no census taken), his charts and all other comments on it correctly note that it was taken in 1861.

20. This article is the second part of a series that began with "Middle-Class Education in England–Boys" (October 1864), in which Martineau agrees that boys' schools need reform but resists the idea that the government should step in to administer the changes.

21. Lillian F. Shankman argues that this article by Anne Thackeray (Aunt Anny to Leslie Stephen's children) had a direct influence on the young Virginia Stephen and in many ways inspired Woolf's *A Room of One's Own* and the development of modern feminism (168–69). In her 1873 revision of the article for a collection of essays of the same title, Thackeray added to her agenda an argument for women's right to vote (168).

Notes to Chapter 3

1. Maxwell was also the publisher of the *Half-Penny Journal, Temple Bar, St. James's Magazine*, and *The Welcome Guest*, all of which Braddon had contributed to or worked on for at least five years before gaining the editorship of her own magazine. Braddon conducted *Belgravia* from 1866 until 1876, when it was sold to another publisher, Chatto and Windus, who replaced Braddon's novels with the works of Charles Reade, Wilkie Collins, and Thomas Hardy (Scheuerle 32).

2. In her recent biography of Braddon, Jennifer Carnell argues that the author was more of a figurehead for *Belgravia* than a hands-on editor and presents evidence indicating that Charles Smith Cheltnam actually reviewed submissions

to the magazine (174–76). Furthermore, Braddon's illness from November 1868 to June 1869 prevented her from completing her *Belgravia* serial, *Bound to John Company*, and certainly from attending to the contents of the magazine (Wolff, *Sensational Victorian* 229). However, it seems clear that whatever Braddon's actual position was concerning the day-to-day business of *Belgravia*, the character, agenda, and philosophy of the magazine were very much under her control. In fact, this periodical is much more closely linked to the personality of its editor than any of the others in this study.

3. Although James generally displays a positive regard for Braddon–affirming that she is an "artist" with a "knowing style" who produces photographs that reflect her "shrewd" observational skills–he claims that her fellow sensationalist Wilkie Collins deserves "a more respectable name" than founder of the genre (593).

4. See, for example, the March 28, 1868 *Punch* cartoon "Sensation Novels" and the May 2, 1863 cartoon about Braddon's *Aurora Floyd*.

5. *Circe* ran in the magazine from March to September 1867 and was supposedly plagiarized from Octave Feuillet's *Dalila*. Interestingly, the *Pall Mall Gazette* was barraged with advertisements for *Circe, Belravia,* and Braddon's other works in the month leading up to Greenwood's assault on her. Maxwell's aggressive ad campaign on Braddon's behalf might have inspired the *Pall Mall's* unwanted attention, but Greenwood may also have been motivated by a personal vendetta against Braddon and Maxwell. He was friends with John Gilby, the spurned literary patron who first supported Braddon's career. Gilby probably had more than a business interest in Braddon, whose relationship with Maxwell led him to completely sever his ties to her. For more on Greenwood's attacks on Braddon, see Wolff's *Sensational Victorian* 208–15.

6. The Wolff Collection at the Harry Ransom Humanities Research Center contains sixteen letters Braddon wrote to Kent between 1865 and 1881. All the letters express her gratitude for his championship of her work.

7. Articles such as "Literature in the Purple" (May 1868), "Literature on the Line" (June 1868), and "Writing for Money" (June 1869) supported Braddon's contention that writing for profit constituted professionalism rather than literary prostitution. These articles followed Braddon's reasoning that only failed novelists would criticize those who were models of professional success.

8. I quote from a copy of this letter contained in the Robert Lee Wolff Collection at the Harry Ransom Humanities Research Center, University of Texas, Austin. The original is housed at the Yale University Library.

9. That Braddon was still considered a champion of women readers and had become much more of a literary authority later in her career is evident in her correspondence with the writer Hall Caine. In November 1901 Caine asked Braddon to serve as an expert witness–as an author "of unquestionable distinction" whose name "would carry weight with the jury"–in a trial to defend his novel, *The Eternal City*, against charges by Mr. Pearson of "The Lady's Magazine" that it was "likely to corrupt" the magazine's female readers (Letter dated November 11, 1901). However, Braddon's draft of her reply indicates that she refused to serve as an expert witness. Her explanation that "when it comes to the question of what kind of story is suited to a Ladies Magazine I find myself unable to pronounce an

opinion. The novelist's scope has widened greatly since I began to write; & subjects which I should not then have dared to approach have now become the common stock of women writers" may indicate her unwillingness to engage in such controversy after having gained a certain measure of respect later in her life (Letter to Hall Caine. No date).

10. Carnell attributes this poem to Braddon herself; however, she mistakenly cites the date as January 1869 (420).

11. Following Mortimer Collins's formulation in "Mrs. Harris" (December 1870), which I examine later in this chapter, *Belgravia*'s illustrations of women reading letters symbolize women reading sensation novels.

12. For another account of the publication of these serials, see Onslow's *Women of the Press* (122–23).

13. With Braddon's three simultaneous serials, the short stories, the nonfiction items she was also writing, and the editorial duties she fulfilled, it is no wonder that the deaths of both her sister and her mother led Braddon to suffer a nervous breakdown in November 1868. As a result she was unable to complete her novel *Bound to John Company*. While another writer took over this novel for her from December 1868 to October 1869, she must have had *Charlotte's Inheritance* completed beforehand since it continued to run and was concluded while she was ill. Braddon told Bulwer-Lytton in 1872 that "for more than six months" after her mother's death "life was a blank, or something worse than a blank, an interval in which imagination ran riot, & I was surrounded by shadows" (Wolff, "Devoted Disciple" 148).

14. All three of these articles were probably written by Braddon. Carnell includes "French Novels" and "Glimpses of Foreign Literature" among her list of Braddon's nonfiction works (421).

15. This advertisement is part of a series of similar ads featuring praise for *Birds of Prey, Circe,* and *Belgravia* taken from a wide range of magazine reviews. I noted ads on September 14 and 21 and on October 5, 12, 19, and 26.

16. The on-line *Athenaeum Index of Reviews* attributes the *Birds of Prey* to William Lush and the review of *Charlotte's Inheritance* to Geraldine Jewsbury.

17. Her use of such a term worked to feminize and emasculate the predominantly male, elite critics who attacked her as unfeminine and low.

18. For more on "Sensationalism in Science," see Onslow's discussion of Patterson (167–72) and Bandish's analysis of the series as a part of the magazine's Bohemian questioning of authority (249–51).

19. Other articles in the series include "Daylight" (August 1868), "Autocracy of the Sun" (November 1868), and "Photospheres" (February 1869). Equally sensational, but not part of the "Sensationalism in Science" series are "Inhabited Planets" (July 1867), "The Cycles of the Worlds" (May 1869), "Does the Earth Grow Sick?" (November 1869), and "Sun Spots" (November 1870).

Notes for Chapter 4

1. Although the women of Langham Place did not adopt the term "feminist," I use it for the sake of convenience and because I believe it accurately describes their magazines and activities.

2. My discussion of *Victoria*'s literary values is indebted to Solveig Robinson's account of the feminist criticism of the *Englishwoman's Review* in "'Amazed at Our Success': The Langham Place Editors and the Emergence of a Feminist Critical Tradition."

3. Pauline Nestor intimates that what she calls the magazine's "restrictive moralism" is directly related to its association with Queen Victoria (102). However, James Stone uses nineteenth-century assessments of the magazine to support his own contention that Nestor's statement fails to account for the responses of contemporary women readers, who got more than a moral lesson from the magazine (76). I would argue that the magazine's tendency toward morality was motivated not by the Queen, but by the magazine's attempt to prove that professional women could maintain their femininity, which, if not signaled by motherhood or charity, was most easily marked by morality.

4. Maria Frawley argues that the magazine's emphasis on the Queen shifts from her status as monarch to her essential embodiment of womanhood and finally tapers off altogether, only to be replaced with depictions of Emily Faithfull herself as the magazine's "queenly center" ("The Editor as Advocate" 97).

5. In fact, Davies claims in a letter to Barbara Bodichon that the prospectus for the magazine caused disagreements that were resolved by eliminating any description of the magazine or address to its readers (March 12, 1863).

6. For more about Taylor's relationship to Victoria Press and *Victoria Magazine*, see Janet Horowitz Murray's "First Duty of Women: Mary Taylor's Writings in *Victoria Magazine*," in *Victorian Periodicals Review* 22 (4) (1989): 141–47.

7. This series includes "Feminine Honesty" (May 1867), "Feminine Knowledge" (June 1867), "Feminine Work" (September 1867), "Feminine Idleness" (November 1867), "Feminine Character" (December 1867), "Marriage" (January 1868), "Feminine Earnings" (March 1868), and "Feminine Respectability" (May 1868).

8. In addition to the involvement of women readers encouraged by the "Correspondence" section, the "Social Science" section asked women to actively participate in social and political activities.

9. After a short stint doing editorial work, Davies devoted herself to improving women's education and is best known as the cofounder and head mistress of Girton College. For more on Davies, see Daphne Bennett's *Emily Davies and the Liberation of Women, 1830–1921* (London: André Deutsch, 1990) and Barbara Stephen's *Emily Davies and Girton College* (London: Constable, 1927, and Westport, Conn.: Hyperion Press, 1976).

10. That the review section was seen as a strength of the magazine is indicated in a quotation Davies pulled from the *Illustrated Times:* "The *Victoria* has sterling qualities and a character of its own. . . . The literary summary is so good that I cannot but suspect in it the hand of the one man of genius whose name I have seen in this serial. I hope the *Victoria* will be able to persevere; if so, it will make a footing for itself" (Letter 337a). Though Davies had no idea "who our genius may be," she was clearly pleased that the portion of the magazine that was so crucial to her was recognized.

11. That Davies already felt a sense of distance from and disdain for Faithfull may well be reflected in her surreptitious use of the degrading nickname "Fido"

to refer to her Langham place partner in private correspondence. Faithfull's scandalous involvement in the Codrington divorce case along with her clashes with other Langhamites about her management of the press and of *Victoria* combined to make her the group outcast. The Codrington divorce case of 1864 was one of the most notorious of the trials made possible by the Divorce Bill of 1857. Faithfull became a pawn who, it was implied, either was the victim of attempted rape by the husband of her friend Helen Codrington or was having a lesbian affair with Helen. Stone and Fredeman explain the effect of the case on Faithfull's reputation and her subsequent rejection by most of her Langhamite colleagues. For an account of the socio-sexual implications of the case, see Martha Vicinus, "Lesbian Perversity and Victorian Marriage: The 1864 Codrington Divorce Trial," *Journal of British Studies* 36 (January 1997): 70–98.

12. Although the book reviews are unattributed and Davies was not the author of all of the notices, her standards guided the contributions.

13. As Esther Schwartz-McKenzie points out, other critics, including Margaret Oliphant, agreed that Thackeray created heroines who were "wrought plainly and without exaggeration" (xxiv). Thackeray's heroines "were *women with commonsense*" and they "projected an idea of what women were that women could appreciate" (ibid.).

14. Though Gaskell's novel turns on some very sensational events, including a murder and subsequent cover-up, *Victoria* embraced it in large part due to the reputation of the novelist. However, the novel also adheres to the magazine's conception of domesticated sensationalism, which I discuss later in this chapter.

15. Clare Simmons discusses this in her introduction to the Broadview edition of Yonge's *The Clever Woman of the Family* (16).

16. The similarities between the June 1863 comment about Gaskell's work—"Not being overcrowded with incident, there is room for the characters to work, and to display a strongly-marked individuality"—and this June 1866 statement that Oliphant's novel—"Not being overcrowded with incident, the characters have room to work, and to display a strongly marked individuality in which the true merit of the story lies" suggest that either the reviews were recycled or the values were so strongly present in the minds of the reviewers that they became repetitive. Interestingly, like Gaskell's novel, Oliphant's contains sensational elements that are "domesticated." I discuss *Victoria*'s endorsement of domesticated sensationalism later in this chapter.

17. I have quoted the brief reviews of Braddon and Wood in their entirety.

18. The level of control exerted by Head is unclear. Robinson claims that he took over the editorship of the magazine, but Stone maintains that while he owned half of the press, Faithfull "alone decided the contents of the magazine" (73).

19. Davies heralded his involvement in the press in 1864: "This is what has been wanted all along, a responsible manager who knows the business. . . . He fully believes in women writers but not in indulging them" (Letter 337f).

20. In August 1865 an article called "A Plea for Prudence" acknowledges the similarities between the themes and plots of sensation novels and the events presented in recent news reports, which have "run a neck-in-neck race with the sensation novelist" (359). *Victoria*, however, concludes that sensation fiction is irresponsible because its characters do not receive the same punishment as England's

criminals, who are "no visionary beings, the creation of a lively imagination, [but] are flesh and blood like ourselves, beings with hearts to break, nerves to agonise, and souls to prepare for the great tribunal of justice" (ibid.).

21. Only "Written for My Daughter" omits this obligatory and often humorous character. However, the advice given to the narrator's daughter could lead the girl to shun romantic involvement altogether and become an "old maid" herself.

BIBLIOGRAPHY

"Adventurous Investigation, An." *Belgravia: A London Magazine* (November 1866): 55–72.

"Advertisement." *Harper's New Monthly Magazine* 1 (June–December 1850).

——. *Harper's New Monthly Magazine* 2 (December 1850–May 1851).

——. *Harper's New Monthly Magazine* 3 (June 1851–November 1851).

——. *Harper's New Monthly Magazine* 4 (December 1851–May 1852).

——. *Harper's New Monthly Magazine* 7 (June 1853–November 1853).

Advertisement for *Birds of Prey* by Mary Elizabeth Braddon. *Athenaeum* (October 5, 1867): 446.

Advertisement for the *Cornhill Magazine. Saturday Review* (January 7, 1860): 32.

Agnew, J. H. "Woman's Offices and Influence." *Harper's New Monthly Magazine* (October 1851): 554–57.

Allen, Frederick L. *Harper's Magazine, 1850–1959: A Centenary Address.* New York: Princeton University Press for the Newcomen Society in North America, 1950.

Altick, Richard. *The English Common Reader.* Chicago: University of Chicago Press, 1957.

"Amateur Music." *Cornhill Magazine* (July 1863): 93–98.

"American Literature." *Harper's New Monthly Magazine* (June 1850): 37.

Archives of Harper and Brothers, 1817–1914, The. In *British Publishers' Archives on Microfilm* in conjunction with the *Index to the Archives of Harper and Brothers 1817–1914*, ed. Christopher Feeney. Cambridge: Chadwick-Healey, 1982.

Armstrong, Nancy. "Postscript: Contemporary Culturalism: How Victorian Is It?" In *Victorian Afterlife: Postmodern Culture Rewrites the Nineteenth-Century,* ed. John Kucich and Dianne F. Sadoff, 311–26. Minneapolis: University of Minnesota Press, 2000.

Arnold, Matthew. "The Literary Influence of Academies." *Cornhill Magazine* (August 1864): 154–72.

Ballaster, Ros, Margaret Beetham, Elizabeth Frazer, and Sandra Hebron. *Women's Worlds: Ideology, Femininity and the Woman's Magazine.* New York: Macmillan, 1991.

Bandish, Cynthia L. "Bakhtin's Dialogism and the Bohemian Meta-narrative of *Belgravia:* A Case Study for Analyzing Periodicals." *Victorian Periodicals Review* 34 (3) (Fall 2001): 239–62.

Barnes, James J. *Authors, Publishers, and Politicians: The Quest for an Anglo-American Copyright Agreement, 1815–1854.* Columbus: Ohio State University Press, 1974.

Baym, Nina. *Novels, Readers, and Reviewers: Responses to Fiction in Antebellum America.* Ithaca, N.Y.: Cornell University Press, 1984.

Beetham, Margaret. *A Magazine of Her Own: The Woman's Magazine 1800–1914.* New York: Routledge, 1996.

Bernstein, Susan. "Ape Anxiety: Sensation Fiction, Evolution, and the Genre Question." *Journal of Victorian Culture* 6 (2) (Autumn 2001): 250–69.

——. "Dirty Reading: Sensation Fiction, Women, and Primitivism." *Criticism: A Quarterly for Literature and the Arts* 36 (2) (Spring 1994): 213–41.

Bevington, Merle Mowray. *The Saturday Review, 1855–1868.* New York: Columbia University Press, 1941.

Blake, Andrew. *Reading Victorian Fiction: The Cultural and Ideological Content of the Nineteenth-Century Novel.* London: Macmillan Press, 1989.

Boucherett, Jessie. "The Work We Have to Do." *Englishwoman's Review* 1 (October 1866): 4–5.

Braddon, Mary Elizabeth. *Birds of Prey. Belgravia: A London Magazine* (November 1866–October 1867).

——. *Charlotte's Inheritance. Belgravia: A London Magazine* (April 1868–February 1869).

——. Editorial note to *Charlotte's Inheritance. Belgravia: A London Magazine* (April 1868): 244.

——. "French Novels." *Belgravia: A London Magazine* (July 1867): 78–81.

——. "In the Firelight." *Belgravia: A London Magazine* (March 1868): 66.

——. Letter to Charles Kent. September 12, 1865. Robert Lee Wolff Collection. Harry Ransom Humanities Research Center, The University of Texas at Austin.

——. Letter to George Sala. No date. Robert Lee Wolff Collection. Harry Ransom Humanities Research Center, The University of Texas at Austin.

——. Letter to Hall Caine. No date. Robert Lee Wolff Collection. Harry Ransom Humanities Research Center, The University of Texas at Austin.

[——]. "A Remonstrance." *Belgravia: A London Magazine* (November 1867): 80–86.

Brake, Laurel. *Subjugated Knowledges: Journalism, Gender, and Literature in the Nineteenth Century.* New York: New York University Press, 1994.

Brantlinger, Patrick. *The Reading Lesson: The Threat of Mass Literacy in Nineteenth-Century British Fiction.* Bloomington: Indiana University Press, 1998.

——. "What Is 'Sensational' about the 'Sensation Novel'?" *Nineteenth-Century Literature* 37 (1) (June 1982): 1–28.

Broomfield, Andrea. "Eliza Lynn Linton, Sarah Grand, and the Spectacle of the Victorian Woman Question: Catch Phrases, Buzzwords and Sound Bites." (Forthcoming). In *English Literature in Transition.*

——. "Much More than an Antifeminist: Eliza Lynn Linton's Contribution to the Rise of Victorian Popular Journalism." *Victorian Literature and Culture* 29 (2) (2001): 267–83.

Byerly, Alison. *Realism, Representation, and the Arts in Nineteenth-Century Literature.*

Cambridge: Cambridge University Press, 1997.

Caine, Hall. Letter to M. E. Braddon. November 11, 1901. Robert Lee Wolff Collection. Harry Ransom Humanities Research Center, The University of Texas at Austin.

Carnell, Jennifer. *The Literary Lives of Mary Elizabeth Braddon: A Study of Her Life and Work*. Hastings, East Sussex, England: Sensation Press, 2000.

Carr, Jean Ferguson. "Writing as a Woman: Dickens, *Hard Times*, and Feminine Discourses." *Dickens Studies Annual* 18 (1989): 161–78.

Casey, Ellen Miller. "Edging Women Out?: Reviews of Women Novelists in the *Athenaeum*, 1860–1900." *Victorian Studies* (Winter 1996): 151–71.

Chapple, J. A. V., and Arthur Pollard, eds. *The Letters of Mrs. Gaskell*. Cambridge: Harvard University Press, 1967.

Charvat, William. *The Profession of Authorship in America, 1800–1870*. New York: Columbia University Press, 1992.

Clarke, Micael M. *Thackeray and Women*. DeKalb: Northern Illinois University Press, 1995.

Colby, Robert A. "'Into the Blue Water': The First Year of *Cornhill Magazine* under Thackeray." *Victorian Periodicals Review* 32 (3) (Fall 1999): 209–22.

Collins, Mortimer. "Mrs. Harris." *Belgravia: A London Magazine* (December 1870): 158–64.

Collins, Wilkie. "Foreword." *Armadale*. New York: Penguin, 1995, 5.

Cook, E. T. "The Jubilee of *The Cornhill*." *Cornhill Magazine* 28 (1910): 8–27.

"*Cornhill* on Men and Women, The." *English Woman's Journal* 12 (November 1863): 178–81.

"Correspondence." *Victoria Magazine* (December 1865): 183.

Cvetkovich, Ann. *Mixed Feelings: Feminism, Mass Culture, and Victorian Sensationalism*. New Brunswick, N.J.: Rutgers University Press, 1992.

David, Deirdre. *Intellectual Women and Victorian Patriarchy: Harriet Martineau, Elizabeth Barrett Browning, George Eliot*. London: Macmillan, 1987.

Davies, Emily. Letter to A. D. [Anna] Richardson. April 10, 1863. *Family Chronicle* 3: 289–90. Girton College Archives, Cambridge.

——. Letter to A. D. [Anna] Richardson. March 15, 1864. *Family Chronicle* 4. Girton College Archives, Cambridge.

——. Letter to Barbara Bodichon. January 14, 1863. Girton College Archives, B309, Cambridge.

——. Letter to Barbara Bodichon. March 12, 1863. Girton College Archives, B313, Cambridge.

——. Letter to Barbara Bodichon. No date. Girton College Archives, B319, Cambridge.

——. Letter 337a. January 2, 1864. *Family Chronicle* 4. Girton College Archives, Cambridge.

——. Letter 337b. January 2, 1864. *Family Chronicle* 4. Girton College Archives, Cambridge.

——. Letter 337f. January 27, 1864. *Family Chronicle* 4. Girton College Archives, Cambridge.

"Day in the Telegraph Office, A." *Belgravia: A London Magazine* (September 1869): 314–18.

Demoor, Marysa. *Their Fair Share: Women, Power and Criticism in the* Athenaeum, *from Millicent Garett [sic] Fawcett to Katherine Mansfield, 1870–1920*. Aldershot, England: Ashgate, 2000.

Dickens, Charles. *Bleak House*. Harper's New Monthly Magazine (April 1852–October 1853).

——. "Preface to the First Edition." *Bleak House*. New York: Penguin, 1985, 41–43.

Dixon, E. S. "A Vision of Animal Existences." *Cornhill Magazine* (March 1862): 311–18.

Dowgray, John Gray Laird. "A History of *Harper's* Literary Magazines, 1850–1900." Ph.D. diss., University of Wisconsin, 1956.

[Doyle, Richard]. "Bird's-Eye View of Society: At Home." *Cornhill Magazine* (April 1861): 497–99.

Eddy, Spencer L. *The Founding of the* Cornhill Magazine. Muncie: Ball State University Press, 1970.

"Editor's Easy Chair." *Harper's New Monthly Magazine* (December 1851): 132.

——. *Harper's New Monthly Magazine* (January 1852): 255.

——. *Harper's New Monthly Magazine* (January 1853): 279.

——. *Harper's New Monthly Magazine* (February 1853): 419–20.

——. *Harper's New Monthly Magazine* (December 1853): 132.

——. *Harper's New Monthly Magazine* (June 1854): 119–20.

Eliot, George. *Romola. Cornhill Magazine* (January 1862–August 1863).

"Elizabeth and Victoria from a Woman's Point of View." *Victoria Magazine* (June 1864): 97–103.

Ellegård, Alvar. *The Readership of the Periodical Press in Mid-Victorian Britain*. Göteborg: Göteborg University Press, 1957.

"Elopement Door, The." *Belgravia: A London Magazine* (July 1869): 115.

Escott, T. H. S. "Literary Bagmanship." *Belgravia: A London Magazine* (February 1871): 508–12.

——. "Vagueness." *Belgravia: A London Magazine* (May 1868): 407–14.

Exman, Eugene. *The Brothers Harper*. New York: Harper and Row, 1965.

——. *The House of Harper: One Hundred and Fifty Years of Publishing*. New York: Harper and Row, 1967.

Faithfull, Emily. "Victoria Press." *English Woman's Journal* 6 (32) (October 1860): 121–26.

——. "Women Compositors." *English Woman's Journal* 8 (43) (September 1861): 37–41.

Feltes, Norman. *Modes of Production of Victorian Novels*. Chicago: University of Chicago Press, 1986.

Fitch, J. G. "The Education of Women." *Victoria Magazine* (March 1864): 436–47.

Flint, Kate. *The Woman Reader, 1837–1914*. Oxford: Clarendon, 1993.

Foley, Brian. "Dickens Revised: 'Bartleby' and *Bleak House*." *Essays in Literature* 12 (2) (Fall 1985): 241–50.

Ford, George H. *Dickens and His Readers*. New York: Norton, 1965.

Frawley, Maria. "The Editor as Advocate: Emily Faithfull and *The Victoria Magazine*." *Victorian Periodicals Review* 31 (1) (Spring 1998): 86–104.

——. "Feminism, Format, and Emily Faithfull's Victoria Press Publications." *Nineteenth-Century Feminisms* 1 (Fall/Winter 1999): 39–63.

Fredeman, William E. "Emily Faithfull and the Victoria Press: An Experiment in Sociological Bibliography." *Library* 29 (1974): 139–64.

Gardner, Joseph. *Dickens in America*. New York: Garland, 1988.

Gaskell, Elizabeth. "Cousin Phillis." *Cornhill Magazine* (November 1863–February 1864).

——. *Wives and Daughters*. *Cornhill Magazine* (August 1864–January 1866).

Gilbert, Pamela K. *Disease, Desire, and the Body in Victorian Women's Popular Novels*. Cambridge: Cambridge University Press, 1997.

——, Aeron Haynie, and Marlene Tromp, eds. *Beyond Sensation: Mary Elizabeth Braddon in Context*. Albany: State University of New York Press, 2000.

Giles, Paul. *Transatlantic Insurrections: British Culture and the Formation of American Literature, 1730–1860*. Philadelphia: University of Pennsylvania Press, 2001.

Gilmore, Michael T. *American Romanticism and the Marketplace*. Chicago: University of Chicago Press, 1985.

Gilmour, Robin. *The Idea of the Gentleman in the Victorian Novel*. London: George Allen and Unwin, 1981.

Glazener, Nancy. *Reading for Realism: The History of a U.S. Literary Institution, 1850–1910*. Durham: Duke University Press, 1997.

Glynn, Jennifer. *Prince of Publishers: A Biography of George Smith*. London: Allison and Busby, 1986.

"Graham versus Reprints." *Graham's Magazine* (May 1851): 280.

[Greenwood, Frederick.] "'Dallila' and 'Circe.'" *Pall Mall Gazette* (September 16, 1867): 9.

——. "Mr Babbington [*sic*] White's 'Circe.'" *Pall Mall Gazette* (September 21, 1867): 4.

——. "Mr. Babington White's New Novel." *Pall Mall Gazette* (September 17, 1867): 3.

Haight, Gordon S., ed. *The George Eliot Letters*. Vol. 3. New Haven, Conn.: Yale University Press, 1955.

Harden, Edgar F., ed. *The Letters and Private Papers of William Makepeace Thackeray: A Supplement to Gordon N. Ray*. Vol. 2. New York: Garland, 1994.

"Harper's Monthly and Weekly." *Putnam's Monthly Magazine* (March 1857): 293–96.

"Harpy, The." *Punchinello* (November 12, 1870): 104.

Harris, Janice H. "Not Suffering and Not Still: Women Writers at the *Cornhill Magazine*, 1860–1900." *Modern Language Quarterly* 47 (4) (1986): 382–92.

Harrison, Frederic. *The Choice of Books and Other Literary Pieces*. London: Macmillan, 1920.

Haywood, Jennifer. *Consuming Pleasures: Active Audiences and Serial Fictions from Dickens to Soap Opera*. Lexington: University Press of Kentucky, 1997.

Herford, Brooke. "Importance of Newspapers to Women." *Victoria Magazine* (December 1866): 176–77.

Herstein, Sheila. "The *English Woman's Journal* and the Langham Place Circle: A Feminist Forum and Its Women Editors." In *Innovators and Preachers: The Role of the Editor in Victorian England*, ed. Joel Wiener, 61–76. London: Greenwood, 1985.

——. "The Langham Place Circle and Feminist Periodicals of the 1860s." *Victorian Periodicals Review* 26 (Spring 1993): 24–27.

Hetherington, Hugh. *Melville's Reviewers: British and American, 1846–1891*. Chapel Hill: University of North Carolina Press, 1961.

Hodgson, W. B. "The Education of Girls, Considered in Connexion [*sic*] with the University Local Examinations." *Victoria Magazine* (July 1864): 250–71.

Houghton, Walter E. "Periodical Literature and the Articulate Classes." In *The Victorian Periodical Press: Samplings and Soundings*, ed. Joanne Shattock and Michael Wolff, 3–28. Toronto: University of Toronto Press, 1982.

——, ed. *The Wellesley Index to Victorian Periodicals, 1824–1900*. Vol. 1. Toronto: University of Toronto Press, 1966.

Hughes, Linda. "Turbulence in the 'Golden Stream': Chaos Theory and the Study of Periodicals." *Victorian Periodicals Review* 22 (Fall 1989): 117–25.

Hughes, Winifred. *The Maniac in the Cellar: Sensation Novels of the 1860s*. Princeton, N.J.: Princeton University Press, 1980.

Huxley, Leonard. "Chronicles of *Cornhill*." *Cornhill Magazine* (March 1922): 364–84.

——. *The House of Smith Elder*. London, 1923.

"Influence of University Degrees on the Education of Women, The." *Victoria Magazine* (July 1863): 260–71.

"Insanity and Its Treatment." *Belgravia: A London Magazine* (February 1870): 478.

Jalland, Patricia. "Victorian Spinsters: Dutiful Daughters, Desperate Rebels, and the Transition to the New Women." In *Exploring Women's Past: Essays in Social History*, ed. Patricia Crawford, 129–70. London: George Allen and Unwin, 1984.

[James, Henry]. "Miss Braddon." *The Nation* 1 (9) (November 9, 1865): 593–94.

[Jewsbury, Geraldine]. Review of *Charlotte's Inheritance* by M. E. Braddon. *Athenaeum* (March 21, 1868): 418.

"Journalism." *Cornhill Magazine* (July 1862): 52–63.

Katz, Susan Leslie. "'Singleness of Heart': Spinsterhood in Victorian Culture." Ph.D. diss., Columbia University, 1988.

Kent, Christopher. "Introduction." In *British Literary Magazines: The Victorian and Edwardian Age, 1837–1913*. Vol. 3, ed. Alvin Sullivan. London: Greenwood, 1983.

King, Margaret. "'Certain Learned Ladies': Trollope's *Can You Forgive Her?* and the Langham Place Circle." In *Victorian Literature and Culture*, ed. John Maynard, Adrienne Munich, and Sandra Donaldson, 307–26. New York: AMS Press, 1993.

King, R. Ashe. "A Tête-à-Tête Social Science Discussion." *Cornhill Magazine* (November 1864): 569–82.

Klancher, Jon P. *The Making of English Reading Audiences, 1790–1832*. Madison: University of Wisconsin Press, 1987.

Lehuu, Isabelle. "Sentimental Figures: Reading *Godey's Lady's Book* in Antebellum America." In *The Culture of Sentiment: Race, Gender, and Sentimentality in Nineteenth-Century America*, ed. Shirley Samuels, 73–91. New York: Oxford University Press, 1992.

Lenard, Mary. "'Mr. Popular Sentiment': Dickens and the Gender Politics of Sentimentalism and Social Reform Literature." *Dickens Studies Annual* 27 (1998): 45–68.

Letter from H. P. to the Editor. *Victoria Magazine* (April 1868): 536–37.

Letter from Henrietta to the Editor. *Victoria Magazine* (August 1867): 336–42.

"Letter to the Proprietors of Harper's Magazine, A." *The American (Whig) Review*

(July 1852): 12–20.

Levine, George. *The Realistic Imagination: English Fiction from Frankenstein to Lady Chatterley.* Chicago: University of Chicago Press, 1981.

Levine, Philippa. "The Humanising Influences of Five O' Clock Tea: Victorian Feminist Periodicals." *Victorian Studies* (Winter 1990): 293–306.

[Lewes, G. H.] "Our Survey of Literature and Science: *Lady Audley's Secret.*" *Cornhill Magazine* (January 1863): 135–36.

[——]. "Our Survey of Literature and Science: *Orley Farm.*" *Cornhill Magazine* (November 1862): 702–4.

[——]. "Publishers before the Age of Printing." *Cornhill Magazine* (January 1864): 26–32.

"Literary Notices." *Harper's New Monthly Magazine* (December 1851): 137, 139.

——. *Harper's New Monthly Magazine* (January 1852): 277.

——. *Harper's New Monthly Magazine* (April 1852): 711.

Lohrli, Anne, ed. *Household Words: A Weekly Journal 1850–1859 Conducted by Charles Dickens.* Toronto: University of Toronto Press, 1973.

[Lush, William]. Review of *Birds of Prey* by M. E. Braddon. *Athenaeum* (October 12, 1867): 461.

Machor, James L. "Historical Hermeneutics and Antebellum Fiction: Gender, Response Theory, and Interpretive Contexts." In *Readers in History,* ed. James L. Machor, 54–84. Baltimore: Johns Hopkins University Press, 1993.

Martineau, Harriet. "Middle-Class Education in England–Girls." *Cornhill Magazine* (November 1864): 549–68.

——. "Nurses Wanted." *Cornhill Magazine* (April 1865): 409–25.

Mattacks, Kate. "After Lady Audley: M. E. Braddon, the Actress and the Act of Writing in *Hostages to Fortune.*" In *Feminist Readings of Victorian Popular Texts: Divergent Femininities,* ed. Emma Liggins and Daniel Duffy, 69–88. Aldershot, England: Ashgate, 2001.

Mays, Kelly J. "The Disease of Reading and Victorian Periodicals." In *Literature in the Marketplace,* ed. John O. Jordan and Robert L. Patten, 165–94. New York: Cambridge University Press, 1995.

McGill, Meredith. *American Literature and the Culture of Reprinting, 1834–1853.* Philadelphia: University of Pennsylvania Press, 2003.

Melville, Herman. "Bartleby, the Scrivener: A Story of Wall Street." *Putnam's Monthly Magazine* (November and December 1853): 546–57, 609–15.

——. "The Town-Ho's Story." *Harper's New Monthly Magazine* (October 1851): 658–65.

"Memorial of Thackeray's School Days, A." *Cornhill Magazine* (January 1865): 118–28.

"Men and Women." *Harper's New Monthly Magazine* (June 1850): 89.

Merish, Lori. *Sentimental Materialism: Gender, Commodity Culture, and Nineteenth-Century American Literature.* Durham: Duke University Press, 2000.

Milne, Gordon. *George William Curtis and the Genteel Tradition.* Bloomington: Indiana University Press, 1956.

"Miss Parkes' *Essays on Woman's Work.*" *Victoria Magazine* (June 1865): 173–78.

Mitchell, Sally. "Sentiment and Suffering: Women's Recreational Reading in the 1860s." *Victorian Studies* (Autumn 1977): 29–43.

Monod, Sylvere. "Esther Summerson, Charles Dickens, and the Reader of *Bleak House*." *Dickens Studies* 5 (1969): 5–25.

"Monthly Record of Current Events." *Harper's New Monthly Magazine* (June 1850): 122.

——. *Harper's New Monthly Magazine* (July 1850): 275.

——. *Harper's New Monthly Magazine* (August 1850): 422.

Mott, Frank Luther. *A History of American Magazines, 1850–1865.* Cambridge: Harvard University Press, 1938, 383–405.

"Mr. Ruskin on Books and Women." *Victoria Magazine* (November and December 1865): 67–76, 131–38.

"National Gallery, The." *Cornhill Magazine* (March 1860): 346–55.

Nestor, Pauline A. "A New Departure in Women's Publishing: *The English Woman's Journal* and *The Victoria Magazine.*" *Victorian Periodicals Review* 15 (1982): 93–106.

Newman, John Henry. *The Idea of a University,* ed. Frank M. Turner. New Haven, Conn.: Yale University Press, 1996.

Newman, Lea Bertani Vozar. *A Reader's Guide to the Short Stories of Herman Melville.* Boston: G. K. Hall, 1986.

North, John S. "The Rationale–Why Read Victorian Periodicals?" In *Victorian Periodicals: A Guide to Research,* ed. J. Don Vann and Rosemary T. Van Arsdel, 3–20. New York: MLA, 1978.

"Novel-Reading." *Putnam's Monthly Magazine* (September 1857): 384–87.

Ohmann, Richard. *Selling Culture: Magazines, Markets, and Class at the Turn of the Century.* New York: Verso, 1996.

[Oliphant, Margaret]. "Novels." *Blackwood's* 102 (September 1867): 257–80.

——. "A Story of a Voice." *Victoria Magazine* (August and September 1863): 302–17, 397–417.

"On the Genius of Charles Dickens." *Knickerbocker* 39 (May 1852): 421–31.

Onslow, Barbara. "Sensationalising Science: Braddon's Marketing of Science in *Belgravia.*" *Victorian Periodicals Review* 35 (2) (Summer 2002): 160–77.

——. *Women of the Press in Nineteenth-Century Britain.* London: Macmillan; New York: St. Martin's Press, 2000.

"Opera 1833–1863, The." *Cornhill Magazine* (September 1863): 295–307.

Oram, Richard W. "'Just a Little Turn of the Circle': Time, Memory, and Repetition in Thackeray's *Roundabout Papers.*" *Studies in the Novel* 13 (Spring–Summer 1981): 156–67.

Parker, Mark. *Literary Magazines and British Romanticism.* Cambridge: Cambridge University Press, 2000.

Perkins, Barbara. "*Harper's Monthly Magazine.*" In *American Literary Magazines: The Eighteenth and Nineteenth Centuries,* ed. Edward E. Chielens, 166–71. Westport, Conn.: Greenwood, 1986.

"Plea for Prudence, A." *Victoria Magazine* (August 1865): 359–62.

Poovey, Mary. *Uneven Developments: The Ideological Work of Gender in Mid-Victorian England.* Chicago: University of Chicago Press, 1988.

Post-Lauria, Sheila. *Correspondent Colorings: Melville in the Marketplace.* Amherst: University of Massachusetts Press, 1996.

Pykett, Lyn. *The "Improper" Feminine: The Women's Sensation Novel and the New Woman Writing.* New York: Routledge, 1992.

——. "Reading the Periodical Press: Text and Context." *Victorian Periodicals Review* 22 (Fall 1989): 100–108.

"Queen as Ruler, The." *Victoria Magazine* (January 1864): 193–201.

[Rae, W. Fraser]. "Sensation Novelists: Miss Braddon." *North British Review* 43 (September 1865): 180–204.

Ray, Gordon N. *Thackeray: The Age of Wisdom, 1847–1863.* New York: Octagon Books, 1972.

——, ed. *The Letters and Private Papers of William Makepeace Thackeray.* Vol. 4. Cambridge: Harvard University Press, 1946.

Reader, W. J. *Professional Men: The Rise of the Professional Classes in Nineteenth-Century England.* London: Weidenfeld and Nicolson, 1966.

Reddie, James Campbell. "Falling in Love." *Cornhill Magazine* (January 1861): 41–47.

Rendall, Jane. "'A Moral Engine'? Feminism, Liberalism, and the *English Woman's Journal.*" In *Equal or Different: Women's Politics 1800–1914,* ed. Jane Rendall, 112–38. Oxford: Basil Blackwood, 1987.

Review of *Bleak House* by Charles Dickens. *Athenaeum* (September 17, 1853): 108–9.

Review of *Bleak House* by Charles Dickens. *Bentley's Miscellany* 34 (1853): 372–75.

Review of *Bleak House* by Charles Dickens. *North American Review* (October 1853): 409–39.

Review of *Can You Forgive Her?* by Anthony Trollope. *Victoria Magazine* (October 1865): 574–75.

Review of *Charlotte's Inheritance* by M. E. Braddon. *Saturday Review* (April 4, 1868): 458–60.

Review of *The Clever Woman of the Family* by Charlotte Yonge. *Victoria Magazine* (April 1865): 573–75.

Review of *A Dark Night's Work* by Elizabeth Gaskell. *Victoria Magazine* (June 1863): 190–91.

Review of *The Gentle Life: Essays in Aid of the Formation of Character* by a Saturday Reviewer. *Victoria Magazine* (February 1864): 383.

Review of *Hard Cash* by Charles Reade. *Victoria Magazine* (February 1864): 380.

Review of *Henry Dunbar* by M. E. Braddon. *Victoria Magazine* (July 1864): 283.

Review of *Little Miss Fairfax. Victoria Magazine* (April 1868): 571–73.

Review of *Margaret Stourton. Victoria Magazine* (September 1863): 477–78.

Review of *Miss Mackenzie* by Anthony Trollope. *Victoria Magazine* (April 1865): 566.

Review of *Miss Marjoribanks* by Margaret Oliphant. *Victoria Magazine* (June 1866): 187.

Review of *Oswald Cray* by Mrs. Henry Wood. *Victoria Magazine* (January 1865): 287.

Review of *Romola* by George Eliot. *Victoria Magazine* (August 1863): 383.

Review of *The Small House at Allington* by Anthony Trollope. *Victoria Magazine* (May 1864): 93–94.

Review of *The Story of Elizabeth* by Anne Thackeray. *Victoria Magazine* (May 1863): 95.

Ritchie, Hester Thackeray, ed. *Thackeray and His Daughter.* New York: Harper and Brothers, 1924.

Robertson-Lorant, Laurie. *Melville: A Biography.* New York: Clarkson Potter, 1996.

Robinson, Solveig C. "'Amazed at Our Success': The Langham Place Editors and the Emergence of a Feminist Critical Tradition." *Victorian Periodicals Review* 29 (2) (Summer 1996): 159–72.

——. "Defining the Nature of Good Literature: Victorian Women of Letters." Ph.D. diss., University of Chicago, 1994.

——. "Editing *Belgravia:* M. E. Braddon's Defense of 'Light Literature.' " *Victorian Periodicals Review* 28 (2) (Summer 1995): 109–22.

Rowbotham, Judith. *Good Girls Make Good Wives: Guidance for Girls in Victorian Fiction.* New York: Basil Blackwell, 1989.

Ruskin, John. *Sesame and Lilies.* New York: Everyman's Library, 1965.

Russell, Edward R. "'Thorough' in Criticism." *Belgravia: A London Magazine* (November 1868): 39–48.

Saintsbury, George. *A History of Nineteenth-Century Literature.* London: Macmillan, 1896.

Sala, George Augustus. "The Cant of Modern Criticism." *Belgravia: A London Magazine* (November 1867): 45–55.

——. "On the Sensational in Literature and Art." *Belgravia: A London Magazine* (February 1868): 449–58.

Sawyer, William. "Summer Reminiscences: From Dora's Letter to Blanche." *Belgravia: A London Magazine* (December 1869): 257.

Schaffer, Talia. *The Forgotten Female Aesthetes: Literary Culture in Late-Victorian England.* Charlottesville: University Press of Virginia, 2000.

Scheuerle, William H. "*Belgravia.*" In *British Literary Magazines: The Victorian and Edwardian Age, 1837–1913.* Vol. 3, ed. Alvin Sullivan, 31–34. London: Greenwood, 1983.

Schmidt, Barbara Quinn. "The *Cornhill Magazine:* The Relationship of Editor, Publisher, Chief Novelist and Audience." Ph.D. diss., Saint Louis University, 1980.

——. "Novelists, Publishers, and Fiction in Middle-Class Magazines: 1860–1880." *Victorian Periodicals Review* 17 (1984): 142–53.

Schor, Naomi. *Reading in Detail: Aesthetics and the Feminine.* New York: Methuen, 1987.

Schwartz-Mckenzie, Esther. "Introduction." v–xxxiii. In *The Story of Elizabeth and Old Kensongton* by Anne Isabella Thackeray. Bristol, England: The Thoemmes Press, 1995.

Scott, Rosemary. "Poetry in the *Cornhill Magazine:* Thackeray's Influence." *Victorian Periodicals Review* 32 (3) (Fall 1999): 269–74.

Senf, Carol. "*Bleak House:* Dickens, Esther, and the Androgynous Mind." *Victorian Newsletter* 64 (Fall 1983): 21–27.

"Sensational Novels." *Victoria Magazine* (March 1868): 455–65.

"Sensationalism in Science: Is the Sun Dying?" *Belgravia: A London Magazine* (July 1868): 71–81.

"Sensationalism in Science: Our Coal Fields." *Belgravia: A London Magazine* (June 1868): 555–60.

Shankman, Lillian F. *Anne Thackeray Ritchie: Journals and Letters.* Columbus: Ohio State University Press, 1994.

"Sharpshooters of the Press, The." *Cornhill Magazine* (February 1863): 238–51.

Shaw, Harry E. *Narrating Reality: Austen, Scott, Eliot.* Ithaca, N.Y.: Cornell University Press, 1999.

Shaw, Margaret L. "Constructing the 'Literate Woman': Nineteenth-Century Reviews and Emerging Literacies." *Dickens Studies Annual* 21 (1992): 195–211.

Sicherman, Barbara. "Reading and Ambition: M. Carey Thomas and Female Heroism." *American Quarterly* 45 (1) (March 1993): 73–103.

——. "Sense and Sensibility: A Case Study of Women's Reading in Late-Victorian America." In *Reading in America,* ed. Cathy N. Davidson, 201–25. Baltimore: Johns Hopkins University Press, 1989.

Simmons, Clare. "Introduction." In *The Clever Woman of the Family* by Charlotte Mary Yonge. Peterborough, Ontario: Broadview Press, 2001, 7–26.

Smith, George. "Our Birth and Parentage." *Cornhill Magazine* (1901): 4–17.

Smith, J. Campbell. "Literary Criticism." *Belgravia: A London Magazine* (April 1867): 225–34.

Smith, Peter. "The *Cornhill Magazine* Number 1." *Review of English Literature* 4 (1963): 23–24.

Solomon, Pearl Chesler. *Dickens and Melville in Their Time.* New York: Columbia University Press, 1975.

"Sonnet to Dickens, Esq." *Harper's New Monthly Magazine* (September 1854): 572.

Sparks, Tabitha. "Fiction Becomes Her: Representations of Female Character in Mary Elizabeth Braddon's *The Doctor's Wife.*" In *Beyond Sensation: Mary Elizabeth Braddon in Context,* ed. Marlene Tromp, Pamela K. Gilbert, and Aeron Haynie, 197–209. Albany: State University of New York Press, 2000.

Stephen, Fitzjames. "Anti-Respectability." *Cornhill Magazine* (September 1863): 282–94.

——. "Competitive Examinations." *Cornhill Magazine* (December 1861): 692–712.

——. "Gentlemen." *Cornhill Magazine* (March 1862): 327–42.

——. "Keeping Up Appearances." *Cornhill Magazine* (September 1861): 305–18.

——. "Marriage Settlements." *Cornhill Magazine* (December 1863): 666–78.

——. "Sentimentalism." *Cornhill Magazine* (July 1864): 65–75.

Stone, James S. *Emily Faithfull: Victorian Champion of Women's Rights.* Toronto: P. D. Meany, 1994.

Sullivan, Alvin, ed. *British Literary Magazines: The Victorian and Edwardian Age, 1837–1913.* Vol. 3. London: Greenwood, 1983.

Sutherland, John. "*Cornhill's* Sales and Payments: The First Decade." *Victorian Periodicals Review* 19 (1986): 106–8.

[Taylor, Mary]. "Feminine Honesty." *Victoria Magazine* (May 1867): 7–13.

——. "Feminine Idleness." *Victoria Magazine* (November 1867): 1–13.

——. "Feminine Knowledge." *Victoria Magazine* (June 1867): 99–108.

——. "Feminine Work." *Victoria Magazine* (September 1867): 403–13.

Teare, Elizabeth. "*Cornhill* Culture." *Victorian Periodicals Review* 33 (2) (Summer 2000): 117–37.

Thackeray, Anne. "Toilers and Spinsters." *Cornhill Magazine* (March 1861): 318–31.

Thackeray, William Makepeace. "The Four Georges." *Cornhill Magazine* (July 1860–September 1860).

——. *Lovel the Widower. Cornhill Magazine* (January 1860–June 1860).

——. *The Newcomes. Harper's New Monthly Magazine* (November 1853–October 1855).

——. "Nil Nisi Bonum." *Cornhill Magazine* (February 1860): 129–34.

——. "Roundabout Papers No. 1: On a Lazy, Idle Boy." *Cornhill Magazine* (January 1860): 124–28.

——. "Roundabout Papers No. 5: Thorns in the Cushion." *Cornhill Magazine* (July 1860): 122–28.

——. "Roundabout Papers No. 11: On a Chalk-Mark on the Door." *Cornhill Magazine* (April 1861): 504–12.

Thompson, Nicola Diane. *Reviewing Sex: Gender and the Reception of Victorian Novels.* New York: New York University Press, 1996.

Tiemersma, Richard R. "Fiction in the *Cornhill Magazine*–January 1860–March 1871." Ph.D. diss., Northwestern University, 1962.

Trollope, Anthony. *Can You Forgive Her?* Oxford: Oxford University Press, 1982.

——. "The Civil Service as a Profession." *Cornhill Magazine* (February 1861): 214–28.

——. *Framley Parsonage. Cornhill Magazine* (January 1860–April 1861).

——. "On English Prose Fiction as a Rational Amusement." In *Four Lectures by Anthony Trollope,* ed. Morris L. Parrish, 91–139. London: Constable, 1978.

Tromp, Marlene. *The Private Rod: Marital Violence, Sensation, and the Law in Victorian Britain.* Charlottesville: University Press of Virginia, 2000.

Tuchman, Gaye, with Nina E. Fortin. *Edging Women Out: Victorian Novelists, Publishers and Social Change.* New Haven, Conn.: Yale University Press, 1989.

Turner, Mark W. "Gendered Issues: Intertextuality and *The Small House at Allington* in *Cornhill Magazine.*" *Victorian Periodicals Review* 26 (Winter 1993): 228–34.

——. "George Eliot v. Frederic Leighton: Whose Text Is It Anyway?" In *From Author to Text: Re-Reading George Eliot's* Romola, ed. Caroline Levine and Mark W. Turner, 17–35. Aldershot, England: Ashgate, 1998.

——. *Trollope and the Magazines: Gendered Issues in Mid-Victorian Britain.* London: Macmillan; New York: St. Martin's Press, 2000.

"Vice of Reading." *Temple Bar* 42 (September 1974): 251–57.

Vicinus, Martha. *Independent Women: Work and Community for Single Women, 1850–1920.* Chicago: University of Chicago Press, 1985.

"Victoria Regina." *Victoria Magazine* (May 1863): 1–2.

Weisbuch, Robert. *Atlantic Double-Cross: American Literature and British Influence in the Age of Emerson.* Chicago: University of Chicago Press, 1986.

Weltman, Sharon Aronofsky. *Ruskin's Mythic Queen.* Athens: Ohio University Press, 1998.

Westwater, Martha. "*The Victoria Magazine.*" In *British Literary Magazines: The Victorian and Edwardian Age, 1837–1913.* Vol. 3, ed. Alvin Sullivan, 443–46. London: Greenwood, 1983.

[Whipple, E. P.] "Novels and Novelists: Charles Dickens." *North American Review* (October 1849): 383–407.

White, Babington. "The Mudie Classics." *Belgravia: A London Magazine* (March 1868): 41–50.

Wolff, Robert Lee. "Devoted Disciple: The Letters of Mary Elizabeth Braddon to Sir Edward Bulwer-Lytton, 1862–1873." *Harvard Library Bulletin* 22 (1974): 5–35, 129–61.

——. *Sensational Victorian: The Life and Fiction of Mary Elizabeth Braddon.* New York: Garland, 1979.

"Word at the Start, A." *Harper's New Monthly Magazine* (June 1850): 1–2.

"Written for My Daughter." *Victoria Magazine* (August and September 1865): 363–78, 441–58.

Wrobel, Arthur. "*Graham's Lady's and Gentleman's Magazine.*" In *American Literary Magazines: The Eighteenth and Nineteenth Centuries,* ed. Edward E. Chielens, 156–61. Westport, Conn.: Greenwood, 1986.

Wynne, Deborah. *The Sensation Novel and the Victorian Family Magazine.* Basingstoke, England, and New York: Palgrave, 2001.

Zboray, Ronald J. *A Fictive People: Antebellum Economic Development and the American Reading Public.* New York: Oxford University Press, 1993.

INDEX